Home In The Village

HOME IN THE VILLAGE

McClellanville in Old St. James Santee Parish

October 12, 2002

For Joe McCurry

Walter Bonner

Walter Bonner

CORINTHIAN
BOOKS

Mt. Pleasant, S. C.

First Edition. First printing, March 2002.

Publisher's Cataloging-in-Publication
(Provided by Quality Books, Inc.)

Bonner, Walter
  Home in the village: McClellanville in Old St. James Santee Parish /
Walter Bonner. – 1ˢᵗ ed.
    p. cm.
    Includes bibliographical references and index.
    LCCN: 2001092439
    ISBN 1-929175-28-0
    1. McClellanville (S.C.)   I. Title
    F279.M13B66 2002   975.7'91
                                            QBI01-200924

Jacket design © 2002 by Rob Johnson Design, Mt. Pleasant, S.C.

Corinthian Books
an imprint of The Côté Literary Group
P.O. Box 1898
Mt. Pleasant, S.C. 29465-1898
(843) 881-6080
www.corinthianbooks.com

Contents

For Beverly Bonner

Acknowledgments

McClellanville, St. James Santee Parish, and all the people therein provided the inspiration for the writing of this book. The author is indebted to the many individuals, resident and nonresident, who made the writing possible by providing encouragement, telling their stories, making available their photographs, giving literary advice, and teaching me how to deal with the computer and other technical aids.

Cousins were a great help. Lloyd Johnson McClellan launched this project by collecting family stories for circulation at a family reunion. Conversations with Richard Dawsey and Edith Dawsey Moses gave me insight into the situation of the family and the community in the 1920s and 1930s. They, and Suzanne ("Sue") Bagnal Britt, passed along tales and lore about the family's earliest experiences in the parish. Lillian Bonner Jamieson, Richard Matteson, and Betty Smith Bonner added written commentary. Harry Mikell Lofton, a younger member of the previous generation, sent some wonderful comment about the family and the community. Young family members Katherine Dawsey Wesslink and Julie Lewis Brinkley told of latter-day happenings. The contributions of these individuals stimulated interest in putting together a cultural history of McClellanville.

The author enjoyed and benefited from long conversations with persons devoted to this favored place — Jack Leland, Bobby Graham, and Agnes Leland Baldwin each gave their time and support on multiple occasions.

Erskine Clarke, Billy Baldwin, and Beverly Bonner gave this author invaluable aid by urging him to delete broad historical material and direct the course of the book toward being a cultural history of the community.

Suzanne (Sue Sue) Britt, daughter of the above Suzanne Bagnall ("Sue") Britt, and a professor of English at Meredith College, consented to edit the first rendition of the book. She did so with a green pen and a ferocity that taught the author to be careful.

Nell Morris, of the Three Rivers Historical Society, has given encouragement from the beginning of the project. Mrs. Morris and her friends, Mildred Johnson and Mary Gregg, gave many helpful suggestions about the manuscript. Robena Medbery made a last reading of the galley proofs and helped me strengthen the end of the book.

Bud Hill, director of the Village Museum, has regularly given moral support and has made available the resources of the museum for study.

The following have been most gracious in allowing the author to look through photograph collections and select ones for publication: Charles Jerry Owens, Lillian Bonner Jamieson, Edith Dawsey Moses, Jean Smith Stroman, Judy Stroman Fortner, Stuart Mackintosh, Rutledge Leland, and Glenn Racine. Their commentary on the subjects of the photographs has been illuminating. Billy Baldwin is thanked, again, for having made a collection of photographs and stories about McClellanville in his book *The Visible Village* and for making those resources available by contributing them to the Village Museum.

I am indebted to my colleague, Dr. Frank Harper, who encouraged me to acquire a computer and learn how to use its components.

Cousin Richard Matteson provided helpful genealogical information on the Lofton and related families.

Special thanks to Dick Côté, Margaret Grace, Lysa Smith, and Diane Anderson at the Côté Literary Group for making the final stages of this project an interesting and pleasant experience.

To all these people I express my thanks and my admiration.

Walter Bonner
March 2002

South Carolina, Craven County, St. James Santee Parish, and McClellanville

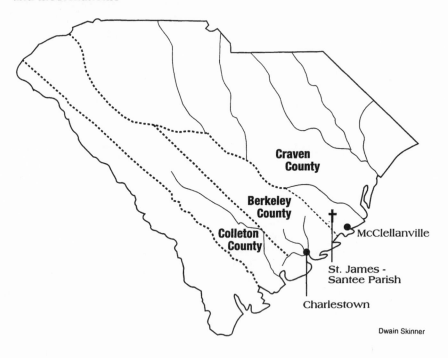

Dwain Skinner

The colony of Carolina was founded with the establishment of Charlestown on the Ashley River in 1670. South Carolina and North Carolina were formally separated in 1729.

The Carolina colony's original counties were established in 1685 and abolished in 1795. McClellanville lies in what was once Craven County.

The Parish of St. James Santee was established in 1706. It was divided in 1754, with the inland portion taking the name St. Stephen Parish. Parishes were abolished by South Carolina's Reconstruction Constitution of 1868, with counties again becoming units of local government throughout the state. McClellanvillle now lies in Charleston County.

Archibald McClellan purchased land on Jeremy Creek in 1771. Richard Tillia Morrison II obtained the neighboring property in the 1840s. In the 1850s, the McClellan and Morrison families began selling lots along the creek. A village appeared and acquired the name McClellanville during the Civil War.

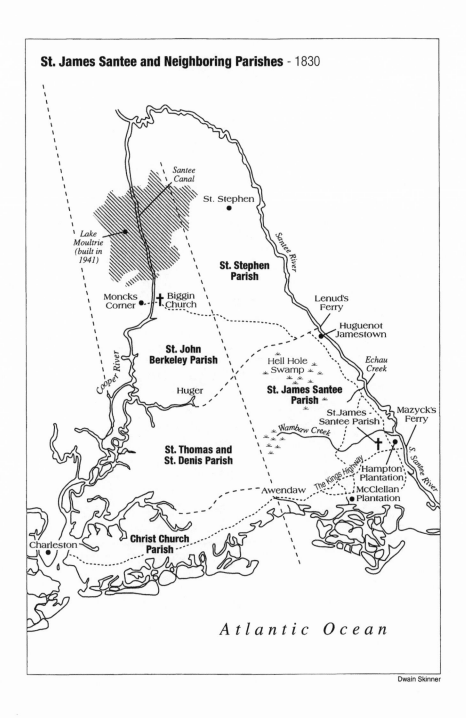

St. James Santee and Neighboring Parishes - 1830

Santee Canal

St. Stephen

Lake Moultrie (built in 1941)

St. Stephen Parish

Santee River

Moncks Corner

✝ *Biggin Church*

Lenud's Ferry

Huguenot Jamestown

St. John Berkeley Parish

Cooper River

Hell Hole Swamp

Echau Creek

Huger

St. James Santee Parish

St.James Santee Parish

Mazyck's Ferry

Wambaw Creek

St. Thomas and St. Denis Parish

✝

S. Santee River

The Kings Highway

Hampton Plantation

Awendaw

McClellan Plantation

Charleston

Christ Church Parish

Atlantic Ocean

Dwain Skinner

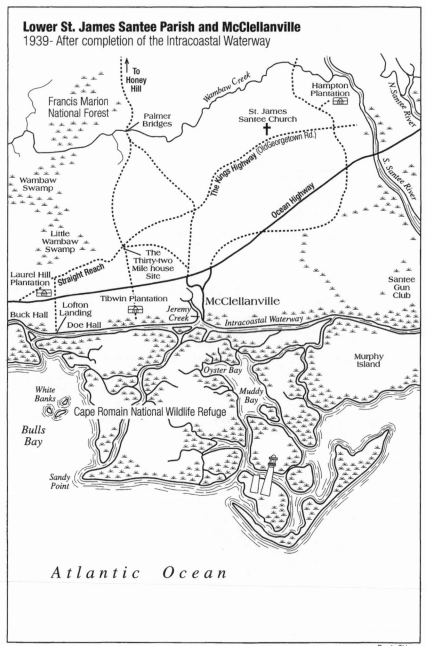

Lower St. James Santee Parish and McClellanville
1939- After completion of the Intracoastal Waterway

To Honey Hill

Francis Marion National Forest

Palmer Bridges

Wambaw Creek

Hampton Plantation

St. James Santee Church

N. Santee River

The Kings Highway (Old Georgetown Rd.)

Ocean Highway

S. Santee River

Wambaw Swamp

Little Wambaw Swamp

The Thirty-two Mile house Site

Laurel Hill Plantation

Straight Reach

Santee Gun Club

Tibwin Plantation

Lofton Landing

Buck Hall

Doe Hall

Jeremy Creek

McClellanville

Intracoastal Waterway

Murphy Island

White Banks

Oyster Bay

Muddy Bay

Cape Romain National Wildlife Refuge

Bulls Bay

Sandy Point

Atlantic   Ocean

Dwain Skinner

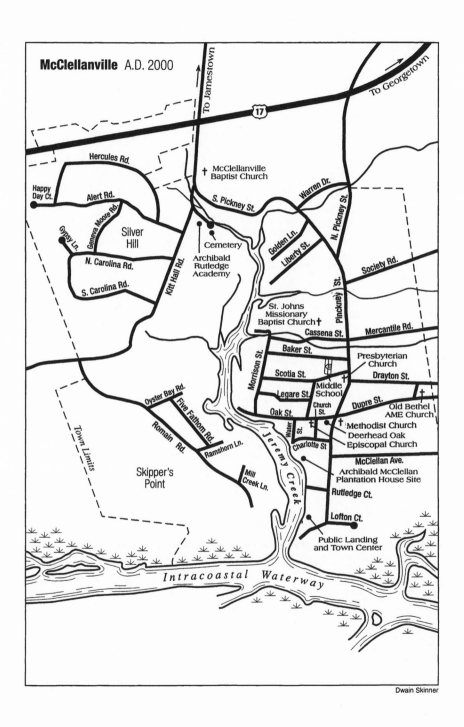

McClellanville A.D. 2000

To Jamestown

To Georgetown

17

Hercules Rd.

† McClellanville
Baptist Church

Happy
Day Ct.

Alert Rd.

S. Pickney St.

Warren Dr.

N. Pickney St.

Geneva Moore Rd.

Gypsy Ln.

Silver
Hill

Cemetery

Golden Ln.

Liberty St.

Society Rd.

N. Carolina Rd.

Archibald
Rutledge
Academy

S. Carolina Rd.

Kitt Hall Rd.

Pinckney St.

St. Johns
Missionary
Baptist Church†

Cassena St.

Mercantile Rd.

Baker St.

Morrison St.

Presbyterian
Church

Scotia St.

Drayton St.

Oyster Bay Rd.

Legare St.

Middle
School

Dupre St.

Five Fathom Rd.

Oak St.

Church
St.

Old Bethel
AME Church

Romain Rd.

Water St.

† Methodist Church

Ramshorn Ln.

Charlotte St

Deerhead Oak
Episcopal Church

Town Limits

Skipper's
Point

Mill
Creek Ln.

Jeremy Creek

McClellan Ave.

Archibald McClellan
Plantation House Site

Rutledge Ct.

Lofton Ct.

Public Landing
and Town Center

Intracoastal Waterway

Dwain Skinner

1

You Want to Live There?

"You want to live there? . . . McClellanville? . . . our home in McClellanville?"

"Well, yes. Yes . . . it's where I've always wanted to be."

Growing up in the 1930s and 1940s, I always loved family visits to McClellanville. We were free to roam around the little coastal village, doing exciting things like climbing oak trees, skipping oyster shells across Jeremy Creek, and playing kick the can. We could build a raft, put up a tree house, and go crabbing. If we ever grew bored, we could seek out and pester our older cousins. We could go out to the farm, sample Aunt Margie's sugar cookies, pick scuppernong grapes from the arbor, and flick the hulls at each other. As we grew older, we could walk from the farm to the landing on Doe Hall Creek, stop along the way to pelt the girls with ripe tomatoes, catch a catfish or a stingray, take a swim, and find that the girls had hidden our clothes. Yet a few more years and we might go flounder-gigging or join a mixed party on a moonlight cruise to Cape Romain.

I was convinced that someone had created McClellanville solely for my entertainment.

This was McClellanville, in old St. James Santee Parish, South Carolina, in the 1930s and 1940s. We were part-time residents in those years and frequent visitors thereafter. It was a delightful place to be, but captivated by the abundance of things to do, and having a host of friendly relatives to visit, I experienced only a part of life there. I did not understand that the community was struggling. These were the second and third decades of economic drought for the community. The place was well into a dormancy that would last at least sixty years (1920 -1980).

With this dormancy, the place was, in effect, saved. It was just as attractive to me in my adult years. I liked family gatherings at Mother's place on Jeremy Creek, shrimp-seining expeditions with colleagues and friends, and lone trips into the creeks to pick up single oysters. I liked gathering pecans, being greeted by name by the proprietor of the one grocery store still operating in town, seeing smoke or mist layering out over fields at the end of a gentle fall day, and finding the rare scotch bonnet shells at Sandy Point on Raccoon Key.

Now we live here and are residents of a changing place. Here and now, at the year 2000, with the town 150 years old and the old parish nearing the 300th anniversary of its founding, the area is being recognized as "beautiful" or "quaint" or "charming" or "a great place to live," and people are moving in. Yet, residents of this village still think of themselves as insiders and as outsiders — members of a close-knit community of people of like mind but detached, and different, from other people in the Carolina Lowcountry. The people persist in a defensive and jingoistic attitude they have displayed for decades. Poverty had a lot to do with keeping their town and their parish quaint, and they are proud that they got along with little help from the outside. Now they worry that newly arriving wealth may bring an end to the life they have known. They fear that an influx of part-time residents and retirees will bring on the thing they fear most — development. They like The Village and the old parish the way it is — pretty much empty and unfinished.

This is about the people who formed the society of the parish and the town throughout the time the place retained its individuality — who these people were and how they got to McClellanville in old St. James Santee Parish — what economic, religious, political, and social forces they believed in and contended with as they built their community — and how they responded to the spirits, the natural beauty and qualities, of the place where they lived.

From the beginning of this village, its people have been interconnected socially, economically, and by marriage. Indeed, it has been hard to tell who is family and who is not in a place where people use the terms "Aunt," "Uncle," and "Cousin" without true relation to kinship. All of them love to talk about people, and in doing so, they tell the story of the community.

2

The Village

Because it is picturesque, uncrowded, and different looking, most people seeing McClellanville for the first time assume that it is an old colonial village. It isn't. It grew up after the Civil War. It is Victorian.

We know that Europeans visited this part of the coast as early as 1526. On August 24, 1526, San Romanus' Day, Lucas de Ayllon named the local point of land Cape San Romano. The Spanish explorer gave us no further information about what he saw. Later, the English explorer, Robert Sandford, tried to change the name of the promontory to Cape Carteret, but the original name lived on as Cape Romain.

The first white man to record his impressions of the area that includes McClellanville and St. James Santee Parish was Angel de Villefane who, in 1561, examined the coast and took possession for his king, Charles I of Spain. The explorer found no convenient harbor and met no natives. Not impressed with what he saw, he gave the place no name. In a secret report to his sovereign, de Villefane dismissed the site as not a good place to settle. He must have been right — 125 years would pass before white people would settle on the nearby Santee River. Another 75 years would go by before anyone would make a home on Jeremy Creek, and an additional 100 years would pass (300 years, altogether, after de Villefane's visit) before a village would be established on the site.

The first white owner of the lands that would become McClellanville was John Whilden, who came to Carolina in 1695. Whilden was among a group of New England Congregationalists who relocated to Carolina after surviving a dangerous war with Indians and after being involved in the infamous Salem witch trials. Their arrival was delayed by shipwreck on Cape Hatteras. Governor Archdale, a Quaker, sent a ship for the New Englanders and invited them to settle in the area called Wappetaw, which is at Wando Neck, about 20 miles from McClellanville.

John Whilden purchased a 490-acre tract on Jeremy Creek in 1705 but, as far as we know, did not occupy it. In 1717, Whilden sold the place to Colonel Thomas Lynch. Lynch had a trading post on the site for at least a few years, probably just until the Seewee Indians died out. Lynch's son, Thomas Lynch, Jr., sold it to George Bennison. The place remained unoccupied until Archibald McClellan (1740-1791) purchased it in 1771 from Bennison's son. Concerned about having title to property held by others, since Carolina was owned by the Lord's Proprietors, McClellan was careful to have his ownership of the land confirmed by a grant from the King of England, George III. The McClellans created a plantation on Jeremy Creek and became the locale's first permanent white residents.

The neighboring property, also with frontage on Jeremy Creek, was acquired in 1850 by Richard Tillia Morrison, Jr. (1816-1910). Morrison, of Scotch-Irish ancestry, was a native of the Wappetaw community and, like John Whilden before him, was a member of the Wappetaw Independent Congregational Church. Morrison moved his family to Alabama

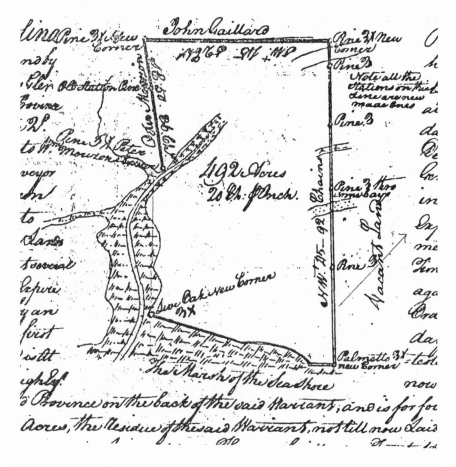

A 1771 plat showing the property that would become McClellanville.

in the 1830s to take ownership of thousands of acres of land. There is an unconfirmed family story that he owned 20,000 acres in Alabama. The Creek Indian uprising induced the family to return, in 1847, to the Carolina Lowcountry. Morrison bought up a number of plantations around Wappetaw and around Buck Hall in St. James Santee Parish, seven miles from The Village, which he would help to establish. He built a cottage on his Jeremy Creek property.

In the 1850s, the McClellan family and the Morrisons

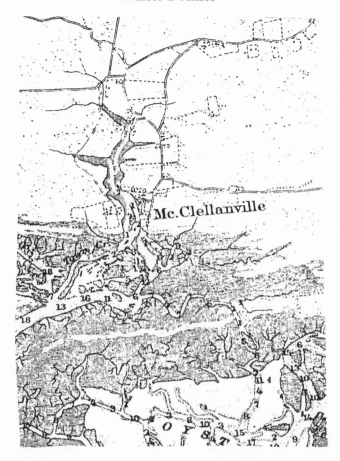

McClellanville in 1896

began offering lots on Jeremy Creek. There were buyers because the great tropical storm of 1822 had blasted Cedar Island at the mouth of the Santee River, destroying the summer homes of the Santee River planters. By 1861, a few summer homes were scattered along Jeremy Creek. The little place
acquired its name during the Civil War. Confederate pickets
stationed there wrote letters to their families, using
"McClellanville" as the return address.

After the war, more families built summer homes in The
Village, and, gradually, these became permanent homes as
people chose to live where there were schools, churches, stores,
social events, and playmates for children. By 1915, the ma-

jority of white residents of the area resided in McClellanville part or all of the time. Because most families had two homes — their rice plantation on the river or their cotton plantation along the marsh plus their place among others on Jeremy Creek — they called McClellanville "The Village." It still is called that today. From 1872 to 1920, McClellanville grew, thanks to the expansion of a few families.

Richard Tillia Morrison, Jr., now often identified as R.T. Morrison II, as there is an R.T. Morrison VII, had eighteen children. His descendants remain numerous and prominent to this day. The McClellans were nearly as prolific and increased in number also. Two other large families were the Lelands and the Grahams. The Lelands were an ecclesiastical family, originally from New England, steeped in Calvinism. The first Leland in the Lowcountry, Aaron Whitney Leland, came to serve as minister of the First (Scots) Presbyterian Church in Charleston. His descendants became ministers and teachers around the area. Many Leland men who were not

The Richard Tillia Morrison II House on Jeremy Creek. This house was replaced by a modern structure in the 1970s.

preachers were named for ministers of the Reformed tradition. There were John Gerardeau Leland, Edwin Cater Leland, and Charlton Henry Leland — all named for preachers who had served Congregational or Presbyterian churches in the Lowcountry. The first Leland in the place that would become McClellanville was J. Hibben Leland, who moved from Mt. Pleasant before the Civil War to teach at the public school. After the war, he also served as magistrate and postmaster. His tribe increased and remained abundant in the community.

The Grahams had a different story, as they came in from the opposite direction, from Horry County. T.W. "Tom Billy" Graham purchased Woodville and Elmwood Plantations on the Santee River after the Civil War. In just a few years, the family was forced to move into McClellanville because their residence at Woodville burned. The Graham family expanded apace with those mentioned above.

Our Lofton family, the family I enjoyed, was established

Pinckney Street ("Main Street") in 1910. The mule-drawn wagon is the only vehicle in sight.

by the arrival of three young brothers in 1872. Connection with the Morrison family allowed two of them, Henry Michael Lofton and John Marion Lofton, to form large branches of the family. Henry Michael Lofton, my great-grandfather, married Susan Ann Morrison during the Civil War. John Marion Lofton and Eliza Ann Morrison married after the war. The youngest of the Lofton boys, Samuel Joseph, married Elizabeth Vinro Moore, but they had no children. (See the appendices for charts of the Lofton family.)

All of the first families in McClellanville had many children over long periods of time. Generations often overlapped. With the production of a second generation of Loftons (my grandfather's), a third generation (my mother's), and then a fourth generation (mine), Lofton descendants were abundant. Our World War II armed forces were strengthened by no less than fourteen members of the Lofton family in McClellanville —twelve men and two women. Of these, two were younger members of the third generation, and twelve were of the fourth generation.

Other families, not quite so large, joined in the formation of the little community. William Peter Beckman, of German extraction, returned to town after the Civil War. He had been stationed in The Village for a while and became enamored of

McClellanville waterfront. All homes except #4 were lost to fires in the 1920s.

The Louis Augustus Whilden House, c. 1860

*Seaside Inn — The Horace Wells Leland House, c. 1875.
Auntie Mame Leland provided accommodations here from
1900 to 1935. Photograph taken about 1910.*

The Hamilton Seabrook House, c. 1878. Photographed in 1920, when it was purchased by Edith Lofton Bonner.

one of the local girls. The Beckmans became mainstays of the Presbyterian Church and were prominent in the community through World War II. Afterwards, becoming teachers or physicians or ministers, the latter generations moved away. No one with the Beckman name remains in the town. The Duke family came later, in the early years of the twentieth century, from the Scotch-Irish stronghold in Williamsburg County. They are still represented in town. The Stromans, originally German-Swiss and Lutheran, took shelter in The Village after losing their properties in Orangeburg County during the disastrous 1920s. Several of them remain.

From the end of the Civil War to World War I, the Santee River plantations declined as rice culture failed. Many of the great houses burned; indeed, today only four (Hampton, The Wedge, Fairfield, Harrietta) are standing on South Santee River. Most of the plantation people moved away, but a few came to McClellanville and stayed for a while. The Lucas, Seabrook, and Doar families were some of these, but no one with those names resides in McClellanville now.

Other families came in, grew quite large, but nearly disappeared. Reverend Prentiss, rector of the Episcopal Church, had twenty-seven children. Only one resident bears the Prentiss name at this time. The Sutlers were numerous for some decades and there were Johnsons and Andersons and Kings. These names disappeared completely, although some of their descendants are present. A few families moved in and out, leaving no trace other than scattered tombstones in the cemetery across Jeremy Creek.

David Doar, who would plant the last rice on the Santee River in 1911, addressed the Agricultural Society of St. James Santee at its meeting on July 4, 1906, the occasion being the 200th anniversary of the creation of the parish. He listed the members of the society of 1860-1861 and listed the members of the society at its reorganization in 1903. In 1860-1861, all eighteen members were Santee River planters. In 1903, only seven of twenty-five members were from Santee River families. The other eighteen, including Henry Michael Lofton and Richard Morrison Lofton, were from families that were newcomers to the parish.

In this new, close, isolated community of like minds, these founders of McClellanville generally found their mates near home. Thus, there appeared men named Morrison Leland and Leland Morrison, as well as Lofton Leland, Leland McClellan, and my grandfather, Richard Morrison Lofton. Keeping track of the different families was made difficult by the tendency of parents to use and reuse name combinations at random. Four persons named Samuel Joseph Lofton lived in or near the community, and none had fathers who bore those names. McClellanville families chose noble, classic names for their daughters: Harrietta, Henrietta, Claudia, and Augusta were frequent choices. There have been two Louise Augusta Loftons, and the combination Margaret Caroline has been used three times in the Lofton family.

Some people, like my mother who was born in 1891 and lived until 1980, knew every one of these individuals and could name them in their proper order, but to us younger folks, it seemed as if the families had been shaken together in a bag and redistributed. So interconnected were these families that the newspaper columnist and wit Jack Leland commented that if you gave one of them a dose of salts they would all go to the bathroom. He also said, "McClellanvillians are all related — by the front door or by the back."

The early members of the community were, as David Doar has written, "drawn together by the calamities which follow war." In the decades following the Civil War, they worked hard, worshipped together, and visited back and forth, developing strong bonds. They were openhearted, generous, kind, and loyal to one another. Also, like the members of any large and happy family, they argued and fought. Interfamily squabbles were nearly always over the schools while fights within individual families were over the inheritance of land.

The local schools were a source of contention into the 1960s. Creighton Frampton, Charleston County superintendent of education for many years, told me that you could always tell who had won election to the school board by seeing who was doing the teaching. "You couldn't straighten out school politics in McClellanville," he said. "One side was always mad."

Elizabeth Vinro Moore, who was raised in a Morrison home and married a Lofton (Samuel Joseph Lofton, 1849-1899), declared that she spent the first half of her life hearing what great crooks the Loftons were and the second half hearing what great crooks the Morrisons were.

This post-Civil War population of McClellanville was built of middle-class individuals. The newcomers were determinedly middle class because being so was part of their value system, their piety. The plantation people who joined them in McClellanville fit right in, for the former rice planters had never had much pretension to aristocracy and now were impoverished by the war and the decline of rice culture. The transition from a parish society led by the rice-planter Episcopalians to one led by the Presbyterian or Methodist cotton farmers was a smooth, nonviolent handoff, a passing of the gavel. The plantation people mixed well and intermarried with the newcomers.

Poverty was the norm for these people in the post-Civil War era, and their situation improved only slowly. The African-Americans who remained in the parish, constituting a 10:1 majority, were in even more desperate straits. Some blacks did take ownership of land and began farming small tracts, but most depended on employment in the homes or on the farms of their previous owners. They lived mainly on the fringes of the plantations and remained in the rural areas as the whites gradually moved into The Village. The "Jim Crow" laws passed by the legislature in the 1890s simply legalized what had always been true: there were two, separate societies.

From the end of the Civil War to the end of World War I, The Village grew slowly, and its financial situation improved to the point that the place could not be called destitute — just poor. The people were able to put together a town with practically every attribute of small towns throughout the country. In fact, it became something of a center of culture.

The school, led by J. Hibben Leland before and after the Civil War, was a magnet for families. The grammar school became a graded school by 1890. In 1904, two decades before high schools opened in many communities around the state, McClellanville High School opened.

When the Presbyterian Church opened in 1872, it was a focus of social and cultural life in the area. The Episcopal Chapel of Ease was consecrated in 1890. The McClellanville Methodist Church, successor to the rural Nazareth Methodist Church, was completed in 1903.

William Peter Beckman operated The Village's first store shortly after the Civil War, but soon there were a number of them, constantly changing hands. One or two physicians practiced in McClellanville at all times. The Bank of McClellanville opened in 1912.

In the 1920s, the town created its own electric power company, using generators owned by the South Carolina Electric and Gas Company. (The generators were turned off at 11:00 PM, so homeowners had to make ready each night.) Beginning in the 1940s, slightly more reliable electric service was brought in by power lines, but when the lines went down in a storm, the lights would be off for up to a week. Over the last two decades, the service has been as dependable as anywhere. Local telephone service was offered as early as 1908, but did not connect to the outside world until the 1930s — folks went to Lu Leland's back porch to make long-distance calls

The great pastime of McClellanvillians was talk, old-fashioned talk about the weather, about who was having a baby, and about what was going on at the school. Talk took place

This South Carolina Electric & Gas Company generator provided the first electrical power for The Village.

The Spray, *captained by Hepburn Morrison, taking formally dressed villagers to Cape Romain, 1908.*

A Cape Romain party, 1928. This group was led by Ludwig Beckman.

in the post office, on the street, in living rooms, and on front porches. As late as the 1970s, McClellanvillians exhibited this love of talk. Leonard Johnson, a North Carolinian and our cousin-in-law, observed: "Here, the people all walk to the post office twice a day even though the mail is put up just once."

Today, in the time of air-conditioning, television, and computers, we have far less social intercourse than did our prede-

Children swimming at Beckman's Beach on Jeremy Creek, 1940s. The Rutledge Leland House can be seen in the background.

Robert Jack McCarley and Rutledge Leland show their bag of ducks, about 1916.

cessors. We also greatly underestimate the capacity of those people to entertain themselves. There was always something to do around the creek: crabbing for the children, fishing and hunting for the youths and adults, swimming, and "Cape Parties" (excursions to Cape Romain). Folks also did a lot of reading. All the girls took music lessons, and there were recitals to attend. Right after World War I, there were enough young men to comprise a baseball team. My father built tennis courts for the town in the 1920s. People turned out to watch McClellanville High's basketball teams, winners of multiple state championships in the 1940s and 1950s. McClellanville was a working village from its start, and remains one, but it has always been a bit of a resort.

In McClellanville, large extended families were the rule. Even unrelated people kept in touch with one another, visiting back and forth, looking out for the sick and disabled. When one elderly bachelor expressed fear of dying alone and of not being found for days, a young boy from the community was recruited to check on the man on a regular basis. Every day the youth opened the old fellow's door and shouted: "Is you dead yet?"

Although the earliest people occupying The Village would not have heard of such a thing, the generations that followed played lots of cards. For women or mixed company, the big game was Bridge. Men, when around their families and in public places, chose Rook, but they would slip off and play poker when they could. Loftons still tell about the time the penny and nickel antes at one game ended up in the Presbyterian Church offering plate.

As Harry Mikell Lofton tells it, "When they were having a Presbyterian Church revival one time, Uncle Tom failed to meet Aunt Mame at the church as promised. Aunt Mame accurately figured he was up to 'Chief Two Moons' place — that is Ozzie McClellan's store — where there was a poker game and plenty of corn whiskey. The boys were all celebrating the revival down the street by playing a little poker and having a few cups of the corn while their wives went to the revival. There were the Chief, Uncle Tom, 'Little Henry' Morrison, 'Commonbreed' Becket Hills, Martin Beckman, Whilden McClellan, 'Bottom Card' Arthur Leland, and 'Dunks' McClellan. All of a sudden, there was a great crack like thunder, and there stood the avenging angel, Aunt Mame Leland Lofton, with a black snake whip, snapping it over their heads. She commanded, 'Hit your knees, boys. Stop playing and start praying.' She scooped up some pennies and nickels from the poker game stating, 'This is for the church collection plate.' She then grabbed Uncle Tom by the ear and dragged him to the car and to the revival. Needless to say, that broke up the poker game for that day, and those old boys were reportedly looking over their shoulders in all poker games to come for a year or so. The Chief barred Uncle Tom from coming for a year. Aunt Mame was one tough Leland when it came to protecting Uncle Tom from evil."

This story from the 1920s or early 1930s was about second-generation and third-generation villagers. While still espousing high standards of personal and public morality, they were drawn to pleasure by the good life of fun and games. It was an ambivalence passed on to subsequent generations. They could not hold true to the pure standards of their predecessors who had been, essentially, immigrants to The Village and, like immigrants everywhere, felt it was important to display religious and ethical unity. Those first families in The Village believed they were creating a holy community. The story also points out a feature of small town life in those days. Almost all the men had nicknames.

Another tale about one of the poker players reveals a great tendency of the people of The Village; they accepted no boundaries, no restrictions on their movements about the land and water. The forests and the marshes were so wide open, so unoccupied, that they all felt they could hunt and fish wherever they chose and whenever they wanted. A story was told of one man who was a notorious night hunter. He did it all the time and everybody knew it, but he could always evade the game wardens. When he died, the game warden came, fully uniformed, to his home to express condolences to the widow. One mourner said to another: "Look, the law finally caught up with old '————.'"

The people of St. James Santee and McClellanville kept a brave front and were determinedly optimistic in every era. Far from being defeatist after the Civil War, they went to work on their new cotton farms, in the forests, or in the creeks. They made a substantial recovery. This attitude would persist and help them survive the agricultural and financial disasters of the 1920s and 1930s. Again, this attitude was a part of their value system, their piety, and their determination to be a part of God's plan.

They were not strangers to grief. Sickness and death were familiar events. They saw tragedy close at hand. The sick were taken care of at home, and when they died, they died at home. The dead were placed in pine boxes made by a local carpenter or in caskets purchased from a village store. The deceased lay for viewing at home in the parlor. There was no funeral parlor in or near The Village. Friends and relatives came to visit before and after the church funeral and the burial service. Some families had burial plots on the grounds of their plantations.

With the arrival of new people in the area and with the founding of the New Wappetaw Presbyterian Church in 1872, there arose a need for a cemetery. The Presbyterians acquired land across Jeremy Creek to establish a burial place. The Methodists obtained adjacent land when their village church opened. People are said to be buried "on the Presbyterian side" or "on the Methodist side," and since there has been a great deal of switching from church to church as families have intermarried or people have gotten mad at ministers, family names on tombstones seem to be distributed at random. They were, in essence, one family and it is fitting that they occupy common ground in the lovely oak grove at the edge of the creek. The feeling is that the dead are in the living company of their kin. One of my cousins insists that if any of us remain to oversee her placement, we should be sure that she is not buried beside a particular kin. Though the two were of different generations, they were close together in age, and they fussed all the time.

Infectious diseases accounted for most illness and death in McClellanville and St. James Santee Parish. Prenatal infant and maternal mortality rates were not much greater than they are now, but overall infant mortality was disastrously high. The "summer diarrhea" was the great killer because neither lay people nor physicians understood the need for fluid replacement. In the first decade of the twentieth century, Thomas Lucas Lofton and Mary Leland Lofton ("Mame") lost four children to summer diarrhea before having two children who matured.

Children who lived to the age of three or four years were, generally, in the clear, but they still had to avoid diphtheria. The communicable throat infection struck communities erratically but with a high mortality rate until immunization became available in the early twentieth century. Measles was not the great killer of whites and blacks as it had been of the Native Americans. Measles had been around Europe long enough to have induced a degree of natural immunity in the whites and blacks. Chicken pox, mumps, and measles became thought of as the routine illnesses or the "usual childhood diseases." Smallpox, the other great killer of the Indians, had been pretty well conquered by the time The Village was founded. The procedure called vaccination served to halt the spread of smallpox epidemics in the United States.

Residents of McClellanville declare there has been little violent crime in the area and blame incidents that have occurred on outsiders. Once, in the relatively prosperous years around World War I, a white man came to town and set up a store in which he sold "Victrolas" and records. He did a lot of business with the blacks and was suspected of selling illegal corn whiskey. One Saturday night, he had a fight with a black customer and died instantly from a knife wound to the neck. The killer was captured the next day by the magistrate and was later tried and sentenced to life in prison. The people of McClellanville felt the killer had done them a favor. A few years later, they secured a pardon for the man, who returned to The Village as something of a hero. For years, the young boys of the town avoided the bloodstained steps of the little store.

It was a group of bad actors from across the swamp who attacked and injured our great-grandfather. Henry Michael Lofton was hale and hearty at the age of seventy-five, but when he tried to stop the "Hell Hole Boys" from attacking one of his servants, he was knifed, leaving one arm paralyzed. Our patriarch was never vigorous thereafter.

Not all violence involved outsiders, however, and local people have been implicated in several incidents. In a western-style shootout, one local man was shot and killed by a storeowner. It seems the transgressor rode into the grocery on horseback, cursing and threatening the proprietor, but the proprietor drew first.

A sad event for the community was the suicide of young Joe Lofton in 1935. This Samuel Joseph Lofton was of the third generation, the son of Henry Michael Lofton, Jr., and Carrie McClellan Lofton. He was my mother's first cousin. Young Joe had recently graduated from The Citadel with an excellent record and was much admired at home. There had been no indications that he was troubled. One rumor suggested he had lost heavily in a poker game, but the tragedy was never explained. His mother, it is said, carried the burden of his death for nearly four decades. It was contrary to the idea that the God of Love has a plan or scheme into which everyone should fit and within which all should contribute. The loss shook the entire village.

Alcoholism was a problem for men in every generation subsequent to that of the founders of The Village. A tradition of self-denial, sermons warning against the evils of alcohol, and legal prohibition of alcohol consumption could not keep young men away from the bottle. Nearly every nuclear family had one or more men affected. Perhaps they felt the prevailing ambivalence concerning pleasure or despaired of making a good living. The society they grew up in was happier and more positive than most, but it had its weaknesses.

From its earliest days to perhaps the 1960s, The Village was a safe place for children, who moved about the town as freely as their parents roamed the forests and marshes. Once they reached puberty, the youths were watched intently but unsuccessfully. At school, the teachers, who often did double duty as Sunday school teachers, took the role of parents, benign but watchful and ready to use the switch or the paddle if one got out of line. Every planned event was chaperoned, making it necessary for older high school and college age young people to do their heavy courting on the sly. I am told they had no trouble making the arrangements.

This good, pleasant, upright society did have its misfits and miscreants. A turn-of-the-century shock for The Village was the rape of a young girl by her own cousins. In the 1930s and 1940s, parents warned their children to stay away from a certain man who was known to have exposed himself to others. McClellanvillians considered these people to be evil beings, for they believed all persons have an evil streak and that the very bad ones had either not been recipients of God's grace or had let themselves fall from grace.

Not all people loved The Village. Some did not find enough to do, while others were disaffected by the petty arguing over the schools or the jealousies prevailing among family members. Mosquitoes, gnats ("no-see-ums"), and ticks discouraged a lot of people. Even now, former residents will ask if my wife, Beverly, is getting along well in The Village. These solicitous inquiries are accompanied by a searching of my face for signs of worry about Beverly, and each inquiry is followed by one of the complaints just mentioned.

By 1920, McClellanville achieved the individuality, personality, and mystique that has held out to this day. Then, agricultural and financial disasters in the 1920s combined to freeze the town and the parish in time. People held on during the '20s, hoping good times would return. The opening of the coastal highway in 1928 promised to bring tourists and other shoppers to The Village, but, in fact, it allowed the villagers to do their shopping in Charleston, which they began to refer to as "town." Residents remained hopeful as the 1930s began but finally had to begin moving out to find work. Census figures show that both the town and the area that was "lower" St. James Santee Parish lost population in the 1930s. McClellanville had been formed in 60 years (1860-1920). It then went dormant for 60 years (1920-1980).

Hot Local Politics

Charleston was home to the aristocrats that Ben Tillman attacked and defeated in his revolution of 1888-90. The city had dominated South Carolina's politics and set the state's cultural tone for over two hundred years but was at odds with the rest of the state after Tillman took over. Everybody else supported Tillman.

Charleston's exclusion from state leadership would last five decades, until Burnet Maybank was elected governor in 1938. During those years, the port city took on the attitude of being standoffish, more cosmopolitan, apart from the communities in the hinterland. In Charleston were a great many people of German extraction plus many Irish Catholics and a good many Jews. These people and the Episcopalians, not a

The Village in 1939

part of the maturation of the mainline Protestant churches, were not so caught up in the agrarian movement and not much interested in prohibition. All around the state, people considered Charleston to be beyond the pale, and Charlestonians were happy to have that distinction.

In 1947, we attended a baseball game in Sumter, where an old friend from the upper state recognized my father and came over to sit with us for a while. In the course of their conversation, Dad commented that people in Moncks Corner and in McClellanville had little in common with folks in Charleston. His friend quickly joked, "Charleston's a foreign country."

Charleston was undeveloped from the industrial standpoint and poverty prevailed. The city was described by one visitor as "a stinking, rotting, unhealthy, poverty-stricken, ill-governed town better known for its vices than its culture." In spite of it, people in McClellanville and other nearby communities went to Charleston to shop. They read the city's venerable *News and Courier* every day. They cursed the old city but looked to it for guidance.

For a while Charleston outdid the rest of the state in fostering political unrest and factionalism. If statewide politics were white-hot, the city's were explosive. Well before the few years of prohibition, Charleston was embroiled in a fight over alcohol sale and consumption. Ben Tillman had insisted on starting the state dispensary system in 1892. This early effort at prohibition lasted until 1907, when it was put to rest, recognized as being entirely corrupt. Through all these years and on through prohibition itself, Charleston had open bars called "Blind Tigers." The existence of these was the focus of the city's political fighting, something for the Charlestonians to concern themselves with since they were removed from the statewide arena.

McClellanville copied Charleston in being a political hot spot. As small as The Village was, it had two Democratic Party clubs: Club One and Club Two. Club One was the stronghold of the Morrisons and the Lelands. Club Two was usually led by the Grahams. The Loftons were loyal to Club One except when involved in family feuds with the Morrisons. The McClellans divided their loyalties between the two factions. Both clubs signed up as many supporters as they could. Lloyd Johnson McClellan recalls that within days after she became eligible by marriage to vote at age sixteen, she was visited by Martin Beckman, who invited her to sign up with Club One.

Town elections were contested regularly, but the school board elections brought the most excitement. The women of McClellanville did not enter into these struggles so avidly. Reminiscences of my mother and her sisters in addition to copies of newspaper articles from old Georgetown and Charleston newspapers reveal that a very pleasant social life was going on in and around The Village. While the men were arguing, the women were supporting one another, and this was true before and after women won the right to vote in 1922. My mother considered the Graham women to be her very best friends. A lot of the politicking that the men did was wasteful and negative, but, to their credit, they were involved in the process. These days we tend to consider local politics unimportant and leave state and national politics to the professionals.

When the United States Supreme Court insisted that representatives of the people be elected under a system that gives equal significance to every vote, the states and counties had to create new subdivisions to which persons could be elected. These have necessarily changed shape and size as populations have shifted. The Charleston County Council has an East Cooper seat, including the areas of Christ Church and St. James Santee Parishes. A representative to the South Carolina House of Representatives serves quite the same area. The area's state senate seat covers a much wider area and seems to change every four years. Presently (2002), the senator for old St. James Santee covers not only the East Cooper part of Charleston County but coastal parts of Georgetown and Horry Counties. Since 1946, no resident of St. James Santee has been elected to any of these bodies. In St. James Santee's present situation, politics is pretty dull. Mt. Pleasant dominates by way of its heavy population density, while McClellanvillians feel abandoned and complain about their taxes.

During the decades of the town's dormancy (1920-1980), hardly any homes were built, most stores and shops closed, and the only business or industry started up was shrimping. On Sundays, you could not buy a cup of coffee, a loaf of bread, or a gallon of gas. It was the classic "quiet village." The only people moving in to stay were a few who had been born and raised there and had been longing to get back. In the '60s and '70s, a few young romantics, singles or couples, dropped out of the "rat race" and moved in to live the "simple life," but they rarely stayed long. In those two decades, two forces profoundly discouraged immigration. The likelihood of school integration suggested to young families that they had better locate in some other district, like Mt. Pleasant. The oil crisis made McClellanville seem even further out of town. And, too, the ever-present mosquitoes discouraged some prospects. On one of my mother's paintings of the Jeremy Creek waterfront, my first cousin once removed added blank verses in which the beauty and serenity of the place are praised. The verses end with the line: "And the mosquitoes keep the place quiet for the natives."

McClellanville is even more atypical now than it was during its formative years. At its beginning, it was just one more small town in a nation of small towns. During the twentieth century, people moved westward and into cities, leaving smaller communities behind. In South Carolina, one might point to Edisto Beach, Rockville, Bluffton, and Murrells Inlet as coastal villages that, for a while, were detached communities where a few families lived and worked. Now, those towns have transformed, turning into resorts where part-time residents play. McClellanville, however, has changed little so far.

Our grandparents and parents, and their fellow residents of The Village, were products of a society that was the norm throughout the South. Their upbringing was like that of the majority of people of our region. They shared the ideals and aspirations of the people of their state and the South. They were remarkably like the the South Carolinian identified in *South Carolina: The WPA Guide to the Palmetto State*, published in 1941. In the book's opening chapter entitled "Who is the South Carolinian?" the essayist actually proposed that behavioral differences are seen on a regional basis in the Palmetto State. Easygoing people are found in the lower state, energetic and industrious people in the up-country, and an "unamalgamated combination of both" exists in the middle of the state. The writer, Louise DuBose, grew up in Clinton, a town in the upper state but near the border of the midsection. DuBose further said that when the geographical differences are minimized, "a composite South Carolinian may emerge."

Her generic South Carolinian has these attributes: Considers possession of wealth secondary to ideas of personal value, has slack economic habits, has personal standards of right and wrong, is well aware of having faults but does not like to hear of them, adheres to traditions of courtesy and dignity, feels honored to help, is neighborly, is dedicated to family, renders service with a scorn for remuneration, is slow to adapt until convinced that some movement is good, and is full of contrasts and antagonisms.

Her South Carolinian sounds familiar to me.

Various commentators, historians, and social scientists have ascribed the above characteristics to the Scotch-Irish people and have added these attributes as well: they are given to extremes of apathy and interest in religion, are suspicious of any authority, and are given to violence. The combined lists pretty well cover the behavioral characteristics of our people, except that our people have not seemed given to violence. The idea that the Scotch-Irish were violent was derived from their history as battlers and fighters in the old country and in the Appalachian Mountains and Piedmont. In the Carolina Lowcountry, the Scotch-Irish behaved rather peacefully and, in race relations, generally took on the paternalistic attitude that the English and the French Huguenots had toward the Blacks.

William Watts Ball, a feisty editor of the *News and Courier* in the 1920s and 1930s, said of his Laurens County relatives: "They are strong and not altogether lovely people. Damn them, they are my people. I am one of them, thank God." That is the way we feel about our people.

3

The Parish

Our family sojourned in Moncks Corner while we grew up. To travel to McClellanville, we could traverse forty miles of country or we could go by way of Charleston, a seventy-mile trip. I preferred the Charleston trip. The roads were paved, there was an exciting ride over the Cooper River Bridge, and there were interesting sights in the harbor. To tell the truth, the Charleston Ice Cream Company was located on Meeting Street, near the Charleston side of the bridge, and my father permitted or promoted stops every time.

Our frequent trips to McClellanville in the 1930s and 1940s gave me opportunities to view the landscape while hearing my parents talk about human efforts in agriculture, politics, religion, and education. I paid not enough attention at the time and, later, found myself wishing I had kept notes about their commentary and made pictures of the scene. Now, I enjoy retracing our route through the country, seeing some of the old landmarks, homes, and bridges. I appreciate the woodland scenes more than I did when I was a boy. I occasionally see a deer or a flock of wild turkeys, and a few years ago I was thrilled to spot a bobcat at the side of the road. I could have benefited more from our slow trips through the forest, traversing much of old St. James Santee Parish. It took a long time for me to understand that people want to be connected to the land and that they desire to feel a part of the history of a place. Now, I go over the old route as often as I can.

On our trips through the country, we first came to Old Moncks Corner, the site of Thomas Moncks' early trading post, situated on high land at the western side of the Cooper River at the point where it divides into Wadboo and Biggin Creeks. At Biggin Creek, the first Santee Canal was made to enter the Cooper River in 1800. Here, also, the Tailrace Canal from Lake Moultrie joined the Cooper River when the Santee-Cooper hydroelectric project was completed in 1941. The 1800 canal was created to assure the transport of cotton and other agricultural goods into Charleston Harbor. The larger canal was dug in 1939-1941 as a part of a project to provide electric power to the Lowcountry and, just as important, to provide jobs in an impoverished area. We boys would get away from school as quickly as we could to watch the creation of the dikes, the powerhouse, and the canal. We watched the mighty Monoghan, an enormous dragline, the largest earth-moving machine made up to that time. We had no idea — indeed, I believe no one imagined — what a difference this project would make to Berkeley County.

Old Moncks Corner was an important place in colonial times because it was an important stop on the Cherokee Trail, the trading path that ran from the Mississippi River, through the mountains of Georgia, through South Carolina, and all the way to the coast at Charleston. South Carolina's Highway 6 follows closely the route of the Cherokee Trail. Starting in Moncks Corner, Highway 6 moves beside the Santee Cooper Lakes, the Santee River, and the Congaree River to Columbia. The trail then went up beside the Saluda River, near the early colonial settlement at Ninety Six, to DeWitts Corner (which became known as Due West and was my father's home), and on through the Piedmont to the mountains. At Moncks Corner, the path started on a high bluff on the Cooper River. Rock outcroppings at the water level gave this place the name "Stony Landing." It is now the site of a state park and home to the Berkeley County Museum.

Stony Landing was the destination of vessels going up the Cooper River, and Moncks Corner was the terminus for South Carolina's first stagecoach line, established in 1766. Old Moncks Corner would ultimately decline in significance, as a public road system was created and, later, as railroad lines were built. A new town grew up at the place where the Cherokee Trail crossed the railroad. The power project that my friends and I "supervised" in the pre-World War II years made the new Moncks Corner a busy place and gave it the basis for burgeoning industrial development and population growth, growth that took place while McClellanville was losing people.

After we crossed the wooden bridges over the Old Santee Canal and over the terminal branches of the Cooper River, we passed the ruins of the parish church of St. John Berkeley Parish, popularly known as "Biggin Church" since it was located near Biggin Creek. St. John Berkeley Parish occupied the central part of the modern Berkeley County. It was settled by people of English origin and Anglican allegiance. The first church on Biggin Hill was built in 1712 and was burned by a forest fire in 1755. It was replaced by a brick structure in 1761 but was burned in 1781 by a retreating British Army unit. The unlucky church was restored after the Revolutionary War but was vandalized during the Civil War and then burned by another forest fire in 1866. Only remnants of the thick walls remain, along with a large cemetery.

From Biggin Church, we moved northeastward to the modern Jamestown, our halfway point. In doing so, we passed through territory that was in St. James Santee Parish before it became part of St. Stephen Parish in 1754. Mostly pineland, the territory had scattered homesteads, all with gardens and outbuildings and a few with small cornfields, but certainly nothing to warrant the term "plantation."

Crossing Highway 41 at Jamestown (in those days, just a crossroad with a store or two plus a railroad station), we were in St. James Santee to stay. The countryside between James- town and McClellanville was, and still is, sparsely settled and rather wild. There were, and still are, pockets of population in unincorporated settlements — Shulerville and Honey Hill — and there are a few tracts of unoccupied land in private hands, but most of the land was taken into the Francis Marion National Forest in the 1930s. In pre-World War II days, the road between Jamestown and McClellanville was noticeably cruder and more difficult than the one we had traversed on the first half of the trip. Low, swampy areas alternated with sandy ridges, and a car could bog down in either. The setting was more beautiful but seemed more dangerous, for this was the road that went near the feared Hell Hole Swamp, the hangout of the Hell Hole Boys, bootleggers who sold corn whiskey.

With two violent events in the late 1920s and early 1930s, the bootleggers of Hell Hole established an enduring reputa- tion of lawlessness for Berkeley County. First, Senator E.J. Dennis was gunned down on the main street of Moncks Cor- ner by an enemy. Second, rival bootleg gangs had a big shootout at the railroad tracks in Moncks Corner. Seven men were killed. My parents, who had just moved our family to Moncks Corner, were shaken. Decades later, the humorist William Price Fox chose Moncks Corner as the locale for some of his tales, one of which was entitled "Moonshine Light, Moonshine Bright."

Moncks Corner had an unsavory reputation, but the boys in Moncks Corner rather looked down on those from around the mythic Hell Hole. We thought they were "hicks," "swamp rats," "country," and were either bootleggers or rustlers of cattle on the open range — an uneducated and violent lot. Yet Honey Hill was an attractive little place, and I always looked forward to passing through it. For a while, it had been a summertime refuge for plantation owners, but the decline of naval stores production and rice planting kept it small. The road through it, on high land, was of white sand. A small store, a small Methodist Church, and eight or ten homes were randomly placed among the pines. The place's distinguishing feature was the uniform whitewashing of the tree trunks around the homes, producing a picturesque village.

In this part of the forest, we could see evidence of logging operations. Tracts of land were clearcut; heavy trucks piled high with timber nearly blocked the road; and the roads were macerated and nearly impassable. In addition, our progress was often halted by herds of cattle standing in the road. The open range remained in effect until the 1950s, and owners allowed their livestock to roam free and forage for themselves. The cows stood dumbly in our path and could not be coaxed or threatened to get out of the way. My father would shout at them, honk the horn, and even nudge them with the car. Nothing would move them except a signal from the bell cow, and she had her own agenda.

In the forest from Jamestown to McClellanville, there were no powerlines or telephone lines. Hardly any vehicles passed through the area, except some mule-drawn wagons and several cars or trucks. The wooden frame houses were small and either unpainted or whitewashed but were mostly well kept and surrounded by the familiar cluster of outbuildings: barns, smokehouses, and toilets.

From Honey Hill, we would descend into Wambaw Swamp, cross a series of wooden bridges (Palmer Bridges), and arrive in "lower" St. James Santee Parish. Immediately, we had to make a choice. If we were going directly to McClellanville, we would stay on the main road (now Highway 45) to cross the Kings Highway and then Highway 17 to enter McClellanville. Very soon, we passed through the "business section" of The Village, consisting of only a few stores. We would pass the school, the Presbyterian and Methodist Churches, and some Victorian homes to reach our home on Jeremy Creek or Aunt Caroline's place (the old Lofton home) on the marsh. It was a very quiet village.

If our destination was Aunt Margie's house at the farm, we would leave Highway 45 and go over Palmer Bridges Road to the Kings Highway. That junction was known as "The Thirty-Two," for it was at the thirty-two-mile mark on the Kings Highway and had been the site of a tavern, a school, and a church in days gone by. Its extensive oak groves and white, sandy roadbeds make this one of the loveliest places in the Lowcountry. From there, we would take the Kings Highway to the southwest. After we rounded a couple of bends, we traversed a 2.2-mile stretch of straight road, called Straight Reach. This portion of the Kings Highway was used as a horse race track in colonial days.

Nearly all of the forest on the McClellanville side of the Wambaw had been Lofton territory. At one time, Henry Michael Lofton owned 11,453 and 1/3 acres of the forest. The passage over Straight Reach was a beautiful drive through a mature forest. None of it was timbered until the 1970s. Before World War II, we would see mature pines bearing slash marks and tin cups for the collection of resin. Workmen took the resin away in large metal containers.

At the end of Straight Reach was Aunt Margie's home, as well as remnants of the old Lofton Community. By the time we arrived, I was ready to hit the ground and get moving. Aunt Margie's farm was self-sufficient. There were fruit and nut trees, a barnyard with cattle and pigs, a cane press, a smokehouse on which were stretched the skins of deer and raccoons, chicken pens, and a garden. The outhouse was a two-seater. A grove of water oaks formed a canopy above the bare front yard. Aunt Margie kept it swept clean, and on the ground, we could play marbles or tease doodlebugs out of their holes. The girls played hopscotch. If we got restless or rowdy, Aunt Margie or our parents would send us off to play elsewhere. From Aunt Margie's home on the Kings Highway, my cousins and I could walk beside fields planted in truck crops to go to Lofton Landing on Doe Hall Creek. A long, hot walk ended when we came from under a canopy of live oaks to stand on a low bluff.

There was the vast marsh — an appealing scene if there ever was one — a few shrimp boats making their way out Five Fathom Creek to Bulls Bay and the ocean, a tugboat on the Intracoastal Waterway moving barges of pulpwood to the paper mill in Georgetown, and the Cape Romain lighthouses in the distance. Our cousins kept a few wooden boats tied up at a rickety dock on Doe Hall Creek. We could go swimming at high tide. In season, the boys would bring in oysters or use

The Cape Romain lighthouses in 1885. The first lighthouse was erected in 1827. The 150-foot-tall light served from 1857 to 1946.

the landing as a base for fishing or flounder-gigging expeditions. We could cross over to the Doe Hall Plantation property next door and see the only indication that Indians had ever been present anywhere along the route from Moncks Corner to the coast: a small oyster shell mound. Such mounds, as well as oyster shell rings in the marsh, were made over a thousand years ago by unknown native Americans.

The things I saw on those trips existed, I believed, for the entertainment of my cousins and me. I did not realize that all these signs of human activity were indicators of desperate efforts by people to keep themselves alive and to keep their holdings intact in difficult times. For this was the 1930s and early '40s, and our part of the country had been battered by the prolonged agricultural depression of the 1920s followed by the Great Depression.

Sometime along the way, I discerned that all was not well with our people and in the country as a whole. My father spoke ominously of hard times. Then, soon after I started attending grammar school in 1937, folks began paying attention to events in Europe. That the Germans were causing trouble was all I knew. Two years later, sitting on the back steps of the school, a couple of us students confidently predicted that the British and the French would save Poland and finish off the Nazis "in two days." Still my father talked about the families in the schools he superintended having trouble making ends meet. After Pearl Harbor, I never heard him doubt that the allies would prevail over the axis powers, but he did suggest that the depression would come back. I began to think of the Great Depression as some infectious disease — it could come on and sweep across the countryside like a plague.

I asked, "Daddy, do you think it will come back?" "Chances are good," he said. Twenty tough years during the prime of his life made him an economic pessimist.

What I saw taking place on those trips in the 1930s and

1940s was the end of an era, the beginning of complete change in the way people made their living. The rural way of life ended for many with the vanishing of the yeoman farmer (the plantation was already long gone) and the decline of small towns. Yet, I did not see, and in retrospect do not believe, that the places I saw on these trips were desolate, as some have said they were. Moncks Corner and McClellanville had taken their licks but were still standing. The countryside in between was depleted of some of its population, but those who remained held on to their precious land and kept their homesteads looking good. They were remarkably confident that better times would be arriving soon. "Underdeveloped" would have been a better term to use in describing the country that we had seen on our trips, and being underdeveloped was its glory.

The war economy and the industrial growth that followed the war allowed the forest community to survive and, eventually, to prosper. Now, as I retrace our rides through the country, I see that most of the forest is owned and managed by the Forest Service. Nearer Moncks Corner, there are new homesteads, prebuilt houses or trailers. Jamestown is now incorporated and holds the "Hellhole Festival" every May. On the McClellanville side of Jamestown, the old, still-scattered homes remain. Though they are old, they are well kept, and one rarely sees a trashy yard. These days, residents drive pickup trucks and sport-utility vehicles. The roads are paved. The concrete bridges are massive and strong, though not rustic and pretty as they used to be.

People long to feel a part of the history of any place, but they need money to survive. Of all the influences that tie people to an area, none is more important than the economic imperative, the need to create wealth. Times change and people have to vary their efforts to keep solvent and hold on to the things they love. Sometimes they pick up and move on. It was, after all, the need to get by or the hope of getting rich that led locals or their ancestors to settle in a certain place.

The Parish

St. James Santee Parish is not a unit of church government or civil government. In using the term "St. James Santee Parish," we refer to the remnant of an area that once had responsibilities in both spheres. This remnant is located about halfway along the coast of South Carolina and consists of an irregularly rhomboidal piece of mainland, about eighteen miles along the coast and twenty miles inland. Attached on the coast are the broad marshes and the narrow barrier islands of Cape Romain.

Even the mainland is low and swampy. Water is everywhere in St. James Santee. The South Santee River is the eastern border of the parish and is reached by driving on U.S. Highway 17 North. This seeming misdirection is explained by two geographical realities: (1) South Carolina's coastline runs not in a north-south direction but from east-northeast to west-southwest and (2) the Santee divides into two rivers (North Santee and South Santee) fifteen miles before it reaches the coast. Between the two rivers is a wide delta, second in size in the United States to the delta of the Mississippi. The Santee is a major river system but is not recognized as such because it has never functioned as a waterway. East of the Mississippi only the Susquehanna River carries more water than the Santee, but our river empties into a shallow bay, which only small boats can cross.

As the parish was originally constituted, its northern or inland border was formed by a bend in the Santee River fifty miles from the coast. When, in 1754, St. Stephen Parish was taken out of St. James Santee, the dividing line was along a public road, which ran from Huger's Bridge on the East Branch of the Cooper River to LeNud's Ferry on the Santee River

The western border of St. James Santee is Awendaw Creek,

Awendaw Bridge. A bridge across Awendaw Creek at this site has always been the gateway to St. James Santee Parish from Christ Church Parish. Photograph and note by Dr. W. H. Johnson, c. 1926.

which is short and narrow but blends into Little Wambaw Swamp and then into Wambaw Swamp

At Cape Romain, the southern border of the parish, inlets lead into a network of tidal creeks in the marsh. Only one of these saltwater creeks — Jeremy Creek at McClellanville — penetrates the mainland for any distance. The creek is deep enough to provide a harbor for the yachts and sailboats that make the journey from the northeast to Florida in the fall and go back in the spring. Those transients use the Atlantic Intra-coastal Waterway, which takes a manmade path alongside the mainland.

The watery boundaries of St. James Santee make it seem to be a sea island, such as those that dot the coastlines of Georgia and South Carolina. It is not an island, but I was not surprised when, in 1992, a second cousin from North Carolina complimented us on the beauty of our marshfront home in McClellanville. She said, "I think your house is the prettiest one on the island."

The Coastal Highway (now U.S. 17), with bridges over the Santee Rivers, was completed in 1928. Before that time, travel in and out of the parish was a major undertaking. The dirt roads were sandy or boggy, the bridges were rickety, and the last stretch of a day-long, forty-mile journey from McClellanville to Charleston was a ferry ride from Mt. Pleasant to the city. Going in the opposite (east-northeast) direction was no easier because the traveler had to ferry across three rivers in making a mere twenty-two-mile trip to Georgetown. As bad as the coastal roads were, they were better than the inland roads because the inland roads had to cross Wambaw Swamp. These roads were impassable for long parts of the year. A map displayed in William Baldwin's novel *The Hard to Catch Mercy* shows an area suspiciously similar to St. James Santee with a swampy area comparable to Wambaw Swamp and a caption stating, "Where the water covers the road in most seasons." We all know that Baldwin was telling how Wambaw Swamp used to flood the dirt road to Honey Hill.

Because the roads were so bad, and because there never was a railroad into McClellanville, freight had to be carried into the parish by boat. But the waterways were not much better than the roads. There was the Santee Path, a water route by which one could go from Charleston Harbor to Santee Bay without going into the ocean, but it wound through a maze of shallow creeks in the marsh behind the barrier islands. In 1950, Thomas Legare ("Nunk") Lofton, my mother's first cousin, had occasion to warn some strangers about one portion of Santee Path. A member of a party of sport fishermen shouted to him, "Is there a lot of water in here?" Nunk stopped gathering oysters, thought about the question for a long time, then shouted back: "Lots of water — but it's spread out real thin."

In the days of sail, a trip from McClellanville to Charleston could take up to a week. When steam engines became available, and even when they were succeeded by the early internal combustion engines, trips to Charleston were overnight affairs. Into the early 1920s, landowners owned shallow draft boats to take furniture and fertilizer to McClellanville and to take their families on shopping trips to Georgetown and Charleston. People who grew up in McClellanville and St. James Santee considered trips to be great undertakings. When, in 1951, my friend Jimmy Bradley and I helped my mother into the car to start a nine-hour drive to Washington, DC, she exclaimed, "Thank goodness, we'll have paved roads all the way!"

Although it may sound illogical, considering what has been recorded about travel in St. James Santee Parish, the main road along the Carolina coast of colonial times passed through the parish. The road was a segment of the Kings Highway, which extended from the New England colonies to Georgia. In St. James Santee, the highway followed the route of a trading path used by the native Americans. The road meandered, keeping on high ground as much as possible, but passing through swampy areas at times. In St. James Santee, it was a rough ride, but George Washington traveled over it while making his presidential tour of the states. Washington breakfasted at Hampton Plantation but did not linger, moving on toward Charleston.

The 1928 highway moved away from the Kings Highway to run closer to McClellanville, so the greater part of the Kings Highway in St. James Santee Parish is still unpaved. The countryside it passes through is heavily wooded and much like it was 200 years ago. Regrettably, the Kings Highway is named Old Georgetown Road, which is correct enough but does not emphasize the road's importance in yesteryear.

Two men and their mule-drawn wagon on The Kings Highway near McClellanville, March 1950.

Because most of lower St. James Santee is low, coastal flooding is common when the bimonthly higher tides occur with the new and full moons. There are patches of land high and dry enough for farming or supporting orchards of pines, but one is never far from low areas where there are cypress or live oak trees. Sandy ridges are scattered about, and on these grow stubby blackjack oaks, like those in the sandhills above South Carolina's fall line. Where the salt marsh meets the mainland, there are subtropical trees and shrubs — palmettos, cedars, wax myrtles, and marsh elders.

The landscape and the seascape provide considerably more variety than is seen in the other parts of the state. There are many sites from which an observer can relish open, natural, and unoccupied vistas. The setting is picturesque, in a haunting sort of way. Isolation and poverty kept St. James Santee in a nearly natural state, and the beauty of it has had a great effect on the men and women of the place.

How the Parish Got Its Owners, Its Borders, and Its Name

One of our sons observed that his grandmother, my mother, always greeted us with cheer and then a quick complaint about her taxes. "Dad," he asked, "why is Grandmother so hung up about taxes? Doesn't everybody pay tax?" I answered, "It's a tradition around here — all these people hate paying taxes."

I have heard persons in every generation complain: "Why should I pay this tax? What do they do for us up here? Nothing!" This attitude, I believe, comes from the parish's situation — geographically detached, economically poor, moved about from one governmental unit to another, and rarely represented in places of power. This parish always has been Carolina's outback.

Here, it is important to explain how St. James Santee and South Carolina's other parishes came and went.

The Fundamental Constitutions, the grand design for Carolina drawn up for the Lord's Proprietors, called for counties to serve as units of government. After the colony had shown a little growth, the proprietors, in 1685, ordered the creation of three rectangular counties — Craven, Berkeley, and Colleton. Later, a fourth county, Granville, would be established in the Beaufort area. In 1685, almost all of the people in the colony resided in and about Charlestown in the central county — Berkeley — which extended from the Stono River in the south to the Seewee River (now Awendaw Creek) in the north. A few white people were daring to live in Colleton County, south of the Stono River, but not one resided in Craven County, which was north of the Seewee River. Craven County had no permanent white residents until that year, 1685, when French Huguenots began moving up the Santee River to create a small community.

Carolina's parishes were created in 1706 at the insistence of the aggressive and politically astute "Goose Creek Men," a faction that came mostly from Barbados and some of whom settled around Goose Creek in Berkeley County. Establishment of the Anglican Church as the state religion had been anticipated in the planning of Carolina, but there had been no move to accomplish this until 1704. The Barbadians were adherents to the Anglican Church and would have used establishment to disenfranchise the Dissenters. The crown intervened to assure that Dissenters had the right to vote and hold office.

Six of Carolina's ten original parishes were given the names of those in Barbados. Two were called St. James and were distinguished from one another by the addition of geographic suffixes — St. James Goose Creek Parish and St. James Santee Parish. (From the beginning, Carolinians rendered the names of these parishes different ways — following the name James

Hampton Plantation on the South Santee River

The Wedge Plantation, South Santee River, about 1921. Constructed in 1826 by William Lucas, son of Jonathan Lucas.

with an apostrophe, a comma, or a colon. Today, we occasionally see a hyphen used at that point. I will use the simplest possible form: St. James Santee.)

St. James Santee was the second of the original ten parishes to receive its charter; only St. Phillips in Charlestown qualified earlier. In all, by the mid-1800s, twenty-three parishes would be established across the Lowcountry and into the midlands.

The parishes were to support the Church of England but soon found themselves responsible for education and for the relief of the poor. In 1716, the parishes were made electoral districts. The organization of a militia came to be a function of the parishes. Properties were recorded as being in such-and-such a county, but even the recording was done in Charlestown. There was nothing left for a county to do, but the proprietary counties existed, on paper, until 1795.

Carolina was nearly lost in the Indian War (Yemassee War), which began in 1715 and lasted over three years. Most of the fighting took place south of Charlestown. When the Yemassees and their allies were vanquished, the victorious Carolinians complained that the proprietors did not support them in the conflict and left them saddled with debt. In 1719, they petitioned their king to take over the colony. He listened and, in what has been called "The First American Revolution," proprietary management ended. Carolina became a crown colony. Not until 1729 did the proprietors give up title to the place in return for title to lands in Virginia, and in that transaction, South Carolina and North Carolina were officially separated.

The Parish Church of St. James Santee, completed in 1772. It was informally known as "The Brick Church" or "The Wambaw Church." This photograph was taken in 1930.

After the Indian War, the colony languished for a decade while damaged plantations were repaired and abandoned   areas were reoccupied. Seeing how weak and vulnerable Carolina was, the colony's new leaders decided to push for population growth by spreading into previously unoccupied areas. "Poor Protestants" from various European countries were invited to occupy any of eleven townships on the frontier.

One of the first townships settled was across the Santee

River from St. James Santee Parish. Beginning in 1732, Scotch-Irish Presbyterians came into Williamsburg Township, and among them was one Archibald McClellan. In 1756, McClellan moved over to participate in the building of a new church for St. James Santee Parish. In 1771, not knowing what Angel de Villefane had said about the place, he set about lending his name to a part of the parish. He bought land and established his plantation on Jeremy Creek.

Some other Carolina townships received settlers who contributed to our particular family. The Stroman (originally Straumann) family, my grandmother's kin, came into Orangeburg Township with the German Swiss. The Bonners, my father's ancestors, came to South Carolina to join Scotch-Irish families who were settling the last township to be occupied, Boonesboro, in what is now Abbeville County. Most of these Scotch-Irish entered Pennsylvania, migrated to Virginia, and then moved down the Great Philadelphia Wagon Road to the "Long Cane" community in Boonesboro. William and Mary Bonner and their three children took a more direct route from Northern Ireland to the Long Cane community. They sailed on the ship *Nancy* to Charlestown in 1765 and joined relatives who had taken the long way to Boonesboro. In 1780, James Bonner, their son, was old enough to join the militia and fight the British.

South Carolina declared its independence in 1776. A second constitution, drawn up during the revolution, deprived Anglican Churches of financial support by way of parish government but left the parishes intact as governmental units. In the upper state, still the frontier at that time, judicial districts served as governmental units.

South Carolina seceded from the United States in 1860 and joined the Confederate States of America in 1861. In an arrangement that did not last long, St. James Santee Parish was in Charleston District, State of South Carolina, Confederate States of America. The post-Civil War Constitution of

August 1865 put all governmental functions under judicial districts, essentially doing away with the parishes. The Reconstruction Constitution of 1868 officially made the parishes a thing of the past, did away with the districts, and turned again to counties as the units of local government. A very large Charleston County was formed from Berkeley and Charleston Districts.

White South Carolinians, who would be called "the Bourbons," regained control of the state in 1876-1877. They were determined to alter some of the political units created during Reconstruction. In 1882, the overlarge Charleston County was divided into Berkeley County and Charleston County, with Berkeley taking over all lands east of the Cooper River. The former St. James Santee lands were now in Berkeley County. The county seat was in Mt. Pleasant, in what had been Christ Church Parish.

But because the Wambaw Swamp effectively separates the coastal and the inland halves of old St. James Santee, the coastal or "lower" portion did not remain in Berkeley County for long. "Lower" St. James Santee and all of Christ Church Parish switched to Charleston County in 1892. "Upper" St. James Santee is in Berkeley County, where Moncks Corner is the county seat. This division along Wambaw Creek, the last cut for St. James Santee, left McClellanville and "lower" St. James Santee dominated by the more populous parts of Charleston County.

Through all these changes, the local people continued to say that they lived in St. James Santee Parish. When Henry Michael Lofton's daughter, Elizabeth Ann, died in 1874, the official records stated that she was buried in St. James Santee Parish. When Henry Lofton ran for the Berkeley County House of Representatives in 1890, a newspaper article told of his being St. James Santee Parish's delegate to the county convention. Wills and deeds continued, for decades, to state that properties were in St. James Santee Parish, adding either

Berkeley or Charleston County. The current residents continue to honor the old parish. There is now a St. James Santee Elementary School, a St. James Santee Health Center, and a St. James Santee Historical Society.

Residents of St. James Santee Parish, founded in 1706 and abolished in 1868, have never let go of the memory of the times when they had their own political division to attend to — and, it seems, will never get used to paying taxes.

4

The People

The small party of Englishmen who founded Carolina intended to establish their base on Port Royal Sound, which was known to have a good harbor, but they came first to Seewee Bay — now called Bulls Bay. The English, unlike de Villefane, found inhabitants present. The Seewee Indians gave the English a warm welcome. (I will use the longer of the two currently accepted forms of spelling, "Seewee" rather than "Sewee," because the longer word better suggests the pronunciation.) Immediately, the Seewees asked the newcomers to protect them from the Westoes, an aggressive nomadic tribe who were rumored to be cannibalistic and who had recently moved near Port Royal Sound. The Seewees brought to the prospective colonists the chief of the Kiawah tribe, who repeated the warning about the Westoes and invited the foreigners to settle in his territory. Thus, the first permanent European settlement in the Carolinas was made in April 1670 at the place they called Albemarle Point, on the Ashley River. Very soon, the proprietors changed the name of the settlement to Charlestown, telling King Charles II that the town was named for him.

The Natives

Today, we have little evidence that the people who greeted the English at Bulls Bay were here at all. Only some pottery fragments and some conch shell implements show they were present. Other Native Americans had moved in and out of the area for up to 12,000 years, some of them leaving the oyster shell rings in the marsh and mounds, such as I saw at Doe Hall Plantation on the mainland.

The Seewees spoke a Sioux dialect and are counted among the Eastern Sioux who had lived in southeastern North America for at least four centuries. In 1670, Sioux tribes occupied most of South Carolina above the Cooper River and up to the Piedmont, with the Catawbas being the largest and the dominant tribe among them. Southeast of the Charleston area were the Muskhogean tribes, whose relatives extended beyond the Mississippi River. In the Piedmont, there was one large Iroquois nation, the Cherokees. At the time the English came on the scene, the Sioux tribes were under pressure from the aggressive and culturally advanced tribes to the south and west. Furthermore, all the coastal tribes, Sioux or Muskhogean, were depleted by tribal warfare, by Spanish slave raids, and by epidemic diseases, especially smallpox, acquired from various European explorers. It is believed that there were no more than 40,000 Native Americans residing in South Carolina when the English came.

The Seewees moved about in lower St. James Santee, some times staying on the coast to fish or gather shellfish and other times living inland where they hunted and grew crops of corn, squash, pumpkins, and other vegetables. In 1701, the English traveler John Lawson found one of their villages on what is now called Awendaw Creek. Indian Field Plantation on the South Santee was so named because it was the site of a major Seewee village. When Angel de Villefane and his Spanish explorers came to look around, the Seewees may have been dwelling at one of their villages away from the coast or may have been hiding out.

Nobody knows how many Seewees there were in 1670. John Lawson reported that they were few in number when he visited in 1701, but he believed they had once been a large tribe. A few years before Lawson's visit, a large number of the Seewees ventured to England to seek an audience with the crown. They wanted to get compensation for losses in trade with some unscrupulous Englishmen, but their inadequate vessels sank not long after they set out to sea. The few survivors were sold as slaves.

The Seewees and their immediate Native American neighbors disappeared. Governor Nathaniel Johnson's report to the crown in 1708 did not mention them. In 1715, when the Yemassee War began, there were fifty-seven of them. There are no indications that the Seewees went to war against the English, but they were not heard from again. The Wando tribe of Christ Church Parish vanished at the same time. The Santees chose to take the side of the Yemassees and harassed, or at least threatened, the Huguenot settlement on the Santee River. They disappeared.

The Seewee people did leave some place names. Jeremy Creek at McClellanville bears the name of their chief, but it is suspected that "Jeremy" was a name given to him by the English. The tribal name was used to identify the body of water where the first English settlers stopped briefly — Seewee Bay — but the name was changed later to Bulls Bay. Likewise, Seewee River had its name changed to Awendaw Creek. Now there is a Seewee Bay, but it is smaller than Bulls Bay and is located in what used to be Christ Church Parish. The poor Seewees were never shown respect.

Some Native American people survived the European takeover of their homeland (the Edistos and the Catawbas exist as organized tribes today and, around the state, descendants of other tribes are gathering to celebrate their past), but there is not a person in old St. James Santee or elsewhere who traces his or her ancestry to the departed Seewees. The Seewees left us no cultural tradition or influence. So completely were they removed that the St. James Santee community bears just traces of their long presence.

The Huguenots

In my youth, I heard tales of a lost colony of French people living way back in the swamps. As we boys sat around telling tales of fish caught or deer killed, the conversation would always get around to snakes and alligators and to whether there were bears and cougars living in the swamp. After that, somebody would claim that an uncle or brother knew for sure that there were French people lost or hiding out in Hell Hole Swamp. They had been seen paddling their dugout canoe, rounding a bend in a creek, and moving out of sight, or they had been heard at a distance. The tales were easy to believe at that time. The French had been there; we knew that for sure.

It was a gallant, inspired, and determined group of French Protestants who made the first white settlement on St. James Santee lands. They have been further characterized as cultured, thrifty, and industrious, but if one were to see the place they moved to, one would think they were unsuspecting suckers and great fools for letting themselves get misdirected to such a wild place.

In 1685, the French began moving onto lands offered by the king and the Lord's Proprietors, settling on bits of high land along the southwest side of the Santee River, about fifteen miles above Santee Bay. Across the river from them stretched hundreds of miles of wilderness plus a still potent and potentially hostile tribe of Santee Indians. Behind them, blocking their way to Charlestown, was Hell Hole Swamp — already known by that name. All around them were strange, dangerous beasts and insects galore. They must have realized that they had been set up as a buffer, an outpost, protecting the central part of the colony. One would think the French would have been angry with their benefactors. They were not angry, for they were refugees, and were relieved if not happy to be there. Torture and death might have been their lot had they remained in their homeland. Also, they must have had a good idea of what they were getting into. Surely they had the advice and encouragement of those Huguenots who had immigrated five years earlier, settling in Charlestown or on the East Branch of the Cooper River. The French did not come up the Santee in a single large boat as the Pilgrims did in landing at Plymouth Rock, nor did they move in a big caravan as the Mormons did on their trek to Utah. The newcomers moved in over a period of three or four years.

There were not many of them. Some say 180 families made homes along the river, but a survey made in 1699 reported only 111 French individuals on Santee out of just 438 French in the entire province. Two years later, John Lawson estimated there were fifty families in the area, which was being called "French Santee." The Huguenots made up for their lack of numbers with a degree of organization and cohesion that others in the province (an unruly mixture of Englishmen — Anglicans and Dissenters — plus many who were unchurched) did not have. The Huguenots had services to sell — many were artisans who could build homes, form tools, or make clothes. They also found themselves to have the balance of power between the rival English factions, both of which first opposed or resented the coming of the French but soon began to court them.

The French were aliens, but they were not just people of one country living in a foreign land — they had no country. They had been run out of France and, although they had lived in an English province for varying times, they were not English subjects. Some of them had abandoned France for England years or decades before coming to the new world, but the majority of those who went up the Santee were among the flood of refugees who rushed out of France after the revocation of the Edict of Nantes in 1685. Most of these immigrants spoke only French when they came and continued to do so, using French in their worship services and ordinary discourse. They quickly saw that there would be advantages in citizenship, and when, in 1697, the English offered naturalization, most of them accepted. Not long thereafter, the French on the Santee would seek membership in the Church of England, a status which would give financial support for their church and give them political power in St. James Santee Parish at its establishment in 1706.

On the Santee, the Huguenots endured. Neither there nor elsewhere in Carolina were they successful in making wine, silk, or olive oil (which is what they were charged to try), but they grew crops and killed game enough for the table, raised cattle and hogs, traded with neighboring Native Americans, began making and selling naval stores, grew crops of indigo, and learned to cultivate rice on inland swamp land. Foreign visitors reported finding them to be happy and rather prosperous though homesick, hoping they might get invited to return to the old country. Of course, they never did go home.

The Huguenots were expected to build a town called Jamestown, but the town never came to be. The French settlers could have selected town lots free of charge but were content to live on their plantations. No more than three homes were built in the proposed village. A church may have been constructed but, if so, it was soon abandoned. A village did appear along little Echaw Creek, a tributary of the Santee, and a Huguenot church was added there. In 1820, Echaw was designated the seat of Craven County. It never functioned as such. Echaw, the town, appears on maps produced as late as 1860. It disappeared into the forest by 1900.

French Santee did not last long. The Huguenots had little high land to work with and were discouraged by the frequent flooding of low areas along the Santee. Their Native American neighbors were disappearing, so there were fewer people to trade with. By 1720, most of the French people were moving up the river to higher land or were totally abandoning the river to live in Charlestown or other parts of Carolina. When, in 1754, the parish was divided into the French Santee half (still called St. James Santee Parish) and the English Santee half (called St. Stephen Parish), there were more people in the new side than in the old. The act of separation called for the wealthier St. Stephen Parish to support the poor people among their former parishioners downstream.

In 1756, work began on the new parish church for St. James Santee. It was placed on the coastal side of Wambaw Creek, where rice plantations were proliferating. The former parish church at Echaw became a "Chapel of Ease," and it held out for a few decades, until nearly all of the French people had cleared out. Services were held in the Chapel of Ease in the early 1800s, but the building fell into disrepair. In 1831, the vestry, seated at the Wambaw church, approved its demolition.

A few French families held on to their properties around Echaw through the end of the Civil War, but the exodus from that part of St. James Santee was complete by 1900. French Santee was no more. In 1861, the DuPre family dismantled its house at Echaw and moved it to the Jeremy Creek waterfront in McClellanville. The house served first as a summer home for the marshfront plantation, Palmetto, and later was the family's primary residence.Because Archibald McClellan's first plantation home burned, the DuPre House is the oldest structure in McClellanville.

In 1911, Santee River planter David Doar made a pilgrimage to Echaw and became a witness to the complete disappearance of the French. He wrote, "It took me a buggy ride of nine hours, through the most Godforsaken, uninhabited, dreary country I have ever seen. The old roads and land-

Nathan Legaré, d. 1801. His Huguenot family became Congregationalists.

marks so blocked and defaced, since I was there 20 years ago, that I was lost more than once. It was a sad ride to me and very depressing to see this old land of the Huguenots, once teeming with plenty and prosperity, with a generous and hospitable people enjoying each other's company and every happiness, now utterly devastated and deserted, given over to beasts, reptiles, and birds, even the forests gone and scarcely a human met with during a day's drive. They say no country is great without its ruins; this is probably true, for it shows a great past, but God forbid that I should witness many more times, such ruins, or go through what I felt, as I stood amid the tangled wilderness where once stood the church of our Parish and of our forefathers, and the crumbling desecrated graves of the sturdy men and gentle, helpful women who worshipped here." (David Doar, recorded in Henry A. M. Smith, "The Inscriptions on the Tombstones at the old Parish Church of St. James's

Santee, Near Echaw Creek," *South Carolina Historical Magazine* 12: 153, 1911.)

There are many people who now think it is not bad that the great forests and swamps of St. James Santee, which have been a part of the Francis Marion National Forest since the 1930s, have been allowed to return to a nearly natural state. And one suspects that the Huguenots were not as happy as was suggested. After all, they left for greener pastures. But Doar's sadness at the absence of the Huguenots is a tribute to the reputation those people established in St. James Santee Parish and the rest of Carolina.

Now I know that the French are extinct in St. James Santee, but they left a tradition of competence, a genteel and civilized attitude, and the myth or mystique of a wealthy and happy society. Folks in the Carolina Lowcountry cherish any Huguenot connection.

The Loftons have French Santee Huguenot ancestors — DuBose, Couillandeau, Bonneau, Sasseau, Videau, DuBliss, Fougereau, Mauze, Burgeaud — but the Huguenots dearest to us did not come from French Santee. Our most direct and favorite French progenitor was Solomon Legare (and we, like those who bear the name, are quick to say that this person had no kinship or resemblance to anyone named *Simon Legree*). Solomon Legare came to Charlestown in 1680 and stayed there. He had married a Dissenter, either in England or in New England, and he and his family kept allegiance to the reformed tradition. His descendants moved to communities where Dissenters were abundant: Colleton County and Christ Church Parish. After the Civil War, they came to St. James Santee Parish where, although the family name has died out, it is used as a given name of individuals.

The Africans

The next people to come to St. James Santee were the Africans, and they did not come willingly.

Slavery in English Carolina was instituted before the first settler came. The Fundamental Constitutions of 1669 provided the legal basis for the practice, which had been followed by all the European nations having colonies in the Caribbean and in South America. Three slaves were among that first boatload of settlers who came to Carolina from Barbados in 1670. More were brought in from Barbados over the next decade. Then large numbers were imported when the English began moving into the countryside and needed hands to till the land or harvest timber. The cultivation of rice created a great demand for labor, and by 1708, when the first counting was made, blacks were in the majority in Carolina. In all, from the age of discovery to the 1800s, at least 10,000,000 West Africans were sold into slavery in the New World. A small fraction, about 400,000, came to the English colonies of North America. In addition, many Indians were enslaved by the Europeans.

Whereas it was the English Barbadians who introduced slavery to the colony, other immigrant groups, including the Huguenots and the Dissenters, also utilized the practice. The Quakers, almost alone, opposed slavery and left the colony when they saw they could not discourage it.

The first slaves in St. James Santee Parish were likely those who accompanied the few white traders who worked in the area. As soon as the Huguenots began making naval stores and planting rice and indigo, they brought in large numbers of laborers, and the place has had a substantial black majority ever since. In 1720, there were in St. James Santee Parish 42 "inhabitants" plus 584 slaves, while the province as a whole was home to 9,000 whites and 12,000 slaves. In 1757, a counting of the population for the purpose of determining the numbers of men who could serve in the militia revealed that there were 35 such white men and 382 slaves in St. James Santee Parish. In St. Stephen Parish, which had been created three years earlier, there were more ablebodied white men (47) and slightly fewer slaves (332).

A roughly 9:1 proportion of blacks to whites would remain in St. James Santee for nearly 200 years, through the eras
of indigo, rice, and cotton and until the collapse of agriculture
in the 1920s. Then there was a wholesale migration of blacks
to northern cities but just a small loss of whites from the area,
followed by six decades of economic stagnation, during which
the population stood still as younger people of both races left
to find work elsewhere. Since 1960, the census has counted
the coastal, or "lower," section of St. James Santee along with
that part of Christ Church Parish that lies between Wando
Neck and Awendaw Creek, an area quite similar to St. James
Santee. The 1960 census showed a 3.5:1 proportion of blacks
to whites in the combined areas. During the 1970s and the
1980s, there was some migration into the combined areas as
people began to use McClellanville and Awendaw as bedroom
communities. By 1990, the ratio of blacks to whites had
dropped to 2.4:1.

The high proportion of blacks to whites, which for so
long existed throughout Carolina's coastal parishes, was a
creation of the plantation system. In St. James Santee, two
sorts of plantations developed: rice plantations appeared along
the Santee River, while indigo and cotton plantations were
built along the marshfront. After the Civil War, the blacks
acquired property and made their homes on the periphery of
the plantations where they had worked. A few followed the
whites, who were steadily moving from their main residences
on plantations to The Village of McClellanville. Thus, there
are pockets of blacks scattered about old St. James Santee.
Homes of black people are concentrated at South Santee and
Germantown, where there were rice plantations on the river,
and at Tibwin and Buck Hall, where there were cotton plantations on the edge of the marsh, and on the outskirts of
McClellanville. Housing is segregated. There is not much
chance this pattern will change because there is little privately
owned land left. Most of it was sold into the national forest
during the Great Depression.

The Africans have had a great influence on every aspect of culture in the Americas, in the United States, in the Carolinas, and in the South Carolina Lowcountry. Their impact has been greatest in places like St. James Santee, where they have been in the majority, and where for generation after generation, they and the white people were constantly in contact, working at the same things and knowing one another intimately, though this was not on an equal or egalitarian basis. The whites were the bosses or leaders, while the blacks were at first slaves and later employees. But the races were at least linked together as the blacks worked on the plantations and farms and in the homes of the white people. Although the history of their relationship might have made the races bitter enemies, a measure of affection developed between them, and this has lasted even though the races began to separate when agriculture collapsed in the 1920s.

The races live apart. Now, however, the blacks are beginning to share political power and influence while they seek equal opportunity in education and employment.

The Rest of the Occupants of St. James Santee

After the entry of the Huguenots, there were no organized or planned migrations of white people into St. James Santee. Throughout the three centuries since the Huguenots arrived, people have moved in and out at random, following different trends or perceived opportunities, hoping to make a fortune or trying to get by. At no time did people rush in. There have been no booms in this parish.

There have been long periods during which people sharing certain economic, social, and religious ideals found themselves living together in St. James Santee. During these times, informal groups of people set the cultural tone in the parish and dominated its political life. To identify these people, I use my own terms: "Aristos" and "Theos." The term "Aristos" is short for "Aristocrats," those who govern because they are members of a small and privileged class. The term "Theos" is a contraction of "Theodemocrats," those who govern a community according to the revealed word of God.

The Aristos held sway from 1706 to the Civil War (1861). The Theos were in charge from the end of the Civil War (1865) to the onslaught of Hurricane Hugo (1989). The change in dominance from the first group to the second did not occur suddenly or violently and did not occur as the result of any mass migrations in or out. The Aristos gradually yielded control to the Theos. Currently, we sense a loosening of control by the Theos. The Theos are sharing leadership with the African Americans, who have stayed in place, and with a new kind of white resident. These newcomers, whom I call the "Neos," are a heterogeneous people and defy characterization as yet.

The Aristos

Beginning in 1706, at the time the Goose Creek Men seized power through the establishment of the Anglican Church, Carolinians began taking ownership of large blocks of previously unoccupied land. A long argument over whether land was owned by the colonists or was rented to them by the proprietors had been decided in the colonists' favor. The province had prospered for a decade. The entrepreneurs of that day, betting on the expansion of population that seemed sure to come, bought up land they did not use right away. Logically, they acquired riverfront or marshfront property, places that could be reached by water.

The Yemassee War delayed development. It took three decades, until the 1730s, for the new regime to bring in more settlers. There followed a new period of prosperity. Plantations began to produce the colony's first great staples — rice and indigo. The entrepreneurs established rice plantations on the South Santee River and used marshfront lands as indigo-producing plantations. St. James Santee became a plantation parish and an Anglican stronghold. In other parishes, such as Christ Church Parish and the several parishes in old Colleton County, many of the plantation people were Dissenters — either Congregationalists or Presbyterians.

The rice-producing plantations that appeared along the South Santee River were successful, though they were never quite as productive as the rice plantations on the Waccamaw River. From the 1730s and 1740s until the Civil War, South Santee was the center of activity in lower St. James Santee Parish. Plantations along the marshfront struggled at first to make indigo or naval stores but would later thrive as cotton producers.

The riverfront plantations were rather self-sufficient. The owners had homes in Charlestown and spent long periods away from the parish. They did spend time together, however, so it can be said that they had a community. They had summer homes on Cedar Island at Santee Bay. They had horse races. They worshipped together, especially after the new parish church was built near Wambaw Creek. They voted at the parish church. They set up a militia. Aside from their service in the militia and on a commission to maintain public roads, local residents were not involved in local government. There was no local government, for all governmental functions were performed in Charlestown. Plantation children were educated at home or went abroad to study. Public education was not high on the list of interests of the plantation people, but by the early 1800s, there were two free schools in the parish.

The plantation system can be faulted for having initiated slavery in Carolina, but the responsibility for slavery cannot be laid at the feet of the Anglicans alone. It must be remembered that slavery was not an action of a single ethnic or religious group nor was it something that happened in a single parish or county. Anglicans were as active as any of the Dissenter groups in providing religious instruction for their slaves.

The Aristos have been criticized for being more interested

in the acquisition of wealth than in the creation of a good society. They were not alone. Europeans of all nationalities and
all church affiliations were in the expansive, acquisitive mode
in that era.

The accomplishments of the Aristos are praiseworthy. From
the beginning, they exhibited the passion and the capacity for
self-rule and self-determination, which have been characteristics of English society. This attitude eventually led to freedom for Carolina and the other North American colonies.
Also, there was a positive side to Anglican acquisitiveness.
They were willing to allow any and all white people to achieve
self-realization, as long as they did it on their own.

The dominance of affairs in St. James Santee Parish by the
Anglicans and their allies came with their ownership of the
land and their relative wealth. They did not constitute nobility, for they did not inherit titles or positions, but they were a
privileged minority. They were a *kind* of aristocracy, so I call
them "Aristos." In St. James Santee, Anglican planters kept
alive the genteel tradition instituted by the Huguenots, and
that influence is felt to this day.

The Theos

The next white people who populated the parish were less
homogenous than the Aristos. They came in at various times,
from different directions, from different national groups, and
from a variety of religious bodies. Some of these people just
showed up and left no record of where they came from. Some
were overseers for the plantation owners, some owned cotton farms, and some were yeoman farmers, teachers, ministers, physicians, innkeepers, cattlemen, lumbermen, producers of naval stores, carpenters, hunters, laborers, and maids.
They were more dispersed around inland areas than were the
plantation people who lived on the Santee River or along the
marsh.

These varied people responded to the social and religious

trends pervading the South to form a homogenous, stable society that lasted a long time and is standing now on its traditions. McClellanville was populated by these people just before, during, and after the Civil War, so society in The Village fairly reflected the ideals and standards of these mainline Protestants — Presbyterians and Methodists. They did indeed think that in the creation of their society, they were honoring the revealed will of God, and they justly deserve the appellation "Theodemocrats."

Some Theodemocrats were created on the spot by the process of religious conversion. Most of St. James Santee Parish's Methodists came from the Anglican Church, which became the Protestant Episcopal Church after the 1780s. Presbyterians began arriving in the mid-1800s and, after the Civil War, began buying up the marshfront plantations and converting them to cotton production. Many Presbyterian immigrants to St. James Santee Parish were descendants of the New England Congregationalists — the old Puritans — who settled at Wappetaw, in the Christ Church Parish area. These families became interconnected and were the major source of population for McClellanville. Our Lofton ancestors joined them.

The Lofton Family

The Loftons provide an example of how these people, the Theodemocrats, came into St. James Santee Parish. We are not certain when the first family members came, where they came from, or what they came to do. We do know that the first Loftons made connections in the parish and that those connections made it possible for their descendants to return and take refuge there after a cataclysmic confrontation with disease and a losing fight with the Union army.

Records of the St. Stephen Episcopal Church reveal that Samuel Herd Lofton, born April 26, 1819, was baptized in that church in July 1819. The records further state that the

boy's father, Samuel Joseph Lofton, was born in South Carolina in 1798. Samuel Herd Lofton's mother was Mary, but her
maiden name and her place and date of birth were not recorded.

In 1822, Samuel Joseph Lofton purchased land in St. James
Santee Parish, Craven County, from Mark Lofton, about whom
we have no further information. Samuel Joseph's 1825 will
gives no clue as to who he was and where he came from but
tells us that his property, including four slaves, was left to his
wife Mary, to his son Samuel Herd, and to a daughter, Harriett
Ann Lofton.

The word passed down to my generation was that Samuel
Joseph Lofton came to the South Carolina Lowcountry from
eastern North Carolina. This association seems likely. A large
family of Loftins lived there, and some have changed the family
name to Lofton.

The originator of this Loftin family was Leonard Loftin,
who was born in Pennsylvania in 1664 and moved to North
Carolina sometime before 1694. He was, therefore, one of
the earliest settlers of that state. The lineage possibly continued as follows: through Benoni Loftin and through Elkannah
Loftin, both of whom remained in North Carolina; through
Samuel Lofton who moved to Ninety-Six District, South
Carolina, after serving as an officer in the American army during the Revolution (and who changed the spelling of the
name); through Samuel Joseph Lofton who lived in St.
Stephen Parish; to the Samuel Herd Lofton who was baptized in St. Stephen Episcopal Church in August 1819. It is
the connection between Samuel Lofton of Ninety-Six and
Samuel Joseph Lofton that is not clear: it is not certain that
one was the father of the other.

We know a lot about Samuel Herd Lofton and his descendants. Samuel Herd Lofton and Susan Ann Lowry of
Christ Church Parish married in 1839. They lived at first in
the Suttons community in Prince Frederick Parish (across the

Santee from Jamestown), but they owned over 3,000 acres of land in St. James Santee and St. Stephen Parishes. Samuel Herd Lofton raised cattle. It was the custom then, and into the mid-twentieth century, to allow cattle to roam freely throughout the forests. Four children, three boys and one girl, were born to the couple while they lived in Suttons. In about 1850, Lofton sold all but a few hundred acres of his rural properties and moved the family to Mt. Pleasant, South Carolina, so the children could attend the Mt. Pleasant Academy. The couple's fifth child, their second girl, was born in Mt. Pleasant on December 31, 1851. Two more sons came later. The Lofton children were

> Henry Michael Lofton – February 9, 1840 – Suttons
> John Marion Lofton – June 16, 1845 – Suttons
> Mary Ann Lofton – November 19, 1847 – Suttons
> Samuel Joseph Lofton – 1849 – Suttons
> Jenny Lulu Lofton – December 31, 1851 – Mt.
>   Pleasant
> Robert G. Lofton –1853 – Mt. Pleasant
> George E. Lofton –1855 – Mt. Pleasant

The Loftons were slaveholders, as Samuel's parents had been. The Lofton household included servants identified as Mary Ann and Joe, and the word "servant" was a euphemism for "slave." Was it coincidental that the Loftons had slaves and children who shared the names Mary Ann and Joe? We do not know.

In 1857, the Loftons began work on a new home. While work progressed, they rented a home owned by Richard Tillia Morrison, Jr., who was planting in both Christ Church and St. James Santee Parishes and who kept a summer home in Mt. Pleasant. In Mt. Pleasant, Samuel Herd Lofton bought and sold beef. A part of his business was the provision of beef to vessels at anchor in Charleston harbor, and that venture would be his undoing.

A Violent Epidemic

In September 1857, a fever struck the small community on Charleston Harbor, afflicting fifty-three persons, and killing twenty-three. The two youngest Lofton boys were the first persons involved, and both died within a few days after onset of the disease. Their mother, Susan Ann, died on September 18, 1857, by which time other households were being affected, and the residents of the town were realizing that something terrible was going on.

When Samuel Lofton showed signs of illness, the local physicians called in a colleague from the Medical College of South Carolina in hopes of learning how the disease started and how it was carried from home to home. Dr. Robert Armstrong Kinloch visited on September 20 and found Mr. Lofton delirious and jaundiced. Lofton died that night. An autopsy the next day revealed anatomical changes confirming the impression that Dr. Kinloch had gotten at the bedside. Mr. Lofton, the consulting physician was sure, died of yellow

Christ Episcopal Church, Mt. Pleasant, in the 1920s. The Lofton monument is the tall obelisk nearest the church.

fever. Years later, in 1900, the remaining members of the Lofton family erected a monument in remembrance of the four members of their family who fell victim to yellow fever. The family erred in the inscription on the monument, missing the date of death by one year.

The inscription on the obelisk, which stands near the Lofton graves at Christ Church, reads:

> In Memory
> of our Father
> Samuel H.
> Mother Susan Ann
> and brothers
> Robert G.
> and George E.
> All died the
> Same week
> In 1858
> God gave,
> He took,
> He will restore
> LOFTON

The townspeople were shocked. Many got out of town as quickly as possible. The dreaded disease had repeatedly attacked southern port cities but had never before come to the healthful summer resort of Mt. Pleasant. Doctor Kinloch continued his study by interviewing family members and examining other people who had been affected by the disease. After the epidemic subsided, he reported to the Medical Society of South Carolina that he was satisfied that the causative agent had been spontaneously generated, arising in piles of rotting leaves. Mt. Pleasant, Dr. Kinloch pointed out, was growing rapidly, with lots being cleared for building. In January 1858, Kinloch published his account of the epidemic in the *Charleston Medical Journal and Review.*

Samuel Lofton Bonner (great-great-great-great-grandson of Samuel Herd Lofton), age 6, at the Lofton family monument, May 2001.

Dr. Kinloch's opinions as to the origin and nature of the yellow fever agent were quickly countered by those of an opponent. Dr. David Hume went to Mt. Pleasant to conduct an independent study, and Hume assured himself that the disease had been brought to Charleston Harbor on one or more ships arriving from Latin America. He suggested that the infectious agent got from ship to shore by wafting through the air on the prevailing southwesterly breezes.

Drs. Kinloch and Hume had previously disagreed over the cause of yellow fever and its mode of transmission. They continued to dispute the subject, publishing four articles apiece on the Mt. Pleasant epidemic and debating the issue before the Medical Society of South Carolina and before Charleston's city council. At stake was whether quarantine rules would continue to require that vessels arriving from the tropics remain at the quarantine anchorage for forty days before moving to the docks where crews could unload cargo. Dr. Hume wanted strict quarantine regulations. Dr. Kinloch emphasized, instead, the need for good drainage and sanitation. The doctors settled nothing and ended up agreeing to disagree in peace, yet they helped prevent the recurrence of the infectious disease in Mt. Pleasant and in Charleston. The Charleston Harbor communities endured only one more epidemic of yellow fever when, in 1863, a blockade-runner brought the disease in from Cuba.

In arguing about the cause and the mode of transmission of the disease that killed the Loftons, Drs. Kinloch and Hume were participating in what has been called the "great medical debate of the nineteenth century." Our Lofton ancestors, however, would not be known as members of the family that revealed to mankind the nature of infectious diseases and of yellow fever in particular.

Drs. Kinloch and Hume did not have the benefit of two monumental discoveries, which would come in the next thirty years. First, the development of a more powerful microscope in the 1860s allowed the visualization of bacteria and proved that tiny living things did not arise from spontaneous generation but reproduced by division. Second, transmission of disease-producing organisms by insects was demonstrated in the 1880s, when English physicians showed that filariasis and malaria are carried by the mosquito. Those two advances in knowledge paved the way for Dr. Walter Reed to prove in 1902 that yellow fever is caused by a submicroscopic agent — a virus — and is transmitted by the mosquito.

We now are sure that the virus reached Charleston Harbor by way of an infected mosquito transported by boat from Latin America. The virus-carrying insect bit a susceptible visitor to the boat and, when the virus invaded his bloodstream, the person became a source of virus for other residents of Mt. Pleasant. Local mosquitoes took care of the spread within The Village. Since Samuel Herd Lofton was affected after others had shown evidence of the disease, it is likely that an employee went to the boat, was bitten by the mosquito, and then carried the virus to shore.

Five Lofton children were orphaned by the epidemic. Henry Michael (17) was attending The Arsenal School in Columbia, which, with The Citadel in Charleston, made up the Military Academy of South Carolina. He previously attended the Kings Mountain Military Academy in York, South Carolina. John Marion (12), Samuel Joseph (8), and Jenny (6) had mild fevers and recovered completely. Mary Ann was not affected. Both of the servants took the fever. Mary Ann survived a mild case, but Joseph was an early fatality.

The surviving children moved to different homes. Henry Michael was old enough to be independent. He withdrew from the Arsenal and began working as an overseer on three Cooper River plantations — Rice Hope, Bene Vente, and Mepkin. An attack of malaria, yet another insect-transmitted disease, induced him to seek other employment. He resigned and took a position as clerk in a store at Suttons, his birthplace. Enjoying that work, he purchased a store of his own at Mars Bluff on the Pee Dee River, and managed it until the Civil War began.

John Marion stayed with the H. S. Tew family, which had lost a child to the yellow fever virus. Just sixteen at the onset of the war, he promptly joined the Confederate army.

Mary Ann lived with the Ferguson family, and Samuel lived with Mrs. Jane Haselden, an aunt by marriage of the Lofton children.

Jenny was the only one of the children to leave the East

Cooper region immediately after the death of her parents. She was taken in and later adopted by Joel and Mary Ann Butler of Amelia Township in Orangeburg District. How the Butlers came to be interested in Jenny is not known, but the move was to Jenny's advantage. The Butlers were wealthy landowners and were childless. In 1869, Jenny married Dr. Charles Rhett Taber of Fort Motte, a prominent physician who served a term as president of the Medical Society of South Carolina. Dr. Taber's 1854 graduation thesis at the Medical College of South Carolina was titled "Yellow Fever," a coincidence but one which likely incited interest between the two people. Jenny kept close contact with her brothers. After Dr. Taber's death, she resided in Columbia, where she and her descendants frequently hosted the Loftons on their trips to the capitol and from which she visited her brothers in McClellanville.

Mary Ann married a Mr. Sams of Beaufort, South Carolina; moved with him to Galveston, Texas; and had two children. Mary Ann died in a house fire.

The three Lofton boys ended up in old St. James Santee Parish. There they participated in the creation of the society of the Theodemocrats and in the growth and development of McClellanville. But, first, two of them went off to war.

The Civil War

Henry Michael Lofton was one of the founders of the Tenth Regiment of South Carolina Volunteers. In 1860, after secession, South Carolina divided into ten military districts, each of which would raise a regiment for defense of the state. Most of the districts did not organize their regiments until after the war began, and the 10th gathered for the first time on May 31, 1861. The unit was composed of men from Georgetown District (now Georgetown, Williamsburg, Horry, and Marion counties) and was commanded by Col. Arthur Middleton Manigault, a graduate of West Point and a planter on the

Henry Michael Lofton
(1840-1917)

Waccamaw River. Henry Lofton, with his military school training, was elected Captain of Company I. They called themselves "The Swamp Fox Guards."

The 10th Regiment, first headquartered on Waccamaw Neck, was responsible for guarding the coast. In April 1862, in a major reorganization of Confederate forces, Company I became Company A of the 26th South Carolina Regiment and in September, became Company C of the 26th Regiment. While still in the 10th Regiment, Henry Michael found time to court Susan Ann Morrison. They married at the Second Presbyterian Church, Charleston on January 30, 1862.

In June 1862, the 26th Regiment helped win the Battle of Secessionville at James Island, South Carolina, after which they guarded the coast from Charleston Harbor to the Santee River. Lofton's company spent three separate stays in McClel-lanville. In May 1863, the 26th regiment was sent to Mississippi in a belated and unsuccessful effort to save Vicksburg from General Ulysses S. Grant. The regiment saw battlefield action at Jackson and Corinth before it returned to Mt. Pleasant

After doing more guard duty, the regiment began seeing the dirty side of war. In May 1864, the 26th was transferred into the Army of Northern Virginia, commanded by Robert E. Lee. The unit was assigned to duty at Petersburg, where it faced a large Union army, led by none other than its old foe General Grant, who was trying to encircle Richmond.

The longest siege in American history was getting under way and Lofton's unit was involved

*Susan Ann Morrison Lofton
(1844-1896)*

in that drawn-out, bitter action for eleven months. After months of wearying trench warfare, the soldiers, especially the Confederates, suffered greatly from exposure, lack of food and water, and disease. The virtually constant firing of small arms plus occasional skirmishes and cannonades kept the atmosphere tense. Lee's once potent army was gradually weakened by disease and desertion.

A story passed down through the Lofton family tells of Captain Lofton's personal encounter with General Lee. It seems Lofton was successful in asking his general to commute the death sentence placed on a youth who had fallen asleep on guard duty. No Confederate records are available to confirm this interaction of our great-grandfather with the famous commander.

John Marion Lofton's 23rd Regiment came to Petersburg also and took up stations near the 26th Regiment. Family accounts do not tell whether the brothers were able to get together, but it is likely that they did. At Petersburg, both regiments distinguished themselves in one of the most famous engagements of the war: The Battle of the Crater. Union Army engineers dug a long tunnel under the Confederate lines and on July 1, 1864, exploded a massive charge of dynamite, creating a great crater. A large contingent of South Carolina's 24th Regiment was killed instantly. The 26th Regiment was immediately beside them, and they, along with the 23rd Regiment and two other Confederate regiments, fought off fourteen Union regiments who attempted to charge through the hole but floundered.

Captain Henry Michael Lofton's account of his military experiences, as written down by his daughter-in-law and his granddaughter, state that he developed tuberculosis rather early in the war and had to give up his command, but he recovered in time to organize another company and return to action. It is more likely that Henry Lofton passed to his family his memory of the reorganization of his regiment plus his memory of an illness he had in Petersburg.

The military archives reveal that he was hospitalized at General Hospital #4, Richmond, Virginia, on July 30, 1864, the diagnosis being "chronic diarrhea and debility." He was transferred on thirty days' furlough to a hospital in Greenville, South Carolina. The sparse records indicate that he was back in command of his company "in the field" in October 1864. The next month, he was sick again and was sent directly to the hospital in Greenville. Inspection reports of January and February 1865 state that he was "absent — sick" each time. The family account states that he was with his unit in Virginia at the end of the war. The 26th Regiment (and the 23rd) surrendered with General Lee at Appomattox.

Disease was the deadly enemy during the Civil War, accounting for twice as many deaths as wounds in battle, and was a great problem for both the Confederate and the Union armed services. Diarrhea was the most prevalent disease of all. The chronic diarrhea suffered by the combatants was not caused by typhoid fever or other specific infections, which the doctors could well recognize. The ailment was more gradual in onset and more intractable. Many men with diar-

rhea suffered also from scurvy, resulting from vitamin C deficiency, and a minority of the physicians learned that both the
scurvy and the diarrhea could be arrested by intake of a diet
that included fresh fruits and vegetables. A great deal of retro-
spective analysis and research suggests that the chronic diarrhea of the Civil War was the result of vitamin deficiency complicated by bacterial overgrowth in the bowel — a disease similar to what is now called tropical sprue.

The accounts put down by my grandmother and my
mother praise Dr. John Y. DuPre, who was the physician/
surgeon of the 26th Regiment, for restoring Henry Lofton's
health. "Old Dr. DuPre dosed him with Cod Liver Oil," both
of them wrote. I believe the good doctor more likely made
Captain Lofton eat his greens and his blackberries, and I wish
the patient had left off mention of Dr. DuPre's therapy. I
suspect that story had a lot to do with my receiving many a
dose of cod liver oil during my childhood. My mother would
give me a dose right now if she could.

John Marion Lofton saw a lot of action and was able to
serve throughout the war, avoiding illness. Because he was
the youngest member of his unit, he became a favorite of his
commanding officer. Marion told his family chronicler that
he had fired his regiment's first and last shots of the conflict,
the first at a Union party raiding the coast near Mt. Pleasant
and the last at an enemy patrol near Appomattox.

What kind of fighting man was Henry Michael Lofton?
The family biographies portray him as determined and resil-
ient, a survivor who fought to the end. However, while the
agonizingly scanty military archives give us good information
about his movements and some information about his illness,
they give no information at all about his conduct in battle or
his skill in leading men. Years after the war, in 1890, he was
elected to the House of Representatives. A brief biography
printed in the *News and Courier* in November 1890 stated
that Lofton was promoted to captain during the war and that

he "was distinguished for his dash and bravery."

Accounts of the times tell us that the defeated Confederates were gathered into their regiments and were instructed to
march back to their states of origin under their own command.
Oral histories place Henry Michael Lofton "near the Virginia
line" at the end of the war and state that from there he walked
to Greenwood, South Carolina, to join his family and "wrest a
living out of what was left."

Back Home

It is believed that Henry Michael and Susan Ann Lofton
and their two children lived at first with her parents. Her
father, Richard Tillia Morrison, Jr., was still planting in Christ
Church Parish, had a home in The Village of Mt. Pleasant,
and was a member of the Wappetaw Independent Congregational Church, but he had already started his move toward
St. James Santee Parish and McClellanville. In the 1850s,
Morrison constructed his plantation home — Laurel Hill —
and his cottage on Jeremy Creek.

Henry Michael Lofton managed somehow, possibly with
the backing of his father-in-law, to lease three plantations at
Andersonville in Christ Church Parish, a community near what
is now Moore's Landing. Henry's brothers, John Marion and
Samuel Joseph, lived with and worked with him. At
Andersonville, Henry joined the Wappetaw Independent
Congregational Church, and he and Susan Anne had three
more children: Louise Augusta; Henry Michael, Jr.; and Julia
Riley. But the family's sojourn in Christ Church Parish ended
unhappily. Having invested all his money in Sea Island cotton,
Henry Lofton "lost it all and had to start from the bottom
again." The Loftons — Henry, Susan, and five children plus
his brothers, John Marion and Samuel Joseph — moved on.

The former St. James Santee Parish that the Loftons settled
in was an almost entirely rural place. In the lower parish,
McClellanville was just becoming a town. In the upper par-

Laurel Hill Plantation, 1850-1989. This photograph was taken in 1972, while the house was abandoned. The house was moved to Doe Hall Plantation and restored, but it was destroyed by Hurricane Hugo.

ish, Echaw was fading away while Honey Hill had ceased to grow. The sparsely settled territory was now a remote part of the large Charleston County.

Henry Lofton obtained 200 acres of land from his father-in-law and established his farm on the Kings Highway near Buck Hall. Desperately needing income, he was receptive to an offer given him by the black Republican legislator, William G. Pinckney, to teach at a school for black children. My great-grandfather's family was sustained while he became a successful farmer and began selling lumber and turpentine.

Here, Henry Michael and Susan Ann Lofton experienced the loss of a child — Elizabeth Ann died at age twelve. Their Lofton family grew, however, with the addition of three more boys: Samuel Joseph, James Armstrong, and Thomas Lucas.

His sons married and moved into homes nearby. With the

*Four genera-
tions of
Richard
Tillia
Morrisons,
1904.
Richard
Tillia
Morrison,
Jr., with
walking
stick, was a
founder of
McClellanville
and, through
his eighteen
children,
ancestor of
many of its
residents.*

Leland and Morrison families nearby, there was soon a need
for an elementary school for white children. The school district was given the Lofton name and it existed for decades.
There was, also, a Lofton post office.

By the time my cousins and I played, swam, and fished at
the Lofton community, most of our relatives had moved on
to McClellanville and the community had lost its name. We
called it "The Farm."

5

How They Made Money
in St. James Santee

Few people became rich in St. James Santee Parish and McClellanville. In no era has a steadily successful economy been established in the area; all have suffered failures, downturns, and recessions. Entire industries have been lost. They rarely made money. Rather, they stayed poor.

The early owners of Carolina expected financial gain. The first wave of settlers consisted of soldiers of fortune hoping to get rich, debtors needing to work themselves free of their burden, and slaves accompanying their masters. These people were not utterly lacking in principle or religious zeal, but their motives were primarily commercial.

Trade with the Native Americans was immediately successful and was the greatest source of income for the colonists well into the eighteenth century. Such trade was so successful that the proprietors could not keep the settlers from dealing with Native Americans and taking most of the profit. Agriculture was slow getting started. Over three decades passed before a reliable staple (rice) was developed and, by the time it was produced profitably, the proprietors were kicked out and the hereditary aristocracy was an impossibility.

The Carolinians did take advantage of things that the land had in abundance: open forests and pine trees. The Indians had kept the underbrush in the forests cleared by systematic burning, providing grazing land for hunting. Settlers promptly used these green mansions for herding cattle and pigs, which they shipped to the land-poor Caribbean islands. In what was the forerunner of the naval stores industry, pine trees were made into staves or lumber, which also found a ready market in the Caribbean. With the successes mentioned and the attraction of settlers by the offer of free land — first 50 acres, then 100 acres, and later 150 acres offered to each free white male — the colony grew.

In St. James Santee, trade was never lucrative, for the Wandos, the Seewees, and the Santees were neither wealthy nor numerous. St. James Santee did have a lot of pine trees and the lumbering and naval stores industries provided a little income for a few of its residents from the beginning to the 1940s. Cattle ranching in the forest was practiced until the 1950s. Indigo production on the riverfront and the marshfront plantations was a source of some wealth for a few decades in the mid-1700s. Rice cultivation on the Santee gave a few in the parish a flirtation with opulence and wealth and

Thomas Lucas Lofton (1882-1959), cattleman and farmer

was a successful occupation from the Revolution until the Civil War. Cotton was the great staple from the Civil War to 1920, when growth of it was abruptly terminated by the boll weevil.

Naval Stores

Many early landowners in St. James Santee produced naval stores: first tar and pitch and then turpentine. Tar and pitch were of early value because they were used as caulking material in the shipping industry. These substances were distilled from dead pine trees, known as "light wood." Pine, living and dead, was one raw material that the parish had in abundance. John Palmer was St. James Santee's first great producer of naval stores, beginning before the Revolution. Palmer lived near Jamestown, in that section which became St. Stephen Parish, but the unincorporated community of Palmerville in upper St. James Santee and the Palmer Bridges over Wambaw Creek were named for him. McClellanvillians are still named for him. The name Palmer is rendered as "Pammer," rhyming with "hammer." This pronunciation is unique to the parish and may be explained by the fact that the original family name was Pamor.

By about 1820, tar and pitch production became unprofitable because ship builders began using other materials and because there was strong competition from naval stores producers in Sweden. At this same time, an extractive industry emerged as producers learned to derive turpentine from resin. Turpentine was used in making lampblack, lamp oil (camphene), paint thinner, wood preservers, and eventually, rubber. Resin was obtained by slashing mature pine trees, collecting the drippings in tin cups, and then pooling the collections for distillation.

The turpentine-producing form of the naval stores industry was founded originally in Jamestown, Virginia, moved into North Carolina, and spread slowly southward. It was, necessarily, a migratory industry because orchards of mature pines were exhausted in five to ten years. Luck thus favored Henry Michael Lofton. When he moved the family into lower St. James Santee in 1872, many acres of pines were available. He acquired thousands of acres, profited nicely, and passed the industry on to his son, James Armstrong Lofton. It could not remain productive, however. As David Doar stated in his history of the parish in 1905, the industry was "now languishing for lack of trees." James Lofton, "Uncle Jimmy," kept the family business alive through 1925, when he sold it to a Mr. Pittman.

The gathering of resin, which I saw on our trips in the 1930s and the World War II years, was the last gasp of the naval stores industry. Advances in methodology, including the extraction of chemicals from pine logs by the pulp and paper mills, made the labor-intensive resin gathering unnecessary. An industry that allowed Henry Michael Lofton to accumulate some wealth was not available to his descendants.

In 1925, the Loftons still had their land. In 1936, other losses forced the family to sell its forestlands to the federal

McClellanville's waterfront in 1952. The large crane was used to transfer timber from Murphy Island onto logging trucks.

government. Other owners did so, and the Francis Marion National Forest came into being. I think now that it was a good thing that the great forest of St. James Santee fell into public hands. The forest is well kept, provides employment for many people, provides a sanctuary for wildlife, and is a beautiful setting for nature lovers.

Rice

Rice was planted in Carolina within a few years after the colony was founded. It had not been anticipated that cultivation of the grain would be successful in the area, and the founders did not provide for it. Individuals experimented on their own and found that rice could be grown in low-lying fields and inland swamps. For several decades, the grain produced in Carolina was used for home consumption. Slowly, planters learned, or were taught by slaves, the superior method of cultivation on riverside marshes and fields with the use of tidal waters to irrigate the crop and control weeds. By 1754, rice was Carolina's largest export. Rice plantations would make South Carolina's Lowcountry the nation's wealthiest region for another eighty or so years.

South Santee rice plantations came into being in the mid-1700s. They were successful but never quite so rich as those on the Waccamaw River, a few miles above Georgetown. St. James Santee can claim one great contribution to rice culture: the parish was the site of the first effective rice mill. Challenged by plantation owners along the Santee River, the English immigrant Jonathan Lucas conceived a water-driven mill for pounding rice. He erected the first one on John Bowman's Peachtree Plantation in 1787. It worked, and copies were made all around the Lowcountry. Lucas became quite wealthy.

Rice planting flourished in the tidewaters of South Carolina from the Savannah River in the south to the Waccamaw, and these plantations specialized in the growth of a particular strain of rice: "Carolina Gold." This tasty and attractive grain, possibly imported from Madagascar, drew the best prices throughout the world. In the 1800s, rice planting remained profitable, even though the state's near monopoly ended with the opening of competitive fields in Louisiana and Texas. The Civil War dealt the industry a severe blow. Fields were damaged, marauding Union soldiers liberated slaves, and overseas marketing was ended by the naval blockade. Most of the plantations ceased to produce rice during the war, and many could not restart when the conflict was over.

After the war, South Carolina's western competitors became dominant, using less labor-intensive methods and growing their crops in open fields on which mechanized equipment could be used. But a few of St. James Santee's rice plantations hung on. The great storm of September 1911 destroyed the last functioning rice fields. Within the next decade or two, most of the old rice plantations would be sold to

Pounding rice at Hampton Plantation

rich northerners to be used as hunting preserves.

In the 1940s, hoping to find a profitable alternative to truck farming, my cousins successfully planted for two years two fields of rice in a low area near the Lofton Landing. Frank Simmons, who had been the engineer on the Lofton's freight boat in earlier years, threshed the product by hand. The boys had no way to market the rice and so divided it among themselves and Frank Simmons. The next year, they went back to planting tomatoes and squash, and all of us ate rice produced in the Southwest.

Cotton

The Lofton family briefly attempted rice production, but cotton farming had much to do with the rise and fall of the family fortunes. The story of cotton is the story of this family and of many others in this community and throughout the South.

Cotton was St. James Santee's staple from about 1865 to 1920, and cotton gave the parish a second glimpse of prosperity. Cotton was first grown in the experimental garden planted by the colony's settlers in 1670. Many decades passed before the Carolinians attempted to grow cotton on a commercial scale, and not until 1747 were the first bags shipped to England. After the emergence of the southeast coast's unique brand of cotton, Sea Island cotton, Carolina planters became enthusiastic about taking on the difficult cultivation and production of the fiber.

Cotton production always was, and still is, a slow process: a long growing season followed by a laborious separation of the fiber from the seed. In the field, cotton needs a lot of hoeing and plowing to protect it from weeds and requires a great amount of costly fertilizer. The early cotton farmers wore out their land in just a few years, but they had land to spare, so they just cleared and made new fields. At length, the growers had to turn to fertilizer.

The famous Sea Island cotton was developed by the process of seed selection in Georgia in 1786. The first fiber of its
sort was shipped from St. Simons Island in 1788. Sea Island
cotton was planted in St. Paul Parish, south of Charleston,
that very year. In 1793, the Revolutionary War hero William
Moultrie planted 150 acres at his Northampton Plantation in
St. Johns Berkeley Parish, a site now covered by Lake Moultrie.
He lost his crop.

David Doar later wrote that the loss was due to the
general's "lack of knowledge of the culture." The failure,
however, was surely related to Sea Island cotton's peculiar
need for a long growing season. The coastal St. James Santee
Parish was at the northern limit of successful growth of this
form of cotton, and Moultrie's plantation was over forty miles
inland, where the growing season is shorter. Sea Island cotton could be grown only along the coast of South Carolina.
Edisto Island was the great center of production. Murphy
Island, at the mouth of the South Santee River, proved to be
the furthest extent of successful cultivation to the northeast.

Sea Island cotton produced black seed, rather than green.
The black seeds were relatively easy to separate from the fibers, but the development of the cotton gin in 1794 greatly
stimulated the cultivation of cotton of all varieties. By 1858,
cotton was king, and Sea Island cotton brought six times
higher prices than most kinds. Its long, thin, silky fibers were
preferred for weaving into clothing. After the Civil War, Sea
Island cotton became St. James Santee's great staple just as
McClellanville was growing into a town.

Growing Sea Island cotton was rather chancy. Crops could
be destroyed by flooding at the times of hurricanes or by the
exceptionally high tides of September when accompanied by
a strong northeasterly wind. Most significantly, the long growing season made Sea Island cotton susceptible to attack by
insects, and it came to pass that St. James Santee's hope for
wealth was wiped out by the Mexican boll weevil. The boll

weevil entered South Carolina in 1919 after a slow march through the Southland beginning in 1897. Farmers learned they could grow short-staple varieties of the plant by careful location and separation of fields, by improved fertilization, and by application of arsenicals, but Sea Island cotton was lost, perhaps forever.

My great-grandfather, Henry Lofton, and my grandfather, Richard Lofton, grew cotton, and while the father prospered from it, the son was impoverished by it.

Henry Lofton's first attempt at growing cotton failed. According to our family history, he "lost everything." He moved to St. James Santee, acquired 200 acres of land from his father-in-law, and finally achieved success in growing cotton, using his profits to buy up timberland for turpentine and lumber production. He also purchased properties along the Kings Highway near his homestead and built homes for his children. Henry Lofton also had summer homes in McClellanville and in Saluda, North Carolina. As McClellanville developed into a year-round townsite, he built homes in The Village for his sons.

My mother, Henry's granddaughter, said of him that when he retired, he was able to sell the timber from his pineland and live out his days in comfort. Dr. Waring signed his death certificate, stating that Henry's occupation was: "capitalist." That was surely an exaggeration, except by St. James Santee's standards.

Richard Morrison Lofton, our grandfather, took over management of the Lofton enterprises in about 1910. He withdrew from the legislature to devote more time to business at home. He was considerably older than his four younger brothers and was the only child in the family who had attended college. He "read law" under a distinguished Charleston lawyer, was admitted to the bar, and served in the legislature. His two sisters, slightly younger than he, idolized him and accepted his direction of family affairs. The girls had been given no financial interest in the businesses or woodlands. Richard's four brothers took responsibilities under his general direction. All of his siblings called him "Big Bubba." If the girls felt offended at having been denied a share of family wealth, they did not show it, as they remained loyal and friendly family members.

Richard's next oldest brother, Henry Michael Lofton, Jr. ("Harry"), took charge of the farming operations and, with Richard, formed a land company to buy and sell properties. Harry also ran a commissary near his residence on the Kings Highway. In 1911 or 1912, Harry moved from the home at the Lofton community and made McClellanville his home until his death in 1925. The land company did not thrive and was allowed to die out in 1915 or 1916. James Armstrong Lofton handled the timberlands, the lumber mill, and the turpentine mill. Samuel Joseph Lofton was involved with the farming but departed to become manager of a Cooper River plantation. Thomas Lucas Lofton, youngest of the group, concentrated on cattle ranching and helped with farming.

To direct the farm, Richard Lofton called home his oldest daughter Margaret — "Aunt Margie" — and her husband, Watus Dawsey. The Dawseys had lived near Gallivants Ferry in Horry County after their marriage in 1910. Watus Dawsey was running two farms there and doing well, but our grandfather thought they were in exile, in the land of the lost, and could not bear to have his daughter remain in such a place. Watus and Margie lived in McClellanville for two years, during which time Watus helped run the farm and served as magistrate, then moved out to Harry Lofton's former home on the Kings Highway. The Dawseys dubbed the place "The Palace," but we always called it "The Farm." At the farm, Margie and Watus raised their large family of six boys and two girls. The farm was one of the two gathering places and activity centers for the Lofton clan, the other being Richard Lofton's home in The Village.

The farm, which Richard Lofton called "My Plantation" in his will, soon fell on hard times. Prices of cotton, even Sea Island cotton, were depressed for several years because of excessive planting throughout the South. As mentioned earlier, the 1911 crop was lost to the great September storm. In 1914, the onset of World War I inhibited overseas shipment and precipitated a cotton panic; prices dropped to the lowest level in history at 5½ cents a pound but recovered partially in 1916. The entrance of the United States into the war effort caused cotton prices to soar in 1917 and 1918, so St. James Santee and the rest of the South enjoyed a reprieve from the economic doldrums. Prices of cotton jumped to an all-time high of 42 cents per pound.

Then came the end of the war and the advent of the boll weevil. In the fall of 1921, the South was feeling the first

The Dawsey House, Lofton Community, near Buck Hall. Constructed in the 1870s, it was abandoned in the 1970s.

effects of a long agricultural depression. Cotton was bringing 5 cents a pound. The Dawseys, like other growers along the coast, had switched to growing short staple cotton but got virtually nothing for it. The family survived on subsistence farming, for which Watus Dawsey was well prepared by his experience in Horry County. They supplied all of their own vegetables, beef, and pork. The boys were happy to provide fish, shrimp, oysters, and crab from the creek, as well as venison and other game from the forest. They grew sugar cane and made their own syrup. Aunt Margie sold milk to dairies in Charleston after setting aside plenty for home use and the production of butter. Our Dawsey cousins recall this era with satisfaction and pride: "We had plenty to eat and shared with relatives and friends. We were better off than most. We just had no money to spend."

During the years between 1910 and 1929, farmers often put a lien on their cotton to finance the large amounts of fertilizer needed to produce the crop. When unable to pay off their liens, they resorted to mortgaging their farms to banks or other financial institutions, to larger fertilizer companies, or to other individuals. By 1920, 21 percent of owner-operated farms were mortgaged, and by 1930, 33 percent were. Poor prices and crop failures forced many small farmers to give up their land in the 1920s. When the Great Depression followed in 1929, large owners began caving in.

The decade of the 1920s was, as Ben Robertson termed it, the "draining time" for the South, for South Carolina, and for St. James Santee. As D.D. Wallace has written in his *Short History of South Carolina*, the setback "affected farmers and all whose income depended on them — all had contracted debts based upon inflated values of land and produce." In Ben Robertson's memoir, *Red Hills and Cotton*, the loss of king cotton is called "the tragedy that saved us" because his Pickens County family had the cohesion and the determination to hunker down and tough it out, to suffer want rather than mortgage property. They came through it stronger than before, but few did so well.

In February 1920, Richard Lofton borrowed $3,000 from J.C. Johnson of Maryland, about whom we have no further information, and mortgaged 899 acres of land, including cleared farmland in and about the Lofton community. Excluded was the strip of fields leading to Lofton Landing. He paid off that mortgage in 1924, after borrowing $7,000 from the Atlantic Savings Bank, using the same properties as collateral. In a year, he repaid $3,500 of that debt, but the other half of the debt outlived him. The Virginia-Carolina Chemical Company loaned the Loftons fertilizer money in 1923 ($1,683.09), 1924 ($2,047.95), and 1925 ($2,138.98). These debts were incorporated into a mortgage of two separate tracts of woodlands of 996 acres and of 150 acres. This debt also outlived Richard Lofton.

Left unencumbered were 8,715 acres of woodlands, the farmlands and homesteads in and about Lofton, the Landing strip, and the turpentine and lumber mill. Furthermore, none of the homes in McClellanville were mortgaged. The family was fortunate to have this abundance of resources to get through these lean years. Many people lost everything.

At Richard Lofton's death in 1928, the appraised values of the properties mentioned were:

Tract	Appraised Value	Mortgage
899 acres	$ 5,394.00	$3,500.00
996 acres	$ 4,982.50 &	$5,870.09
&150 acres	$ 375.00	
8,715 acres	$43,575.00	$0

The mortgages were not satisfied until 1936, when all of these tracts were sold to the United States Forest Service for inclusion in the Francis Marion National Forest. The payment, $40,337.15, illustrates the near one-third decline in property values over the eight years from Richard Lofton's death to the sale of the land. The agricultural recession and the Great Depression had taken their toll.

The surviving Lofton men — Jimmy, Sammy, and Tom — made the decision to sell to the Forest Service. They pondered over their alternatives at length and finally met at the farm to make up their minds. Richard Dawsey remembers watching and listening in as the men walked about the front yard for three hours. None really wanted the land to go out of the family, but it was a liability to them at the time: there wasn't much timber left, production of turpentine had ceased, and there were taxes to pay. They would still own their homes and the cleared farmland. Tom, who herded his cattle on the open range, could still do so even if the forest was owned by the government. Jimmy and Sammy were in favor of selling immediately, but Tom wasn't sure and requested a further delay, saying he thought a better offer might come along.

Despite any uncertainties among the men, they sold. The proceeds were divided five ways, with each of five Lofton families receiving $8,067.43. Henry Michael Lofton, Jr.'s, family had to pay off a debt of $2,935.05, and the Richard Lofton estate paid $6,435.05. A rumor circulated later among the family that the International Paper Company had come to Uncle Jimmy a few weeks after the sale with an offer of $10 an acre. That story is to be doubted because the amount so far exceeded the appraised value.

As I grew up, I was aware that the Loftons had once owned a large amount of land now in the National Forest. Considering how much pride people had in land ownership in that era, I suspect the family members were embarrassed by the loss. My mother never mentioned it to me or to my sister and brother, but all her life she placed great importance on avoiding debt and holding on to property. I never heard the subject aired until I got curious in the 1990s and went about asking folks what they knew about it.

My cousin Richard Dawsey, the oldest surviving member

of our cousinhood and the cousin most knowledgeable about the matter, thinks Richard Lofton tried hard and was a skillful grower of cotton but was simply overwhelmed by the economic decline that impoverished the entire South. No one else has been so forgiving. Richard's sister Edith believes that our grandfather "paid more attention to politics and neglected his farm." Relatives from other family units were more critical. Cater Leland, son of Richard's sister Louise Augusta, said that Richard "ran the Lofton businesses or ran them in the ground." Another nephew, Harry Mikell Lofton, son of James Armstrong Lofton (Uncle Jimmy), is of the opinion that "Big Bubba must have been a terrible manager because the great Lofton estate, largest in the state at that time, was lost on his watch."

To Richard Lofton's credit, he and his brother, Henry Michael, Jr., ("Uncle Harry") kept all the debt on their shoulders. The other three boys had no debt. The three surviving boys could have retained the unencumbered 8,715 acres of forestland but chose to sell it. Uncle Jimmy and Uncle Sammy essentially retired on the proceeds, living off the interest on their shares. Jimmy served in the legislature, but Sammy was quite inactive. Tom continued to do his truck farming and ranching for another two decades.

I think they did the right thing in selling, for they could make no money from management of the land. Keeping the land for division among descendants would have been nice for my generation but would not have helped the financially strapped families right then. Now the forest is publicly owned and we can enjoy it as much as ever.

Who is to say, to judge, as we look back through our retrospectoscope, that Richard Lofton was negligent or foolish? If it were possible to change things, I would want our grandfather to have ceased cotton farming at about 1920. He might have seen the handwriting on the wall and gotten along well enough on income generated in his little law practice, from rental or sale of small portions of the land, and from sale of timber from time to time. But cotton farming was the reason people had farms at all. Because he liked it and, perhaps out of loyalty to the Dawsey family which had been drawn into the situation, he persisted in trying to grow cotton. I think he kept hoping that cotton would pay off.

In 1927, he tried for the last time. Over the beauty of a field of short-staple cotton ready for the picking, he was heard to exult, "Now isn't that beautiful." Richard Lofton died in April 1928, and Richard Dawsey is proud to say, "We buried Pa with his last crop of cotton."

Truck Farming

The agricultural activity I saw during the 1930s and the 1940s was "truck farming." Practitioners of that kind of farming did not call themselves "planters" but "farmers." They were landowners trying to hold on to their homesteads. Truck farming evolved into "agribusiness," but in St. James Santee, it was not successful.

Truck farming came into significance with the growth of American cities after the Civil War and got its name long before there was such thing as the internal-combustion-engine-powered vehicle we call a "truck." Farms in outlying communities trucked their vegetables and fruit to markets by wagon or by train. Farmers in Delaware, Maryland, and Virginia became greengrocers to the big cities in the Northeast, and Florida growers began shipping to the same areas. When cotton farming became unprofitable in St. James Santee, the landowners turned to truck farming. They were lucky to find an opportunity to sell their produce, a slot in time between shippings from the Middle Atlantic states and Florida. Clemson University's agricultural extension program helped farmers change to the new methods of growing and marketing.

The Dawsey boys would load up a truck with cucumbers and depart for a market in New York City. They made such trips with loads of sweet corn, cabbages, potatoes, beans, cantaloupes, and watermelons. Tomatoes were the big money crop, greatly depended upon but unreliable due to uncontrollable factors. A late freeze could kill the plants, or cool weather in Florida could delay shipping of the crop, thus depressing prices. At tomato-picking time, there was frantic activity. The fully grown but still green and the slightly ripened tomatoes were gathered in the fields and brought to the packing shed for grading and packing. From there, they were taken to market by large trucks owned by middlemen. We younger children were allowed to help, or at least to hang around in the fields and in the shed, and sometimes would get ten cents for the damage we did. The tomato harvest ended abruptly. Great amounts of tomatoes not ready for picking were left in the fields to be gleaned by the family or by the workers, who were mostly black residents of Buck Hall Community.

Successful truck farming required careful planting, cultivation, harvesting, and marketing. Timing of each phase had to be just right. Many of South Carolina's farmers were unable to keep the pace, especially when challenged by the labor shortages and the droughts, floods, and freezes that occurred from time to time. Many had inadequate capital with which to buy tractors or other laborsaving equipment. Truck farming began to evolve everywhere into a function of agribusiness, which involved leasing or buying large amounts of land, purchasing farm equipment, and hiring migrant labor. The era of the family farm was coming to an end.

With his Horry County experience in tobacco cultivation, Watus Dawsey set out to grow the weed. James Armstrong Lofton tried as well, and the two built and shared use of a curing barn, carrying the product to market in Mullins. After several years, the families gave it up. Moist soil and damp air were not good for tobacco.

The Dawseys did pretty well. The farm stayed in production until 1953, when Watus died of carcinoma of the stomach. By that time, his sons, my cousins, had moved into other lines of work. The fields were rented to the Thomas family, Virginians who moved into St. James Santee after World War II. Later, the Morrisons sold the rest of what had been Laurel Hill Plantation to the Heath family of Christ Church Parish. For almost three decades, the Thomases and then the Heaths, two agribusiness families, did all the farming between Awendaw Creek and the Santee River. The Thomases kept at it until 1985, by which time the young men of their family moved into different occupations. The Heaths did not re-plant after Hurricane Hugo damaged their fields in September 1989.

Agriculture, the main business of St. James Santee for over 250 years, was a thing of the past. Will it ever return, to become a source of livelihood for people of the parish? There are stirrings. In 1996, the former Pinch Gut Farm, about two miles northeast of McClellanville on Highway 17, became Patriot Farm (the change in name indicative of a change in expectations around the area) and has enjoyed successful seasons as a you-pick-it strawberry farm. In 1997, some members of the Thomas family rented fields at Laurel Hill from the Heaths and began growing vegetables while setting up a vegetable and fruit stand at the roadside.

Seafood

T-shirts sold at the annual Lowcountry Shrimp Festival proclaim "McClellanville: Seafood Capital of the World." This is a monumental exaggeration, but the message does indicate how important seafood has been to the town since the end of World War II. The boys and girls who returned from World War II scratched out a living by "going in the creek," the local term for any activity on the water: fishing, shrimping, clamming, crabbing, or oystering, either in the tidal creeks or in the ocean, whether for commerce or entertainment.

Oystering has been going on for thousands of years. Unknown Native Americans, who lived in the area long before the Seewees did, left mounds and rings of oyster shells at the edges of the marshes. White men gathered oysters for their own consumption until after the Civil War, when they began shipping them to faraway places. Bulls Bay oysters, famous for their saltiness and flavor, were favorites in the cities of the Northeast. The people of McClellanville are confident that their oysters are superior to those of Chesapeake Bay and those of the Gulf Coast.

Until the 1960s, there was an oyster factory near Buck Hall. Now the place is the site of an upscale development. Every house at the place called "Shellmore" was destroyed by Hurricane Hugo, then quickly replaced. Elsewhere, many families or individuals gathered and shucked the bivalves. Every time we went to McClellanville in season, my father would purchase a gallon can of shucked oysters. We had a lot of oyster stew and considered the finding of a tiny crab in the stew to be a sure sign of good luck. "I got the crab," we'd shout, striving to be first at detecting one. Regrettably, one can't buy shucked oysters now. Labor costs are too high, and the gatherers can sell the unopened oysters to seafood restaurants and raw bars in Mt. Pleasant, Charleston, Murrells Inlet, and Myrtle Beach.

June Dawsey (Watus Woodson Dawsey, Jr.), the eldest of our cousinhood, had an oyster shed at Tibwin. He was the distributor for some of the gatherers of the area. June, it seems, had a knack for getting others to do the work. June held the shellfishing rights on Tibwin Creek, Doe Hall Creek, Sandy Point Creek, and on the beautiful White Banks in Bulls Bay. After June's death from lung cancer, his brother Ellis Dawsey kept the rights. He did not take to oystering but became proficient at "scratching" clams and made a good living at it. He was joined by James and Lloyd McClellan (Lloyd, a girl, being another of our cousins) and by Mel Lofton, a member of the previous generation. Mel would drive up from his Sullivans

Island home to join the others at Lofton Landing. As James McClellan's eyesight failed, he and Lloyd were replaced by Dewey McClellan, their son, so three generations of Loftons were scratching clams, drinking coffee, and doing a lot of talking on White Banks.

It was not to last. A television news reporter visited the site and featured Ellis and Mel as the last practitioners of clam scratching; other people employed large clam dredges, which tore up the creek bottoms. The two men were, the reporter said, a dying breed. His comment was prophetic, for those two clammers would not last much longer. Both died of lung cancer.

A few years before the clammers ceased working, the Landing was sold to my orthopedic colleague, Bright McConnell. He allowed Ellis and the others to continue using the old base of operations. When I complimented him on his generosity, Bright answered, "They came with the property, didn't they?"

When Bright McConnell took over Lofton Landing he found it in a nearly natural state — that is, in need of a lot of clearing and cleaning up. Lanie Moses Youngman, Ellis Dawsey's niece and my first cousin once removed, visited the place a couple of years later and said: "They cleaned up that place like no Lofton ever could."

Crabbing

Kids have been catching crabs with hand lines and dip nets for as long as anyone can remember, but their method could hardly be adapted to the commercial scale. Aspiring commercial crabbers, most often youths trying to pick up a few bucks, put out trot lines and moved back and forth along the lines to net the crabs just like the kids did. The work was hard and the catch small, so no one in St. James Santee made a living at crabbing until well after World War II, when the development of the crab pot made it productive. Patterned somewhat like the classic lobster pot, crab pots were designed and used by the watermen of Chesapeake Bay before they appeared all along the South Atlantic and the Gulf coasts. Now, as one motors about in the marshes of St. James Santee, one has to dodge the floats marking the location of crab pots in every stretch of creek.

In 1963, the Maryland Crab Company came to town and set up a processing plant. In 1984, the business was taken over by a family from Georgetown and renamed the South Carolina Crab Company. The business occupies half of the dock and buildings formerly owned by the Thomas family, the other portion having been taken over by the Leland family's Carolina Seafood Company, which has enjoyed continual growth. A small management staff carries out the steaming of the crabs in great vats, and the crabmeat is "picked" by hand by a cluster of workers, mostly female. The product is expensive. A pound of white crab meat retails for about $16 (claw meat $12-$14), but people are willing to pay for it because production of that amount of crab meat at home would take at least three hours and create a big mess.

Barges take the remains away from the crab factory on Jeremy Creek and dump the refuse on the edges of creeks across the Inland Waterway, providing a feast for gulls and other scavengers, but the tides bring an unfortunate amount of unsightly shell back into Jeremy Creek. With crab shells, oil slicks, and other flotsam abounding, McClellanville's home creek is not so scenic as it was years ago. I do not complain; McClellanville is still a working village, not a retirement community or resort. The independent operators are young men who own a good-sized motor boat and a number of pots. They are assigned no leases but put their pots wherever they can find an opening. They work at crabbing year round but do best during the warmer months. The independence appeals to these men.

The Lofton family's brief effort at crabbing on a commercial basis ended violently. Ellis and James Dawsey, as youths, tried crabbing using trot lines in Doe Hall Creek. They argued over who was doing the most work — the effort ended in a toe-to-toe fight in their batteau.

In the last few years, three different producers in and around McClellanville are preparing soft-shell crabs for market. The crabbers sell crustaceans ready to molt to the producers, who carry the crabs through vats of different salinity to end up with the desired soft-shell. It takes a lot of work and expense, but prices are good, suggesting that this will be a successful addition to the economy of The Village and St. James Santee.

Shrimping

Commercial shrimping, a late introduction to McClellanville's seafood industry, has been the biggest source of income for The Village and St. James Santee Parish from the 1940s into the '90s.

Prior to 1935, people cast nets in tidal creeks to catch shrimp for the table. That summer, a small flotilla of fifteen boats, owned and operated by Portuguese sailors based in Brunswick, Georgia, came to Jeremy Creek. Using a barge as their base of operations, the Portuguese made hauls for shrimp in Santee Bay, Bulls Bay, and in the ocean. Young natives of McClellanville saw how to gather shrimp on a commercial scale, which consisted of preparing the nets and rigging the boats. The Portuguese moved on after that one season, but the local industry was conceived by their efforts.

In October 1946, according to an article in the *News and Courier*, fifty shrimp boats worked out of four docks in McClellanville. Many of these boats were from Georgia or North Carolina, but locally owned boats worked among them as well. The brothers Thomas Legare ("Nunk") Lofton and Mel Lofton, my mother's first cousins, owned small butthead boats obtained from military surplus. Other relatives served as

Shrimp boats at harbor on Jeremy Creek, 1996.

strikers on those or, preferably, on larger and better-equipped boats. Over the next few decades, shrimpers moved along the Atlantic and Gulf coasts to take advantage of the catch available in the different areas. Bigger boats became the norm. Men lived on them for months. At times, young men from McClellanville would be shrimping out of Rockville, South Carolina, or out of ports in Florida and even in Texas. When Santee Bay and Bulls Bay opened for shrimping each September, boats from other ports would congregate in McClellanville. One stormy day, I counted ninety-three shrimp boats in port.

The Leland, Duke, and Thomas families were major

The East Wind, *McClellanville's first locally owned shrimp boat, about 1935.*

owner-operators, processors, and shippers of shrimp and other varieties of seafood. Their docks were busy with women who headed the shrimp and men who graded and packed the catch for shipping. The dock owners also sold fuel and ice to independent operators.

About the time truck farming ceased at Lofton, our cousin James Dawsey began to crew on shrimp boats. He took interest in repairing damaged nets, became proficient at the work, and then became a designer and producer of nets, working at home and for two marine supply houses in Charleston. Shrimpers from all along the coast depended on his work. His expertise was the subject of an article in *Sandlapper* magazine.

Shrimping turned out to be a "sometimes thing." No McClellanvillians became wealthy doing it. Catches have varied greatly from year to year, depending on whether the crop survived the one or two long cold snaps that seem to recur each year. Nets are damaged or destroyed as they snag objects on the ocean floor. Profit margins have fallen because fuel costs rose greatly after war broke out in the Mideast in 1973, and labor costs have risen steadily. In recent years, the industry has been hit by competition in the form of pond-raised shrimp imported from low-wage countries in Central and South America. Even more ominously, shrimpers have been buffeted by criticism from environmentalists who decry the destruction of sea turtles, small fish, and other marine life in the "by-catch" taken with each drag of the net. The McClellanville-based fleet is growing smaller, and we no longer see the September influx of vessels from other ports. Many predict that commercial shrimping, in the Portuguese manner, is a dying industry.

If the Lofton family's response to these constrictions on shrimping is any indication of its future, then we may see the end of it. Dewey McClellan, cousin Lloyd's son, was the last owner of a shrimp boat. He sold out in 1989 to enter the heat-

The Vacio de Gama, *one of the Portugese shrimp boats in McClellanville, 1935.*

ing and air conditioning business, just in time for Hurricane Hugo to provide him with a lot of work. Presently, the only member of the Lofton clan involved in the seafood industry is Dewey's younger brother, Dickie, who works as a striker on a local boat. Other people in the community are holding on as best they can. They love the work, for they love the independence and the joy of working in a beautiful environment. I've heard many of them say, "It's so nice out there, you don't want to come in."

Whatever happens, the town can thank the Portuguese sailors for keeping St. James Santee and McClellanville alive over the last six or seven decades and for giving the town its present identity as "that charming little seafood town." And while the Lofton family has virtually abandoned the seafood industry, we have provided a visual reminder of the presence of the Portuguese in McClellanville. Richard Lofton, Jr., a professional artist, did a fine watercolor of the pioneer shrimp boats, gaily painted, attractive, tied up side to side at a catwalk on the creek. The nearest boat bears the name *Vacio De Gama*. My mother, an amateur who became a good watercolorist and who had no compunctions about copying her brother's work, turned out dozens of copies of the painting during the 1950s, '60s, and '70s. She had a few especially popular paintings, and when anyone expressed interest in one, she would produce it in short order. She took $10 for each and was truly worried when we teased that the Internal Revenue Service would catch up with her. Almost every home in The Village has one of my mother's paintings of the *Vacio De Gama*, or had one before Hurricane Hugo's flood.

Where People Are Working Now

For now, McClellanville is a working village. While it is home to retirees and part-time residents, the place is heavily populated by young people in need of employment. Some drive to Charleston, but those who want to live *and* work in old St. James Santee are finding their jobs in service. The United States Forest Service employs some young people at its headquarters in The Village. Some work with the United States Fish and Wildlife Service, which has a large reservation at South Santee.

The private service sector has grown rapidly and provided income for people who live in the parish. Now, at the end of the twentieth century, there are three restaurants in and around town, as well as three filling stations that also sell fast food. Police, firefighters, and emergency medical technicians are stationed in town around the clock. There is a furniture store on the highway. Telephone services have expanded, adding provision of cable and satellite television service.

This growth and development in the service sector had its start in the 1980s and flourished after Hurricane Hugo. It is providing The Village and St. James Santee with just a tinge of prosperity. But many people are not prosperous, and their properties are at risk of being sold to wealthy nonresidents.

6

Religion: Theology Mattered
in St. James Santee

S ome may think that the parish enjoyed golden ages of
wealth during the heydays of rice and cotton planting,
but it was never thus. The parish's residents were never
able to lay up treasures on earth. They tried, instead, to lay up
treasures in heaven. Observations from the ends of my parents' lives illustrate their spirituality.

"Now I lay me down to sleep. I pray Thee, Lord, my
soul to keep." Sitting at my mother's bedside in the intensive
care unit, I heard her recite the familiar prayer time after time.
She was misinterpreting my comments or making irrelevant
ones: "Take the trash out, will you, Daddy?" I tried to focus
her attention on realistic matters, inviting her to look at a tiny
ceramic Christmas tree the nurses allowed us to place on her
bedside table. "How beautiful," she said, and then said, "How
beautiful" repeatedly as I tried to engage her in conversation
about our relatives. Without stimulation, she would quickly
revert to the child's prayer.

This was the fifth day after her heart attack. Her confusion was alarming because it began abruptly and unexpect-

edly. She felt well after the initial pain subsided, and until this day, had been as alert and cheerful as always through her 89 years. We knew she was in danger because damage to the conducting system of her heart had necessitated installation of a cardiac pacemaker, but her confusion was the first indication that she was not doing well. Although we began preparing for her care at home as she rallied a bit the next day, she died later that evening.

Ten years earlier, I watched Mother trying to coax my father into lucidity. A stroke had paralyzed his nondominant (left) side and put him in bed for the last two and a half years of his life. He could speak, but he rarely said anything meaningful. I was thoroughly surprised and depressed when I heard him say one day, quite succinctly, "Walter, I think I'm about as bad off as a man can be."

Through the many months of my father's disability, Mother did a good job of keeping him comfortable and content. She sat with him for hours at a time, doing handwork while talking to him as if they were in a two-way conversation. To get him to speak at all, she would comment on or ask questions about religious topics. One day, she asked him to recite the names of the books of the Old Testament for me. He named them all in order without a slip: "Genesis, Exodus . . . Haggai, Zechariah, Malachi." Mother smiled triumphantly. She asked the first question in the Westminster Shorter Catechism: "What is the chief end of man?" Without hesitation he answered, "The chief end of man is to glorify God and enjoy Him forever."

These last things my parents said were statements of faith. Their malfunctioning brains were able to come up with religious quotations. Religion, education, and family were their life-long interests. Throughout their lifetimes, religious observance was a central feature of life in the South, in South Carolina, and in St. James Santee. They lived amongst people who aspired to build a society rooted in the Judeo-Christian system of values and a reformed Protestant lifestyle.

The religion my parents espoused was a blend of beliefs and practices that had formed during the Protestant Reformation. Their life together traced or repeated the course taken by Protestant churches from their arrival in North America to the mid-twentieth century. Their marriage re-enacted the merger of Protestant Christians into a unit, single in spirit if not in creed and document. The churches they came from joined forces throughout the South to create the church of the Theos.

Our Methodist mother, raised in the Lowcountry, where there had been an abundance of churches and a variety of religious influences over a long time, thought of God as a close, personal friend. She walked and talked with Him. Our father came from a close-knit Presbyterian community of the upper state, people who still felt they were immigrants, different from those around them. They wanted to make clear statements as to what they believed and so held on to doctrines that had been elaborated during the Reformation. Their statements said that God is different from us. He is a mighty and sovereign ruler. They acknowledged that He is the God of grace and of love because He revealed this in the person of Jesus Christ, but He is still separate from us — holy — very much the God of the Old Testament.

In marriage, my parents managed to change their ideas about various matters so that they could coexist and be good mates and parents. In the same manner, the ideas their churches had about God and religion blended to produce the unique, evangelical, Protestant religion that pervaded the South and dominated religious affairs in St. James Santee and the entire South from Civil War times to the present.

Religious Diversity

Carolina was founded at a time when the Christian church was dividing and subdividing. Martin Luther's reformation in Germany 150 years earlier succeeded because a spirit of freedom prevailed and because people desired to live lives of personal piety. Luther's study of scripture convinced him that the church itself did not convey salvation of individuals but that people are saved by faith and by the unmerited grace of God. Second-generation reformers carried Luther's ideas throughout northern Europe and the British Isles. Many Protestant churches emerged, some on a national basis, some founded on a particular ideal or concept about worship or personal piety, and some being the product of charismatic leaders.

In France and Geneva, John Calvin systematized Luther's doctrines and added to them the idea of the sovereignty of God: that God is in control of all affairs and that we ought to live our lives accordingly. Calvinism was adopted by the French Protestants — our Huguenots — and by churches that would be called "Reformed" on the continent and "Presbyterian" in the British Isles and by Baptist churches in both areas. Although the Church of England retained an Episcopal form of government and a liturgical form of worship, it was heavily influenced by Calvinism. Subdivisions of the Church of England, such as the Congregational church, were strongly Calvinistic.

During Queen Elizabeth's long reign (1558-1603), a movement developed that had great effect on religious life in England and throughout her colonies. The Puritans, greatly influenced by the reformers but coming from the membership of the Church of England, began to stress purity of action in the church and in their personal lives. They considered the Bible to be all-important as the source of direction for personal conduct and for organization, discipline, and worship in the church. They were Sabbatarians. In worship, they desired simplicity, placing emphasis on the glorification of God rather than on the pleasing of the senses. Many opposed the use of the Apostles' Creed and the Gloria Patri and objected to kneeling in worship. They wanted the altar made into a communion table and placed in the middle of the sanctuary to show that the service of communion is not an exclusive privilege of the clergy. They opposed the use of rings in the wedding service. Most significantly, they desired separation of church from the state and wanted either a representative church government or no structure at all.

The Church of England tolerated most of the variances desired by the Puritans, but it would not accept a change in the form of church government. The established church took the position that the Bible, tradition, and reason were of equal importance in developing rules of worship and organization and thus retained the form of government that had existed for over 1,500 years.

Elizabeth's successor, James I, was the first of the Stuart monarchs. Raised in Scotland with a Presbyterian background, he was nominally Protestant, but he was the son of Mary, Queen of Scots, a Roman Catholic. He was attracted to Catholicism, but, as king, attempted to hold to the middle ground offered by the Church of England. During his reign (1603-1625), the Puritans succeeded in founding the Congregational Church.

James' great contribution to church life was the publication of a new translation of the Bible in English known as the "Authorized Version" or "King James Version." This was the holy book of the English-speaking Protestant Christendom, and its contents became the language of society in the mother country and its colonies. Generations of families have kept these Bibles. Ours, the one the Loftons are listed in, was printed in Belfast, Ireland in 1702. As of this time — the year 2002 — the last entries are the names Samuel Lofton Bonner, born September 10, 1995, and Amelia Grace Bonner, born August 13, 1998, son and daughter of David and Cynthia Bonner. This Bible was first owned by the Millar family. It passed on to the Stromans, then to the Loftons, then to the Johnsons, and finally to the Bonners.

The second Stuart king was Charles I, son of James, who ruled from 1625 until 1649. Charles attempted stricter enforcement of laws requiring worship in the Church of England, while also advancing the cause of the Roman Catholic Church. In England, the Puritans and other separatist groups organized in opposition. Similarly, in Scotland, there was hostility between those loyal to King Charles and the "Covenanters," those who wanted to preserve the Presbyterian Church government. The English Parliament became increasingly hostile to the crown, and the ensuing civil war lasted until 1649, ending with the beheading of King Charles.

Oliver Cromwell, military leader of the forces opposed to the king, served as Lord Protector from 1653 until his death in 1658. Freedom of worship was granted to all groups other than the Church of England and the Roman Catholic Church. However, Cromwell began to dispute with the English and Scottish Presbyterians and purged them from his parliament. This was a time of religious strife, in which animosities were created that still exist to this day, but it was also a time of experimentation. Multitudes of religious sects appeared and disappeared. One group appearing at this time that came to be of importance in America was the Quakers. The Quakers occupied the middle colonies of America and, later, invited our Scotch-Irish ancestors to join them.

Restoration and the Carolina Colony

After Cromwell's death there arose a reaction to Puritan piety. The people yearned for the relative freedom and entertainment they enjoyed under the monarchy. Parliamentary rule could not endure, and, in 1660, the monarchy was restored with the crowning of Charles II, son of Charles I. Puritanism was cast aside in a frenzy of upper-class self-indulgence. It was during this time that "Merry Old England," as it was known in this era, founded the colony of Carolina.

Charles II attempted to make all Christians worship according to the standards of the Church of England. In 1662, Parliament, faithful to the king, passed the Act of Uniformity. In 1664, the lawmakers further constricted religious observance and labeled all who refused to participate in the approved way "Dissenters." In 1673, Dissenters were forbidden to hold military or civil office unless they took communion in the Church of England. At the same time, Charles attempted to make the Church of England serve as the official Church of Scotland by changing Scotland's church to an Episcopal form of government. The result was discord and rebellion, for the Covenanters would not hear of it. Rather paradoxically, England under Charles II continued the policy of several previous regimes in providing sanctuary for French Huguenot refugees.

Charles II died in 1685 and was succeeded by his brother James II. James enforced Charles II's policies with vigor. In Scotland, the Covenanters, who never accepted domination by the Church of England, were hunted down and killed in large numbers so that the first year of James' reign is remembered in Scotland as "the killing time."

Thus, James became the object of a popular rebellion. He was driven from the throne and replaced by co-regents, William of Orange and his wife Mary. William was raised in the Reformed tradition of the Dutch church. In England, he functioned within the Church of England, the established church of the land. The Presbyterian Church was established in Scotland. In both countries, freedom of worship was extended to all religious groups. Even so, the right to vote, hold political office, and attend universities was limited to members of the established church.

The concessions made following "The Glorious Rebellion" still did not satisfy Scotland's most uncompromising Calvinists. Demanding separation of church and state, they set up their own church, the Reformed Presbyterian Church.

In a later schism, Reverend Ebenezer Erskine and others led a faction out of the Reformed Presbyterian Church to create the Associate Reformed Presbyterian Church. This new group adhered to an even purer style of Calvinism. The Associate Reformed Presbyterians were among the Lowland Scots who migrated to Northern Ireland after William of Orange's defeat of King James II's Catholic armies. Displeased with the English who lured them there, and having made enemies of the native Irish, a great many of these Lowland Scots migrated to the Americas after about 1725. In America, they came to be known as the "Scotch-Irish." These were the people who would, by various routes, come to McClellanville and contribute to the formation of the Theodemocratic society.

The Scotch-Irish brought with them a religious intensity and a love of their churches, whether Presbyterian, Reformed Presbyterian, or Associate Reformed Presbyterian. They had become enthusiastic students of the Bible and religion and of secular affairs as well. While they demanded separation of church and state, they endeavored to create a society of Puritan ideals. Rather than build beautiful sanctuaries or create music, statuary, or paintings, they wanted to glorify their sovereign God Almighty through the beauty of their lives. They tried to be God's people and they were in many ways, but they often fell into self-satisfied narrow-mindedness. They were believers in progress, for they felt that they were the movers and shakers in God's plans for His kingdom, yet they accepted some ideas or standards as being irrevocable. Wherever they roamed, they carried these contradictions with them. They had a lot to do with setting the moral tone and way of life in the places they settled down, including McClellanville.

In whatever part of Carolina the Scotch-Irish settled, they found themselves in a society that was, at its beginning, endowed with the ideal of religious diversity. In having freedom of worship, the colony was ahead of society in England. This founding principle was the creation of one of the Lord's Proprietors.

Lord Ashley Cooper was the most dynamic of the proprietors. He took the lead in getting the colony settled, and he arranged to have his personal physician and secretary, John Locke, draw up the blueprint for the government of Carolina. Locke's product, the Fundamental Constitutions, contained provisions for religious tolerance. All would be free to worship in any manner they pleased if they would affirm that there is a God and that He is to be worshipped and would answer thus when asked to comment. Any seven persons, including slaves, could establish a church of their choice. These religious standards were the most liberal features of the Fundamental Constitutions. In other respects, it was a most conservative and backward-looking work. The great reputations of Dr. Locke and Lord Ashley rest on other accomplishments. Locke distinguished himself in philosophy and the study of the mind, while Lord Ashley is best known as the author of the writ of habeas corpus in its present form. Lord Ashley's stand for religious tolerance was not a late development for him. During the English Civil War, he managed to serve both the parliamentary and the royal governments, and he kept his head.

During the proprietary era (1670-1719), about half of Carolina's settlers, and exactly half of the governors of Carolina, were Dissenters — a mixture of Presbyterians, Baptists, Quakers, and other denominations. The Dissenters and the Anglicans mixed quite well for the first twelve or fifteen years, but as the population grew, there appeared suspicions and animosities similar to those that existed in the mother country. The groups divided on a geographical basis. The Dissenters tended to gather southwest of Charlestown while the Anglicans remained in and about the newly forming city.

Next the Huguenots immigrated, first into Charlestown and to Orange Quarter on a branch of the Cooper River and then into St. James Santee.

The Huguenots upset the balance of power. The majority joined the Church of England. Why they chose to abandon or deviate from the Reformed faith they had fought so hard for in France is a question that has been much debated. The best answer is that they did not think that the two churches were remarkably different. Both the Huguenot and the Anglican Churches were Protestant and anti-Roman Catholic. Both had liturgical forms of worship. Furthermore, the French felt kindly toward the English for having taken them in when they were being chased out of France. From the practical standpoint, the French gained financial support for their churches and gained the right to vote and hold political office.

It is also true that not all Dissenters welcomed the Huguenots. Some were downright hostile to them. The group of New England Congregationalists located in the Wando Neck area protested to Governor Archdale (a Dissenter himself) the close proximity of the French. These contentious Christians were none other than the forerunners of many Theodemocrats of St. James Santee and McClellanville.

In the first years of the eighteenth century, the Anglican party became the dominant population and sought to disenfranchise the Dissenters. They initiated legislation that would later establish the Church of England in Carolina and restrict political activity to members of that communion. With Ashley Cooper (who became the Earl of Shaftesbury before he died) and other original proprietors out of the way, they had little difficulty winning their point. After initial denials by the proprietors and the crown, the Church of England was made the established church of Carolina in 1706 and parishes were created. Political activity of non-Anglicans, however, was not curtailed.

From then on, there was little religious squabbling in Carolina. The colonists concerned themselves with fighting off the French and the Spanish and with eradicating pirates. In 1715, the Carolinians began the long and dangerous war with the local Indians. Carolina's townships were created in the 1730s. Land and freedom were offered to people of various religious groups from Scotland, Wales, Ireland, Switzerland, Germany, and England itself. In Carolina — now divided into South Carolina and North Carolina — religious pluralism prevailed.

The Great Awakening

As South Carolina's population began to grow and disperse throughout the territory, a surge of interest in religion occurred. The Great Awakening began in the 1740s and continued through the American Revolution. Jonathan Edwards, the Calvinist minister, figured prominently in the movement in the northeastern colonies. In South Carolina, the movement was begun by the missionary activity of John and Charles Wesley and George Whitefield, ministers of the Church of England but the founders of Methodism. The movement promoted Puritan ideals of the Christian life but laid greater emphasis on free will than did the Calvinistic churches and sects. Methodism encouraged believers to seek a personal relationship with God, beginning with an individual conversion experience.

The Great Awakening started a revivalist movement in the entire nation, especially in the South. Methodists became more Calvinistic, while Presbyterians became more comfortable with the idea of free will. Baptist and Lutheran Churches held similar beliefs. The Church of England became the Protestant Episcopal Church after the Revolution. It lost membership, to the Methodists especially, but endured and held a moderate Protestant position, much like the others.

Thus, in the South, there was near uniformity or homogeneity in religion from the early 1800s through World War II. There have been Roman Catholic and Jewish congregations in most communities, but these have been too few in number to detract the Protestants from their course together.

The Protestant churches did maintain some individuality in worship. An informal style marked the evangelical churches — the Methodists and the Baptists. At the other extreme were liturgical churches — the Episcopalians and the Lutherans. In between were the semiformal Presbyterians.

The beliefs of the Protestants were doctrinaire. They were Trinitarians. They held that Jesus is the head of the church and that the congregation constituted the living body of Christ. They adored the Bible as the inspired word of God. They participated in a strong congregational life: churches were activity centers in small communities, such as McClellanville, but also in municipalities. Ministers could come and go, but the heart of the churches was the people. At home, the people read religious magazines and tracts. The Protestants of the South were devoted to the idea of separation of church and state, but they also favored the creation of a Christian community or society. Being great Sabbatarians, they passed laws (South Carolina's Blue Laws) that sometimes restricted the activity of the few who held corporate worship services on Saturdays.

Individuals with other ideas than those held by the majority generally kept their thoughts to themselves or, at least, did not attack the majority. It was widely known that Dr. James Waring, Henry Michael Lofton's physician in the early 1900s, did not believe in the virgin birth. The doctor attended the Episcopal Church in McClellanville, supported it financially, and was friendly with its members, but he would quietly leave the worship service when communion was served.

There was virtually no difference in the lives of the Episcopalians and Presbyterians. At weddings and other social events, the hosts would serve both "Episcopal punch" (spiked) and "Presbyterian punch" (non-alcoholic), but that provided the only means of telling who was a member of what.

By 1800, the Methodist Church was the largest in the United States. Presbyterian and other reformed churches had grown vigorously as a result of immigration before and after the Revolution. The first Scots to come to Carolina in the early 1700s were those who had supported the Stuart kings. Many were well-to-do merchants or shippers. Though they were Presbyterians, they tended to be loyal to the United Kingdom after Union in 1707 and generally remained loyalists during the Revolution. The Scots Presbyterian Church (now First Scots Presbyterian) opposed the rebellion. The Scotch-Irish were a different breed of churchmen, bitterly opposed to the Stuarts and to anything British. They had been fighting the British along the border between England and Scotland for generations. They were quite ready to take the American side in the Revolution.

In about 1830, there began another surge in interest in religion, giving birth to the Great American Revival. Presbyterians were the source of much of the "old-fashioned revivalism," which characterized the movement, but gradually yielded leadership to the Methodists, the Baptists, and other evangelical churches. Presbyterians thus failed to grow as much as the others did. Today, in most of the South, a friendly sea of Baptists surrounds the other white churchmen. St. James Santee was unusual in this regard. In St. James Santee, there were Huguenots, then Episcopalians, then Methodists, then Presbyterians, but no Baptist church appeared until after World War II.

The Morrisons came from a Scotch-Irish Presbyterian family in Maryland. The first R.T. Morrison moved down to Christ Church Parish, married Elizabeth Ann Legare, and became a member of the Wappetaw Independent Congregational Church.

The Lelands, originally English, moved to New England from where Aaron Whitney Leland came to become minister of the First (Scots) Presbyterian Church in Charleston. His descendants carried their Calvinism on to Christ Church Parish and then into St. James Santee.

New Wappetaw Presbyterian Church in 1930. It was constructed in 1875. The original steeple was on the left side.

The Grahams came from Scotland, where they belonged to the Presbyterian Church. Because they found no Reformed congregations while they stayed in Horry County, they joined the Methodist Church and remained Methodists in McClellanville.

The McClellans, originally Scotch-Irish and Presbyterian, became Episcopalian after Archibald McClellan settled in St. James Santee in the 1760s, but his descendants reverted to Presbyterianism or became Methodists when churches of those denominations appeared in McClellanville.

Since World War II, shifts of population and advances in mass communication and travel have promoted a trend toward religious pluralism. Church affiliation is still the standard, but there are more religious bodies to affiliate with. Evangelical churches, especially, have multiplied and grown in membership. People move freely from one church to an-

*Reverend Ludwig Beckman, Jr.,
in 1930.*

other and are no longer identified by their church membership. These days, churches compete with secular entertainment for the loyalty of their people. In St. James Santee, as the apostle Paul warned, the people may fall under the influence of the elemental spirits (the natural spirits) of the place.

In the Churches

Although he had never been a Presbyterian, and did not remain one for long, Captain Henry Michael Lofton was a founding father of the New Wappetaw Presbyterian Church of McClellanville. Lofton is listed as one of its first elders.

Henry Lofton's forebears, as mentioned earlier, were Episcopalians turned Methodists. He remained a Methodist until he relocated to Christ Church Parish after the Civil War. There, he joined and held office in the Wappetaw Independent Congregational Church, the church Susan Ann Morrison Lofton had grown up in. But the Wappetaw community was much changed from its pre-war state. It was depleted of able men, and its plantations had been laid waste or neglected. People were moving away. The Congregational Church had been vandalized. It became evident that there would be no recovery for the weakened congregation. Henry and Susan Ann moved to their permanent home six miles southwest of McClellanville. In 1872, Henry Lofton made the motion to dissolve the church and divide its assets between the Mt. Pleasant Presbyterian Church and a newly forming church in McClellanville, later named the New Wappetaw Presbyterian Church.

The church building at Wappetaw gradually disintegrated. The historian Petrona McIver, who watched it deteriorate through her teenage years, wrote: "I remember the ruins of the church as a crumbling shell. A wooden structure of plain design, it never fell but just seemed to settle lower and lower until it just disappeared."

The old building lasted long enough to give Henry Michael Lofton the scare of his life, the story of which he told repeatedly to his children. Returning alone to his home at Buck Hall from a meeting in Mt. Pleasant, Lofton encountered a severe thunderstorm and chose to take shelter in the dark old church. He pushed the door open and entered. Immediately the stillness was shattered by a scream, and a dark figure rushed past him and out through the cemetery. He learned, later, that the figure was a crazed woman who often used the church as her sanctuary.

When the McClellanville congregation elected its officers at an organizational meeting, leadership roles went to four patriarchs. Elected elders were R. T. Morrison; R. T. Morrison, Jr.; J. Hibben Leland; and Aaron Whitney Leland. As far as we know, Henry Lofton did not feel slighted. Henry, his brothers, and their families were active members at New Wappetaw. Henry made and kept a pledge of financial support. The congregation gathered funds and was soon able to plan construction of a sanctuary. The building, which is still used today, was dedicated on December 20, 1874, at ceremonies presided over by the Reverend Doctors John Girardeau and Gilbert Brackett, representing Charleston Presbytery. The first worship service at New Wappetaw Presbyterian Church was held in the completed sanctuary on June 20, 1875.

Henry Lofton's conversion to Presbyterianism did not last. A little more than a decade after the founding of the New Wappetaw Presbyterian Church, he and Susan Ann had a major conflict with the establishment.

I always heard that Henry Lofton left the Presbyterian Church because he did not like the way the Presbyterian preacher buried his wife. That bit of family lore was in error. Susan Ann, who lived to 1896, was buried in the Methodist part of the cemetery after services led by a Methodist minister. An earlier conflict with the Presbyterian sanhedrin led Susan Ann and Henry from one church to the other.

A June 7, 1885, entry in the minutes of the New Wappetaw Presbyterian Church states:

> Charleston Presbytery at its most recent meeting in Charleston adopted the following paper: 'This Presbytery has learned with sorrow of troubles which exist in New Wappetaw Church, that impair the efficiency of that church and hinder the progress of the redeemer's kingdom in that community. Therefore be it resolved that a commission of Presbytery be appointed to visit said church and make inquiries into the nature of those difficulties, and with full power to take such action in the premises, as under the law of our church their wisdom might suggest.'

A search of the minutes reveals that the above action was taken and that the commission consisted of the Reverends John L. Girardeau, C. S. Vedden, and W. T. Thompson, plus elder J.A. Enslow. From then, however, minutes are quiet about the matter. If the commission visited or took any action, we do not know. New Wappetaw's minutes never reveal *what* was going on but do tell us *who* was doing the arguing.

A March 14, 1886, entry says:

The following letter from Mrs. Susan Ann Lofton was read by the moderator:

McClellanville, SC
March 14, 1886
To the session of New Wappetaw Church
Gentlemen:

The unchristlike and official misconduct of R. T. Morrison, Jr., J. B. Morrison, and A. W. Leland towards my family necessitates my removal from your church. You will, therefore, according to the laws of the church, grant me an immediate dismissal from your "roll" of membership, and by so doing oblige,
Yours Respectfully,
Mrs. S. A. Lofton

Richard Tillia Morrison, Jr., was her father. J. B. Morrison was her brother. What prompted my great-grandmother to make such strong charges against her own people?

Because Susan Ann Morrison included the term "official" in her letter, the session sent her word that she should "bring charges and specifications" against the officers. Mrs. Lofton replied on March 31, 1886:

To the session of New Wappetaw Church
Gentlemen:

In reply to your communication of the 14th I would respectfully state that when I made the request for dismissal from the church I was under the misapprehension that it was not necessary for me to give my reasons in order to ask a dismissal. I did not intend then to prosecute and will not now prosecute any charges against the officials of the church. All that I want is an honorable discharge from the church to which I am entitled as a member in good and regular standing.
Sincerely,
Mrs. S. A. Lofton

That ended official recording on the matter, and we will likely never find out what the spat was about. It may have been a purely ecclesiastical matter — perhaps the gang of three thwarted Henry Lofton's desire to serve as an elder in that church. Maybe the leaders accused the Loftons of not meeting their financial commitment. It is entirely possible that the disagreement had its origin over properties, for the lands and the schools were the things people fussed about. The residents of St. James Santee argued with one another but came back together to worship, to marry or bury one another, and to feel united against the outside world.

Susan Ann and Henry Michael Lofton did not secure a new church home immediately. They worshipped nowhere for six years but, being religious people, they allowed themselves to be led to a new congregation. Their son Richard and daughter-in-law Edith were continuing to attend New Wappetaw Presbyterian Church. Edith suggested that her in-laws try attending Methodist worship services and offered to go with them, resulting in Henry's branch of the Lofton family

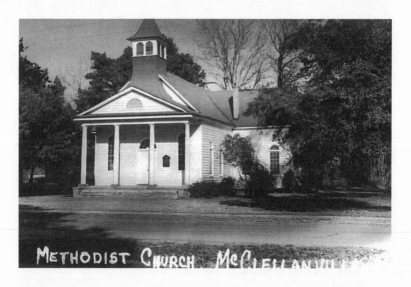

The Methodist Church, constructed 1902. Photographed in 1946.

St. James Santee Episcopal Chapel of Ease, consecrated in 1890. Photographed in 2000.

moving back to Methodism. John Marion Lofton and family remained in the Presbyterian Church.

The McClellanville Methodist Church was organized in 1885 and erected its sanctuary in 1903. The congregation came from the old Nazareth Church at the Thirty-two and from some who moved from the Episcopal and Presbyterian Churches. In the same era, Episcopalians were moving in from the Santee River plantations and found it appropriate to build a Chapel of Ease in McClellanville. First services were held there in 1888. Those churches would last as the only houses of worship for white citizens until the McClellanville Baptist Church organized after World War II. In the 1990s, a Pentecostal Holiness Church opened outside town limits. Black citizens created Bethel African Methodist Church after the Civil War and later organized the Missionary Baptist Church. Bethel Church has been replaced by a modern sanctuary located out of town, so the original building is called "Old Bethel."

Membership in the Episcopal, Methodist, and Presbyte-

McClellanville Baptist Church, constructed 1941. Photographed in 1946.

rian congregations of McClellanville was determined more by whom one married than by attraction to any religious standard or doctrine. Families, of course, tended to remain in the church they started in.

Henry Toomer Morrison caused a stir when he left the Presbyterian fold and joined the Episcopal Church in 1910. He had attended an Episcopal college (Hobart) and married an Episcopalian, so his ties to the church were strong, and he saw no reason he should not change. His brothers objected for a while but ultimately conceded that there were enough Morrisons to go around.

The Grahams and the McClellans are mostly Methodist. The majority of the descendants of the Santee River planters attend the Episcopal Church, but marriage has replaced the old family names (Lucas, Rutledge, Doar, and Seabrook) with non-indigenous surnames.

In The Village there has been friendly acceptance of one another. The Presbyterians and the Methodists have functioned as one in many ways — youth groups have met together, scout troops have included youths from both churches, women's circles have had joint projects, and summer Bible schools have alternated between the two buildings. Individual members of the Episcopal Church have joined in many of these functions. The growing Baptist congregation has met with the others in joint worship services.

The religious interconnections of the DuPre family provide an example of ecumenism. Reverend Daniel DuPre, a signer of the Ordinance of Secession,

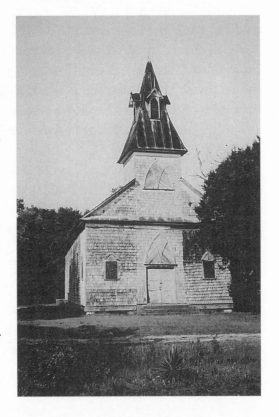

Old Bethel African Methodist Episcopal Church, built about 1872.

came from a Huguenot family and was a member of the Episcopal Church. He was attracted to Methodism, joined that church, and was ordained a Methodist minister. His career was spent moving about Methodist churches in the Lowcountry. He often preached at the Wappetaw Independent Congregational Church. After the Civil War, he was a frequent guest minister in the Presbyterian pulpit and served as interim pastor of New Wappetaw Presbyterian Church for one short period.

Reverend DuPre named a son (Andrew Hibben DuPre) for the Methodist minister Andrew Hibben. Andrew Hibben DuPre's son, John Young DuPre, married Helen Laval, another Huguenot descendent. Mrs. DuPre sang at my mother's wedding in the McClellanville Methodist Church. In turn, her daughter, Helen Laval DuPre Satterlee, showed the ecumenism of her ancestors. The younger Helen was a member of the St. James Santee Episcopal Church, a member of the ladies' circle at the New Wappetaw Presbyterian Church, and a frequent participant at functions of the McClellanville Methodist Church.

Membership in McClellanville churches has held steady since its losses in the 1920s and 1930s. Churches are an important part of this community but, these days, the public or visible lives of its citizens are not so interwoven with church membership. People are not identified as member of a certain church. One hears less of "the Presbyterians" or of "the Methodist women." Observation of the Sabbath is not so routine in this era of prosperity, as food and entertainment is readily available, travel is easy, and the beauty of the environment (some of the spirits of the place) frequently beckon people out of doors.

7

Around the Beach

The *Charleston Courier* of February 1, 1862, announced the marriage of Captain Henry Michael Lofton of Marion District and Miss Susan Ann Morrison of St. James Santee on January 30, 1862. The Reverend Doctor Thomas Smyth conducted the services at the Second Presbyterian Church in Charleston. The couple's first child, Richard Morrison Lofton, was born a scant but proper nine months later on October 27, 1862.

Richard Lofton's early years were much affected by the war. His father was necessarily absent for most of the first two-and-a-half years of his life. When the siege of Charleston threatened residents of the city, Richard and his mother moved to Greenwood, South Carolina. At Greenwood, his mother delivered her second child, Elizabeth Ann. When the war ended, the refugees were guided back to the Lowcountry by Henry Lofton, who had walked to Greenwood from the Appomatox, Virginia, area.

The family resided at Andersonville Plantation in old Christ Church Parish for about five years during Henry Lofton's unsuccessful attempt at raising Sea Island cotton. Richard's siblings, Louise Augusta, Julia Riley, and Henry Michael, Jr., joined the family before they moved on to St. James Santee. Richard grew up at the Lofton's new home on the Kings Highway near the Laurel Hill plantation of Richard Tillia Morrison, Jr., and near Buck Hall. His sister, Elizabeth Ann, died at age twelve, but he gained three more brothers: Samuel Joseph, James Armstrong, and Thomas Lucas.

Richard was taught at home and at a small elementary school. By 1879, Henry Michael Lofton was prosperous enough to enroll Richard in the Carolina Military Institute (CMI) of Charlotte, North Carolina. Colonel John P. Thomas founded the institute in 1872. CMI was essentially The Citadel in exile, for Federal troops still occupied The Citadel in Charleston and denied the re-opening of the college. The school in Charlotte used the buildings and grounds of the former North Carolina Military Institute, founded in 1856 by Colonel H. D. Hill, later a Confederate general. CMI provided instruction in mathematics, physical sciences, history, ethics, modern languages, ancient languages, commercial subjects, and military science. The school's catalog stated that it "adheres itself primarily to the youth of the Carolinas. Its discipline is military in character, but the system pursued at the institute is based on agreements and appeals to the sense of honor and to the sentiment of duty." Thus, my grandfather followed in Henry Michael Lofton's footsteps as a participant in the South's tradition of romantic militarism.

The majority of students were South Carolinians. A smaller number hailed from North Carolina, and there were a few from Georgia and Virginia plus a scattering from the northeast. Richard's classmate and roommate, Jacob Paul Stroman, came from Springfield, South Carolina.

Cadet Lofton did well at the military school. He rose to third-ranking officer in the corps of cadets and was third academically in his 1882 graduating class. Graduation ceremonies in June 1882 turned out to be an emotional event because the institution was closing its doors. The Citadel in Charleston was to return to life. Federal troops had moved out, and the South Carolina legislature, dominated by white, native South Carolinians, promptly moved to re-open the school with John P. Thomas at its head. At CMI's closing exercises, each senior provided an address or presentation. An article in Charleston's *News and Courier* covered every aspect of the program and reported that "Cadet R. M. Lofton's production deserved special mention." His subject was "Lessons of Bacon's Life," a review of the career and thought of Francis Bacon.

Richard returned to South Carolina to work with his father, but he soon sought a profession. He sojourned in Charleston where he read law with the prominent attorney and state senator, Robert Barnwell. Barnwell thought highly of the young man and offered an assistantship, but Richard chose to return to old St. James Santee. He found a wife in Charleston, for there he renewed acquaintance with Lillian Edith Stroman, whom he had met on trips to the home of his former roommate.

The Stromans were from a family of German Swiss Protestants who settled in Orangeburg Township in the 1730s. Edith's great-grandfather established a cotton plantation at Rocky Swamp, midway between Springfield and Norway, South Carolina. Her grandfather was one of about 150 South Carolinians who, in 1861, owned one hundred or more slaves. The plantation was greatly weakened by the war and was damaged further by marauding soldiers under General Sherman, but the home survived. Though it was in the direct path of the invading army, the place was not burned. Edith's father was able to make the farm productive within a few years and did well enough to send his children off for secondary education.

Edith did not have an easy childhood. Her mother died two months after her birth. Her father remarried, and there are indications that Edith's stepmother preferred the children's removal. Edith moved about from relative to relative, spending much time with her mother's family in Charleston. Ultimately, she came under the care of her Aunt Harriett Millar, a connection that set the stage for a long association of "Aunt Hattie" with the Lofton family. In Charleston, Edith attended Memminger High School, one of the few high schools for girls in the southern states. In June 1884, at

Richard Morrison Lofton in the uniform of the Carolina Military Institute.

age sixteen, she received her diploma. When she and Richard married at Rocky Swamp Methodist Church on December 17, 1884, Edith was barely seventeen years old.

Richard and Edith settled in McClellanville, where Richard worked with his father's farming, lumbering, and turpentine-making projects. He was admitted to the South Carolina bar on May 26, 1885, by the signing of the role of attorneys at the Supreme Court in Columbia.

Lillian Edith Stroman, graduation photograph, Memminger High School, 1885.

The couple's first child, Margaret Caroline, was born on October 8, 1885. Soon thereafter, Edith suffered from post-partum depression. It was necessary to move her to the farm at Lofton so that she could be cared for by her mother-in-law. She recovered quickly but remained at Lofton almost two years and, during that time, taught at a small school on "Oil Hill," near the thirty-two-mile house.

Edith had no more children until February 21, 1889. The arrival of that child, Susie May, necessitated the acquisition of a larger home on the marsh overlooking Cape Romain. There, in the new home, Edith would deliver seven more children, the ninth and last being her only son, Richard Morrison Lofton, Jr., born March 23, 1908. One girl, Charlotte, died soon after birth on October 22, 1900.

Richard purchased the marshfront home from the New Wappetaw Presbyterian Church, which had some kind of structure there as a home for the minister. We are not sure whether that house remained and was added to or whether it was torn down. Some of our older cousins recall hearing that the Loftons moved a small house from the family plantation to the spot around the beach. What is certain is that a small two-story house was the center of the home and that wings were added to each side and to the rear. Patched together as it was, "Around the Beach" looked typical of McClellanville homes, but it could not be called Victorian, as it lacked the gables so dominant on the large houses designed and built between the Civil War and World War I. It was not trimmed in the so-called "gingerbread" style. Society columns in Charleston and Georgetown newspapers described the Lofton home not in terms like "beautiful" or "elegant" but as "spacious."

What was spacious and beautiful was the view from the house. Richard and Edith Lofton and children looked out across the widest sea marsh on the East Coast of the United States. The afternoon sun illuminated the lighthouses of Cape Romain, which stand nearly five miles from the mainland and

"Around the Beach." The Richard Morrison Lofton home, 1892-1989.

were both built in the 1800s. At night, as the family sat on the porch, they watched Cape Romain light blink regularly. A full moon rising over high tide sent a wavering band of light through the marsh. Edith Lofton told her children it was a fairy path.

In front of the house was a sparse lawn of Charleston grass, fronted by a white picket fence, beyond which were live oaks draped with Spanish moss. Before the days of motor vehicles, an oyster-shell-covered public street ended beyond the oaks, and there were benches on which townspeople could sit (mosquitoes permitting) to enjoy the view. Over the marsh, gulls and terns called gently as they wheeled over the smaller creeks. Late in the day, cicadas sounded, and the slow decrescendo of their buzzing spoke of peace and contentment. The place welcomed and called one back.

At its edge, the marsh soil was firm and sandy for thirty or forty yards before turning into dark, soft mud. This rim of the marsh, which flooded only on the highest tides, supported a scant growth of short and stubby spartina grass. There were broad areas of bare sand. Boys and girls could walk on this marsh, herd fiddler crabs across it when it was dry, or catch blue crabs on it when it was flooded.

Sandy, light-colored marsh soil such as that in front of the old Lofton home was found at intervals from Jeremy Creek to a point several miles northeast. Villagers called all of this "the beach," even though it was very different from the true beach on the ocean shore. The Lofton homestead was said to be "around the beach." When playing at our home on Jeremy Creek or anywhere else in The Village, we would sooner or later decide to "go around the beach."

In the backyard were a carriage house and a smoke house. There was a grove of pecan trees; there were grapevines bearing scuppernongs and blue grapes; and there was a vegetable garden. In 1898, my grandfather enlarged the place by purchasing the contiguous piece of marshfront from Mr. Ozzie McClellan. The added property extends eastward along the marsh, ending about a quarter of a mile away where a small creek penetrates inland. This thin strip, designated high land on the tax map, is actually quite low. It is often flooded by tides above the normal 5.2-foot level. Called "the pasture," the area was grazing land for cattle and horses but at times, it bore crops such as beans and corn. Most important, it was a playground for generations of children from all around The Village.

The creek at the end of the pasture acquired the name "Cooter Pen Creek" because Richard Lofton, Jr., and Binks DuPre established on it a holding pen for terrapins. The two aspired to sell these to restaurateurs in New York just as some of their ancestors sold terrapins to transatlantic vessels in the days of sail. Beverly and I took ownership of the end of the pasture in 1971 when Mother deeded over to me the remnant she owned, which included cleared land and the woods at the edge of Cooter Pen Creek. She inherited that section when she and her siblings divided the property in 1931, following her mother's death. Mother drew the short straw and thus took ownership of the terminal portion of the property. I proposed we name our place "The Cooter Pen," but Beverly vetoed the idea and we settled on "Short Straw."

The Lofton homestead included about fifteen acres of high land and seventy-five acres of marsh. In Richard Lofton's day, owners held clear title to the marsh out to the low-water mark of the nearest creek. Now, owners of waterfront property hold title to the marsh and pay tax on it, but the state controls use of it.

"Around the Beach" was not a massive property, and the house was not imposing, but it looked like it belonged there. The view was arresting. During Richard Lofton's terminal illness in 1928, his friend John Shokes visited frequently. An oysterman and farmer of mixed black-and-white parentage, Mr. Shokes was a contemporary of our grandfather. They sat together on the porch, swapping stories. Several times John Shokes commented, "Richard, you have the whole 'bottry' here," comparing the view with that from Charleston's famous Battery, where the Ashley and the Cooper Rivers converge.

As long as Edith Lofton lived, the grounds were beautiful because she enjoyed planting and gardening, bringing specimens from the Stroman place in Springfield. My mother would proudly identify her mother's plantings. Inside, the house was well-kept and well-outfitted, again because Mother Edith liked things to look good.

For most of their lives, Richard and Edith made do with oil lamps for illumination. In the 1920s, the electrical service in the Lofton house was primitive. A single bare bulb suspended from the center of the ceiling was all that was provided in any room. In some rooms, the wiring put in place in the 1920s stayed in use to the end. It is remarkable that Hurricane Hugo beat an electric fire to the destruction of the old place.

Comforts that we take for granted were absent from the Lofton house while the original residents lived there. There was no such thing as central heating. Some of the downstairs rooms had fireplaces, but the children's rooms had none. They took hot water bottles and heated flannel sheets to bed. In the 1950s, Caroline Lofton Johnson installed gas heaters in the few rooms she used. Window screens were another late addition to the comfort of living in The Village. Most homes were not provided with them until after World War II. People got by with the use of mosquito cloth when the insects were abundant after heavy rains and when the frequent northeasterly winds blew them in off the marsh. I vividly remember having the protective cloth draped around the youth bed I slept in on more than one visit to "Around the Beach."

The water supply was from a shallow well outfitted with a hand pump or from a cistern that collected rain water off the roof. The pump water was exceedingly hard and tasted a little like Epsom salts. Even worse, the minerals in the water tended to precipitate on exposure to tea, especially when chilled. One had to hustle in making, adding ice to, and drinking one's tea to keep from seeing an unappetizing brown flocculate collect at the bottom of the glass. The girls hoarded the cistern water to use in washing their hair. The family bathed indoors with water heated in the kitchen. For toilet facilities, they used slop jars or the outhouse.

During that time, "Around the Beach" was also home to other residents. The children had a teacher, music instructor, and governess in the person of Edith's maiden aunt, Hattie Millar. Cousin Ernest Leland lived there for months at a time, as did Richard's youngest brother, Tom. The family cook, Maum Ellen, lived in an apartment in the rear wing.

Margaret Harriett Millar, known as "Aunt Hattie," came to live with the Loftons in May 1902. It was she who raised Edith Stroman after Edith's mother died. Aunt Hattie, born in Charleston on March 30, 1845, was a Civil War spinster. Her first beau died in battle. A second was killed in a fall from a horse. At "Around the Beach," Hattie was the children's home teacher and piano teacher as well, taking in pupils from the community. Less than two months after Hattie took residence, the Lofton's sixth surviving daughter joined the family circle. Caroline Juliet was born on June 16, 1902. As soon as the newcomer moved out of her mother's room, she moved in with Aunt Hattie and became more than Hattie's charge or responsibility. Caroline, everyone knew, was "Aunt Hattie's girl."

The children also got considerable instruction from Maum Ellen, who lived in the rear apartment. The cook and housekeeper for the family, she was the third in command. The children were made to help by setting tables, cleaning house, and doing yard work. Ellen was less effective in teaching them

The Lofton family, about 1906. Children, front: Mary ("Teen"), Augusta, Caroline. Children, rear: Frances, Susie, Margie, Edith. Seated: Richard and Edith Stroman Lofton.

how to cook or, perhaps, did it all herself. None of the girls was interested in or skilled at cooking when she managed her own home. All of them were busy doing other things.

Richard and Edith's family had a busy social life. There were birthdays and holidays; recitals and church events; outdoor activities, such as boating, swimming, crabbing, and horseback riding; and dances and overnight parties at homes in The Village or around the parish. In that Victorian age, girls were closely supervised or chaperoned. When swimming, girls had to wear long outfits. At home, they could swim only in the confines of the boathouse where Richard Lofton kept his freight boat. Under his supervision, the girls rode horses sidesaddle. On Sunday afternoons, the Loftons had musicales. The girls would play, and all would sing. Neighbors and relatives came in to participate.

On occasion, the family traveled to Charleston. While Richard served in the legislature, they visited Columbia to attend various events. In the summer, they spent weeks at their grandfather's place in Saluda, North Carolina. This annual sojourn was at the command of the patriarch. The children preferred to stay in McClellanville, where they had free run and had relatives and friends to play with.

When Richard Morrison Lofton, Jr., was born on May 23, 1908, he had seven older sisters to

Richard Morrison Lofton, Jr.
(1908-1966)

look after him: Mary Evelyn (Teen), 3; Caroline Juliet (Caroline), 6; Louise Augusta (Augusta), 10; Frances Havergal (Frances), 14; Lillian Edith (Weenie), 17; Susie May (Susie), 19; and Margaret Caroline (Margie) 22.

The lives of the Lofton children were continually centered at "Around the Beach." After the three older girls had finished college, they still spent much time at home. The younger girls were present and in constant attendance to their brother. Young Richard, "Dick," and his closest sister, Teen, were naturally allied by their ages and remained so until Dick died of lung cancer in 1966. They were given ownership of the house and its original lot after their mother's death. The two retained ownership but gave Caroline a life interest in the home as she remained in The Village.

Six of the Lofton girls married, but only three married to Richard's complete satisfaction. Margie's marriage to Watus Dawsey in 1910 took place in spite of Richard's opposition and his refusal to attend the service. No others dared marry until Susie and Luther Bagnal wed at the McClellanville Methodist Church in 1917. Uncle Luther always bragged that he survived Richard Lofton's intense scrutiny when he came to The Village to ask for Susie's hand. My father's wish to marry daughter Edith met with Richard's approval, perhaps because Dad waited a good and proper five years to pop the question. Augusta's marriage to Maurice Matteson, after a courtship of over two years, was smiled upon. Pa was not happy about Frances' betrothal to Robert Kennon, and his displeasure intensified when Caroline announced she would marry Sergeant Dewey Johnson and she wanted to get in on Frances' planned home wedding. The double wedding at home came off, nonetheless, and received much attention in the weekly news account of McClellanville happenings.

The "Around the Beach" home remained a sort of communal dwelling after Richard and Edith Lofton died, people coming and going. The one unmarried sister, Teen, moved to Winston-Salem, North Carolina, to study nursing, but Frances and her husband, Robert Kennon, with daughter Mary Frances, moved in right away. Caroline Lofton Johnson followed, bringing her children, Harriet and Lloyd, and they resided in the rear wing. Sergeant Dewey Johnson lived at his station on Sullivans Island and would spend weekends at "Around the Beach." In 1940, the Kennons built a home of their own on Pinckney Street, The Village's main street. The Johnsons moved into the front of the house, and the rear wing was torn down. After Dewey Johnson's death in 1957, Caroline was alone for a few years but was joined by her grandson Richard McClellan and her granddaughter Gail, as well as Gail's husband Ashley Fuller and children Wesley and Caroline.

8

Ma and Pa

(each pronounced with a nasal "a," as in apple)

The elder Richard Lofton was a busy man. As a young man, he helped his father oversee the sawmill and the production of turpentine. He was an attorney but, all his life, considered planting to be his main occupation. When the patriarch, Henry Michael Lofton, retired in 1912, he put Richard in charge of the Lofton enterprises. All the boys had equal financial interests in the operations. Richard's siblings had no qualms about granting leadership to their older brother, who was a college graduate, an attorney, and a former legislator.

Richard Lofton's law practice primarily consisted of transferring titles and settling disputes over property lines for people of the community, but he did try cases in the courts at Charleston and Georgetown. At that time, both medicine and law, it should be stated, were part-time occupations of those who practiced in rural areas. In 1907, he represented the Audubon Society in its claim against a group of men who were killing snowy egrets at Blake's Reserve, a freshwater impoundment on the property of the Santee Gun Club. The egret was in danger of being exterminated by hunters, who would collect

Clubhouse of the Santee Gun Club, built in 1905.

and sell the bird's tail feathers for insertion in women's hats. The birds of St. James Santee made up one of the last breeding colonies along the coast. Attorney Lofton won the case.

Service in the legislature took more of his time. During most of his years as a representative, the legislative sessions in the state capitol were quite brief; sessions began a few days after the general election in early November and adjourned by Christmas time. Still, there were legislative delegation meetings to attend in Charleston and occasional trips to Columbia to take part in committee meetings. Richard Lofton's other public political activities included service on the local school board for as many years as possible (trying to keep control from slipping into the hands of the Grahams) and being a leader in Club One of McClellanville's Democratic Party. On the nonpublic or private side of politics, Richard Lofton frequently hosted dignitaries from around the state, who loved to come to St. James Santee to hunt and fish.

In his earliest years, Richard Lofton was a member of the Wappetaw Independent Congregational Church in the old Christ Church Parish. When the family moved to St. James

Santee, he attended the New Wappetaw Presbyterian Church in McClellanville. While a student at Carolina Military Institute, Richard moved his membership to the First Presbyterian Church, Charlotte. By the time he completed his military college education, studied law, married, and returned to The Village, his mother and father were embroiled in their dispute with the elders of the McClellanville church. Still, Richard moved his membership back to New Wappetaw, and Edith joined with him. After a few years, Edith took the initiative in leading her in-laws to involvement in regular worship services. She suggested, and Henry Michael Lofton agreed, that the family join the McClellanville Methodist Church. Richard and Edith moved their memberships in 1898.

It was a small new church, and its membership was comprised of a few who came from old Nazareth Church congregation, some who converted from the Episcopal Church, and a few new arrivals in the area. They used the public school as a site to hold services until a small sanctuary, still in use today, was constructed in 1902. Richard became a leader of the flock. When a regular minister or supply minister was not available, he stood in as the preacher. He officiated at marriages and conducted funerals. Richard Dawsey observed that our grandfather "liked preaching even better than lawyering." In the dark and discouraging days of the 1920s, Richard Lofton was a pillar of the church. Reverend J. O. McClellan credits Lofton with keeping the church alive in that time.

The Lofton family attended church school and worship services every Sunday. In the little Methodist church, the family, except Aunt Hattie and Caroline who chose the Episcopal service, sat in the front pews on the left-hand side. Richard Lofton had a strong baritone voice and loved to sing the descants along with the hymn singers. Thomasine Graham Harvin remembers with pleasure how he would sound out the descant "In the wildwood" when the congregation sang "The Little Brown Church in the Dell." It made the worshippers smile.

Depending upon which cousin one talks to, Richard Lofton was either manly and kind, a role model for men and boys, or stern and overbearing. Most descriptions come, of course, from people who were children or young adults at the time, and my observation is that the young normally find adult males to be frightening. Harry Mikell Lofton, Richard's nephew, says he never saw his uncle smile and that his uncle's prayers at church were so intoned and so powerful as to make "a young boy frightened of an unknown deity."

At times though, our grandfather could loosen up. He enjoyed the outdoors and was an avid hunter. He sailed in the regatta at Rockville, with a daughter crewing for him. He owned one of the first automobiles to challenge the parish's boggy roads and, later, in the 1920s gained the reputation of being an aggressive, impatient driver. He refused to remain behind someone on the road but instead put the pedal to the floorboard and charged past, frightening his passengers. Once he led a group of men skinny-dipping. One stifling hot day, he and others were waiting at Lofton Landing for delivery of fertilizer. Someone regretted that a swim was not possible because they had no bathing trunks, at which Richard Lofton peeled off his clothes and dove in.

Edith Stroman Lofton – "Ma"

Our grandmother was a genteel person, greatly loved and respected for her kindness, industry, and good cheer. Although she had necessarily moved about in her childhood, she had not considered herself abandoned or neglected and was devoted to both the Stroman and Millar families. She was an avid correspondent, and she wrote chronicles of the two families and of Henry Michael Lofton, her father-in-law.

She attended Presbyterian churches with her Millar family in Charleston, and she went to a Methodist church with the Stromans in Springfield. In her own home, she was a reader of scripture and included all house, yard, and field workers in the family's devotional exercises. Her children were encouraged to take part in all church activities. In her last years, after all the children except Teen had left home, she had Bible reading and prayer services with Maum Ellen and with servants who came over from neighboring households.

She took part in many of the women's reform movements of the era. She was a member of the Women's Missionary Union, the Women's Christian Temperance Union, and the Order of the Eastern Star. Her objection to the consumption of alcohol derived not only from her religious or ideological stand but also from observation of its effect on her in-laws and other residents of The Village. Later in life, she held to her stand for temperance even while she became a brewer of beer. Her brother, Dr. Jacob Paul Stroman, Richard's old college roommate, advised that she consume a non-intoxicating amount every day to stimulate her appetite. She brewed her own on the back of the porch to avoid having to purchase it at a local store. Lillian Bonner Jamieson remembers that it "smelled bad."

Edith Lofton played piano and sang, but a malady common in the Stroman family gradually took away her skills. She developed presbycusis, or nerve deafness. This form of hearing loss becomes apparent in middle age and progresses to varying degrees in different individuals. Hers was profound. Her brother, Dr. Stroman, was equally deaf and had to use an earhorn in communicating with his patients. In the next generation, my mother was the only one of seven children to be impaired. She could not carry on a conversation by telephone. Of my cousinhood only my brother Henry uses hearing aids. I cannot hear the ticking of our car's direction signal nor pick up all the directions Beverly gives me.

Reverend Ludwig Beckman's autobiography recalls how much trouble Edith Lofton had communicating. "Ludie" Beckman, Harrington Morrison, and others attended a party given by Augusta Lofton at "Around the Beach." At the end,

Mrs. Lofton said to each departing boy, "Thanks for coming. I'm glad you enjoyed it." Harrington immediately realized he had left his hat, but when he went back and asked for it, she said, "Thanks for coming. I'm glad you enjoyed it." He retrieved the hat the next day. They lived, as the incident also shows, in a polite society.

At home, Edith Lofton was a constant instructor of her children, and she exhorted them to do good work at school. She encouraged good penmanship and saw that the children had books to read. She taught them Greek and Roman mythology and showed them how to recognize the constellations in the night sky. Stargazing was a source of pleasure for the family. The front porch of the home faced directly south where Scorpio shines brightly in the summer. Then, with just a step into the yard, they could view the other quadrants in a dark sky.

Edith Lofton managed a sprawling household that swarmed with young people. As the 1911-1920 decade began, Margie, Susie, and Edith were young adults in their early twenties, teaching school at various places around the state, and coming home as often as possible. Teenagers Frances and Augusta were doing well in school and both later went off to college. Caroline, Mary (Teen), and Dick were growing up fast. Miss Edith had Aunt Hattie Millar's mature presence to guide her and had house servants and a yard man to do a lot of the work. They were happy and cordial people living upright lives in accord with their religious beliefs.

However, the family suffered sad misfortunes from time to time. The village home of Thomas and Mame Lofton burned. The younger Loftons had to move to "Around the Beach," and it was there that one of their first three children died. A letter from Hattie Millar to a distant relative tells of the sadness and despair felt by family members: "The poor child cries incessantly, and nothing can be done."

In those days, people accepted the fact that life was tough.

Illness and death were seen up close, at hand, in the home. They grieved and lamented life's harshness, but they accepted it as natural, recovered from these disappointments, and went on with their lives, sustained by their concept of progress and by confidence in God's providence. No death of a family member could have dissuaded them from the belief that things always turn out right. However, it was the death of an institution that struck family finances a blow, turning our people's interest from farming, business, and politics to education and the arts.

The Bank of McClellanville

Richard Morrison Lofton was the founder and president of the Bank of McClellanville, incorporated October 29, 1912. John Marion Lofton, Jr., Richard's nephew, served as cashier, and Richard's daughters worked from time to time as tellers. Teen Lofton was proud that she could serve as a teller. "I

The post office and bank, photographed in 1946. The bank, which closed in 1926, is next to the truck in this photo.

could really count that money," she remembered. She also said that Edith (my mother) was best at it. "Your mother was Pa's favorite," Teen told me.

The story of the Bank of McClellanville is the story of small town banking in the first third of the 1900s.

As the century began, the nation was recovering from a recession, and people were in an optimistic mood. In South Carolina, there was economic growth throughout the first decade of the twentieth century. With the beginnings of electric power production, there was growth of manufacturing. Better roads and railroads enhanced travel. The state remained greatly dependent on agriculture, but tobacco and cotton prices were up. Farmers began to diversify a little under the influence of graduates of Clemson College and were better off than they had been since the Civil War. Even so, fifty percent of the state's farmers were tenants rather than landowners, and a high percentage of those who owned land often took liens on their crops to buy fertilizer.

In 1900, the United States Congress strengthened the gold standard. The South Carolina Banker's Association organized in 1901. In 1906, the state established the position of bank examiner. Banking, previously looked upon as money-grubbing by an agricultural society, became respectable and profitable. Sproat and Schweikart state in their history of banking in South Carolina, "By 1910, banking had become one of the most enticing and lucrative businesses in the state." (Sproat, John G. and Larry Schweikart, *Making Change: South Carolina Banking in the Twentieth Century* [Columbia: South Carolina Bankers Association] 1990.)

Banking got a further boost in 1913 when the founding of the Federal Reserve System made banking safer for depositors and for the bankers. With the economic picture otherwise bright, the state withstood the collapse of the cotton market, which occurred when shipping lanes were disrupted at the onset of World War I. Between 1915 and 1920, four hundred state-chartered banks were established in South Carolina. Nearly half of the new banks were in towns with populations fewer than 1,000. As M. K. D. Kann observed in her unpublished Ph.D. thesis, "South Carolina in the Jazz Age," banks were established "in nearly every hamlet from Chappels to Cades."

A great shakedown occurred with the arrival of the boll weevil and the onset of the agricultural depression of the 1920s. The wartime boom ended abruptly. Incomes fell drastically. Two samples of figures having to do with cotton production show how terrible the blow was. In 1920, cotton production in South Carolina cost $250,000,000 but earned only $140,000,000. In Williamsburg County, cotton production fell from 37,000 bales in 1920 to only 2,700 bales in 1921. The state barely escaped economic collapse.

Over the next several years, farm land values dropped from an average of $52 per acre to $25 per acre. Many farms were sold for taxes, and many more were heavily mortgaged. In 1921, twenty-one percent of South Carolina's owner-operated farms were mortgaged. By 1930, thirty-three percent were mortgaged. Farmers borrowed money to live on. In 1929, eighty-five percent of tenants were debtors, and seventy percent of landowners were debtors. Tenant farmers began leaving the land, the whites moving mainly to nearby towns or cities and the blacks migrating to the big cities of the North and the Midwest.

Those who borrowed money and those who lent money were equally at risk. Family farms and woodlands fell into the hands of banks, fertilizer companies, and pulp-and-paper companies. Businesses went into receivership or went out of business. Banks failed. In South Carolina, there were 225 bank failures in the years 1920-1929. Only 112 South Carolina banks closed during 1930-1934, the era during which the Great Depression forced closure of many banks throughout the nation. In South Carolina and the rest of the South, the

Great Depression was an anticlimax to the destructive effects of the loss of cotton. Entire communities suffered as a result of these losses.

State officials attempted to help the small-town banks by reviewing their records and suggesting a course of action: reorganization, merger, or closure. Quite often, the recommendation was closure. Everywhere the closing of the banks heralded the passing of the heyday of the small town.

Richard Lofton's bank was incorporated on October 29, 1912, and closed on April 13, 1925. Reports of the bank for 1914-1919 and for 1924 are on record at the South Carolina Bank Commission offices. The sale of $15,000 in stock established the bank. By 1919, the bank had assets and liabilities of $60,837.78. Assets included loans of $46,050.33, and liabilities included deposits totaling $38,112.72 — a healthy situation. In 1924, the total assets and liabilities were down to $39,589.33, and there was a dangerously high loan ($32,163.17) to deposit ($16,948.73) ratio. The bank's health was dependent on the economic well-being of its loan holders. That year's report listed an ominous item under liabilities: bills payable — $3,000. As we know, the little bank did not survive.

In 1993-1994, as I sought information about the Bank of McClellanville, I found few people who knew it had ever existed. Where had it been located? Older residents told me that the bank and the post office shared a neat little building situated on the east side of Pinckney Street, directly across from the center of the school. No structure is there now. What had become of it? Cousin Lloyd checked around and found that the bank building still lives. Mr. Mackintosh, the postmaster, bought the building and moved it behind his home on Scotia Street. He added a room and offered it for rental. It still looks attractive.

Those people who knew that the bank had existed assured me that they had never heard anyone express strong feelings of loss or direct any resentment against officials of the bank. Bobby Graham remembers that he lost the few dollars he had been saving toward a new bicycle and that his sister Lyda lost all of her $2.00. Graham, who became a professor of economics at the University of South Carolina, believes the bank failure was discouraging to the community but that it brought no great financial loss to the people.

Word circulated that the bank would re-open, but it never did. An article in the April 1926 *News and Courier* reported that account holders would get at least half of their money back. Perhaps some got more from the sale of the bank's property.

The bank undoubtedly failed because the loan holders were not able to pay their debts. Maybe people around town were not mad at Richard Lofton because they realized that the bank's directors could have foreclosed on some of their properties. Maybe people accepted word that the demise of the bank was caused by the hard times. Yet, I wonder. While I grew up in Moncks Corner during the 1930s and the 1940s, I repeatedly heard unkind remarks about people involved with that town's failed bank. People were especially resentful of one businessman who, it was said, precipitated the bank's collapse by getting all of his money out. He did seem to have a big house, big cars, and a lot of servants. Tall tales were told about the size of the bankroll he kept in his pocket. I was thrilled one day to be able to count out $19.75 in change to the $20.00 bill he proffered when I collected for the *News and Courier.*

The big loser in the closing of the Bank of McClellanville was surely Richard Morrison Lofton. The other stockholders were losers also, and those relatives and friends might have borne some resentment in silence. It is satisfying to me to know that Richard Lofton retained enough good will in the community and in Charleston County to win re-election to the legislature in 1926. He kept plugging.

The Twenties

The Lofton family took four economic blows. Richard's struggle to continue making cotton succeeded only in developing a large debt. The bank failed. There was not as much law to practice. The forest industries produced less cash flow, as most of the lumber was sold during Henry Michael Lofton's last years and turpentine production had ceased. Our grandfather continued his public career. He remained chairman of the school board and secured funds for the erection of the building still used as a middle school. He led an effort to bring a railroad to town but could not get people to put up the necessary money. He also supported creation of the Ocean Highway.

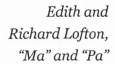

Edith and Richard Lofton, "Ma" and "Pa"

Somehow Richard and Edith were able to send two more children to college. Teen was a dropout at Lander and at the University of South Carolina but, later, in the 1930s, became a registered nurse. Richard Lofton, Jr., graduated from The Citadel in 1928.

On July 1, 1922, Richard Lofton signed a will bequeathing all his property, real and personal, to his wife Edith. My mother wrote the document and witnessed it along with her brother-in-law Maurice Matteson and her great-aunt, Hattie Millar. What prompted his making the will at that particular time is unknown.

He lived in apparently good health for six more years, giving my older cousins and other relatives opportunities to develop strong opinions about him. The boys found him strong, handsome, and commanding. They were proud that he did a lot to help other people. Richard Lofton was, they say, "a fine man." His son, Uncle Dick, used a famous figure of literature and film to characterize Richard Lofton. "If you want to know what my father was like," Dick said in 1966, "go see the movie *To Kill a Mockingbird*. He was exactly like Atticus Finch." Nephew Harry Mikell Lofton shares a different image. Harry remembers a stern-looking man with a lion's mane of white hair who never smiled. Harry often accompanied his father, Uncle Jimmy, on trips around the beach to talk with Big Bubba. "The subject was always the mortgage that could not be met."

Richard made a partial comeback in farming in 1926 and 1927. He ran successfully for a seat in the legislature in 1926. He remained a leader at the McClellanville Methodist Church and attended the Methodist State Conference in December 1927. He kept telling his brothers that the mortgage could be paid off by the mid-1930s. In the spring of 1928, a digestive disorder interrupted his service in the legislature. It was soon evident that he had cancer, and he began to decline rapidly. Near the end of his life, he revised his will, leaving his landing property and "plantation" to his son and leaving the inland half of the farm to his one unmarried daughter. Again, my mother drafted the will. Richard Lofton signed the document with a shaky hand, and he died three days later, on April 19, 1928, just weeks before Richard Lofton, Jr.'s, graduation from The Citadel.

Judge Clarence Lunz, a cousin-in-law, probated the will. The warrant of appraisement does not give the value of the real property but of the personal property he owned:

1 wagon	$ 20.00
1 cart	$ 10.00
Plows	$ 15.00
50 sheep	$ 75.00
20 head of cattle	$300.00
2 mules	$150.00
1 horse	$ 50.00
1 Ford automobile	$ 75.00

Besides the homestead, his real estate included the landing and farm properties, the mortgaged lands mentioned above, plus a number of smaller tracts of land scattered around St. James Santee. We have no record of the value of these.

Edith Lofton was left poor but not in debt. She had the home place, and she held title to some forty-four acres of land remaining from the Stroman place at Springfield. At that point, she might have given over to despair. She had come from a family of wealthy landowners, but her brother lost nearly all of that estate to taxes. She had married the handsome scion of a wealthy Lowcountry family, but he managed to lose much of the estate entrusted to him. Her husband was dead. Aunt Hattie was dead. She was deaf and had no way to support herself.

What she did have was a supportive family. Daughter Teen lived with her. The other children came as often as they could, and grandchildren stayed for long periods of time. The Dawsey family was self-sufficient and kept Ma supplied with their bounty of milk, meats, and vegetables. Richard Dawsey kept the yard and garden. Edith (Lillian Edith) Dawsey cherishes the memory of the months she spent as a companion to her grandmother. Each afternoon, Ma would get out her good china, and they would have tea. Sometimes they would share the ritual with Ma's neighbors and friends. Thoughtful neighbors helped. The Grahams left their back light on every night.

Edith Lofton wore mourning clothes, but it did not appear as though she felt sorry for herself. She remained active in the church. She wrote a long chronicle of the life of Aunt Hattie Millar. She carried on an active correspondence with those children who lived away from The Village. If she ever lost her bright outlook on life, she never showed it. She did, however, fall gravely ill in 1930. My sister and my cousins watched Dr. Jake Stroman's visits with anxiety. The liquid medicines he brought were dark and smelly, they remember. Ma died on May 28, 1930.

9

Romantic Victorians

McClellanville experienced its own kind of golden age in the first two decades of the twentieth century. By 1900, the town had reached the size at which it would remain for about eighty years. Its major institutions were in place or would be within a few years. Its people had worked themselves up from abject poverty to being just a little prosperous, and its casual way of life was established. One occasional visitor said of the town in that era, "McClellanville is a little like heaven. It's hard to get to, but when you get to it, you don't want to leave." The Village of those decades is the McClellanville that people still look back to.

Children who grew up during those years had authoritative but doting parents and had grandparents, aunts, and uncles living nearby or even in their homes. They had abundant cousins. Out-of-town friends visited for long periods of time. They visited other families in town, went to church, attended school, played, and did chores. They had arguments like everybody else and inconveniences and difficulties in abundance, but they were greatly satisfied about their place in the

Picnic party in a 1905 REO (Oldsmobile) about 1908. This car was used to bring mail to The Village about three times a week.

Well-dressed young adults on the waterfront, 1917.

Young women in their buggy, Pinckney Street, 1908.

great scheme of things. They had community. The town had
a Victorian appearance and a Victorian moral atmosphere,
but the place effected a reversal of time on the people. The
Victorians became romantics.

They loved The Village. Some of them had to move away,
but throughout their lives they were dedicated to the people
and institutions of the community. Those who could come
back to live there did return. Many of them lived until the
1980s – when the place began to lose its individuality but
gained the attention of people of the outside world.

By 1900, the people who had come to McClellanville after the Civil War had produced large families. There were
two branches of the Lofton family — Henry Michael Lofton's
and John Marion Lofton's. The Morrisons, the Lelands, the
Grahams, the McClellans, the Beckmans, and others had
grown apace, and intermarriage among them had produced
the complex cousinhood that thwarted the efforts of outsiders to keep them all straight.

The stories told about one particular family group, the family I heard most about, can tell the lives of these people.

Harry Mikell Lofton, a first cousin of those who grew up at "Around the Beach," and who may be suspected of favoritism, wrote of them: "All of their (Richard and Edith Lofton's) female offspring and the only male, Dick, were in my opinion, about the most talented, intelligent, impressive family I have ever known anywhere. Frances Kennon was a stern taskmaster. She had much to do with making for me any successes I ever accomplished. She was my high school English teacher. Caroline was a sweetheart. Margie was a saint. Cousins Edith, Susie, Augusta, and Teen were brilliant and talented. Dick was a truly great artist. All that family were brilliant performers in life."

The Lofton girls bordered on being pretty. Caroline was the best looking, and her mother called her "my flower girl." Margie, the oldest, was a bit shy and retiring, but the rest were outgoing, fond of socializing. All of them filled their moments with productive activity, if nothing more than knitting or tatting. They read a lot and played the piano. Teen and Caroline wrote poetry. The girls were never reticent to share or demonstrate their talent when requested to.

The six girls who married did so later in life than was the custom in that time. They had education, social advantages, and skills which, along with the fact that they were closely chaperoned and supervised by their parents, might have made them a bit daunting to prospective suitors. Richard Morrison Lofton's stature and bearing may have frightened off a few prospects.

"Margie" Lofton

The Memminger Normal School yearbook of 1907 shows Margaret Caroline Lofton neatly attired in her school uniform, attractive but looking somewhat surprised or camera shy. The photograph correctly portrays her nature, for she was the most reserved of the Lofton children, but she was a very active person, enjoyed company, had a mind of her own, and was tough and resourceful. She created and held together the largest family unit, provided an informal meeting place for us, was an uncomplaining hostess to long-term visitors, and kept a jar of sugar cookies for the children. As a youth, Margie sailed with her father in the regatta at Rockville. She enjoyed playing games until the end of her days, and Chinese checkers was her favorite. She would also play card games such as Rook or Authors, played with one or two people.

From very early on, she was called by two names — "Margie" and "Monnie" — and she was known by both of these names for the rest of her life. We would speak of "Aunt Margie" when talking to someone from outside the family. Among ourselves, Margie was "Monnie." For grandchildren, "Monnie" meant "Grandmother," for children it meant "Mother," for her husband it meant "Margie," for siblings it meant "Sister," and for nieces and nephews it meant "Aunt Margie."

After graduation from Memminger Normal, she taught at the little school in the Lofton community. At the McClellanville Methodist Church, she was introduced to Watus Woodson Dawsey, a brother-in-law of the minister. Watus was a tobacco farmer from Horry County. She decided to marry him, but Richard Lofton was not pleased. It may have been that Edith was not happy about Margie's choice either, but she did not complain.

Why Margie's beau did not suit Richard we do not know. Watus was not without financial or religious qualifications. He owned two farms. He was from a religious family; his sister was married to the minister of the local church and his brother was a Methodist minister, who later became a bishop. Perhaps Richard could not bear the thought of Margie having to move to the "Independent Republic of Horry." (Horry County always seemed different from the rest of the

Lowcountry: Most of Horry's settlers had no ties to Charleston but went directly up the Waccamaw River or drifted down from North Carolina.) One possibility is that Richard had a professional in mind, like himself, or a person of wealth and high position.

Nevertheless, Margie made up her mind to proceed with the marriage, and if she ever regretted doing so, she kept the thought to herself. Her father, it is said, did not attend the wedding. Margie moved to Horry County and there gave birth to the first member of our generation. Watus Woodson Dawsey, Jr., called "June" all his life, was born on February 11, 1911. The rest of the Dawsey children were, however, born in the more acceptable area of the old St. James Santee Parish. Richard Lofton made peace with the Dawseys and convinced them they should take residence at Henry Michael Lofton, Jr.'s, place in the Lofton Community. Watus would be in charge of the farm. Henry Michael, Jr. ("Uncle Harry"), was planning to retire from farming and move to McClellanville. Richard was busy starting up his bank.

The Dawseys' return was an agricultural and economic mistake and one that might have been foreseen. The boll weevil was on the march across the South. The farm depended on cotton production for most of its cash income, so it came to pass that the operation was badly hurt by the boll weevil. The agricultural depression of the 1920s followed. In that situation, Margie showed her determination and industry. She managed the household, kept the garden, secured income by selling milk, and gathered enough pecans each fall to pay the taxes on the place. The children were made to continue their schooling, and she provided their medical care, using home remedies. When a rattlesnake bit one boy on his leg, she scored the site with her knife and sucked the poison out. Margie had a lot to do with getting the family through the hard times.

One of her granddaughters has worried that "Monnie was not much honored." That observation probably derives from the undeniable fact that the matriarch was service-oriented; she did a lot for other people and did not require so much of them. Her strength and her goodness did not escape recognition, however. Harry Mikell Lofton, her first cousin, thought she was saintly. Daughter-in-law Carolyn Dawsey admired Monnie for never saying bad things about people and for having endurance and determination. Lloyd Johnson McClellan appreciated Monnie's playfulness.

Susie Lofton

Born on February 21, 1889, Susie May Lofton was the first of the Lofton children born at the family's residence, "Around the Beach." She grew up to be a happy, friendly person. All her life, Susie kept up with her nieces and nephews and endeared herself to us by seeking us out to talk about what we were doing.

Susie graduated from Winthrop College in 1910 and, for six years, moved about, teaching school in small towns in South Carolina. In 1915, at Greeleyville, she met the man she would marry, a lumberman named Luther Bagnal. Luther dared to make the trip to McClellanville to ask for Susie's hand in marriage. In later years, Luther enjoyed telling how he had to cross three rivers on ferries, gradually make his way over muddy roads, and face Richard Lofton. He was successful.

Richard and Edith Lofton may not have raised their girls to be Southern Belles, but

Susie Mae Lofton Bagnal, 1920

they did want them to be ladies. They were proper, well-be-
haved, courteous women, but they were not formal and never
haughty. They did not take themselves too seriously. Susie
illustrated her Victorian upbringing and her ability to laugh
at herself in comments she made, late in life, to a granddaughter. She told of her wedding, the reception, and her honey-
moon. The couple spent their first night in a Charleston ho-
tel. "I had to send Luther out for some warm milk," she recalled. Then, slapping her thigh and laughing out loud, she
added, "It was two weeks before I knew him," and meant
this in the biblical sense.

The Bagnals lived in Columbia for a few years, then made
their permanent residence in Winston-Salem, North Carolina. There, Susie continued Richard and Edith Lofton's practice of taking in friends or relatives for long periods of time.
Acquaintances from Columbia or relations from McClellanville
showed up at her door, sometimes without advance notice,
and were invited to stay until they made arrangements elsewhere. Younger sister Teen, younger brother Dick, and
nephew June Dawsey resided with her for months, mixing in
with the four Bagnal children. Later, in post-World War II
years, the Bagnals' beach house at Garden City Beach, South
Carolina, was a gathering place for all of us. Aunt Susie visited McClellanville frequently to keep herself informed about
the social life of the place and to tell her children and grandchildren stories of The Village.

In some places and at some times, Southern girls were
trained and expected to be void of ideas and opinions. That
was not true of the Lofton girls. They had plenty of ideas
and, with limited exceptions, expressed their opinions and
stood their ground when necessary, as illustrated by Susie's
relationship with her husband. A small businessman, Luther
Bagnal was one of the South's first white Republicans in the
modern era. Until the end of his life, you could depend upon
a conversation with him to include at least one blast at Franklin

Delano Roosevelt. Susie was in no hurry to convert to Republicanism. For a long time, she canceled Luther's vote by pulling the Democrat lever. She was an avid reader and a collector of poems. I found her to be an unyielding opponent at Monopoly. A granddaughter admired her for having played "ferocious" Scrabble.

Susie was a thrifty homemaker, often doing wash by hand, and spending little money on herself. Luther had to force her to buy a new outfit from time to time. She took care of her shrubs. Depending on whom one talks to, Susie was an accomplished cook or a reluctant one. Her granddaughter observed that on the cook's day off, Susie went to the farmers' market early, bought fresh produce, and spent the whole day cooking. But Susie's daughter, Suzanne Bagnal Britt, remembers that when Susie was left on her own, she would open cans of Campbell's tomato soup.

The children who grew up at "Around the Beach" were imbued with a positive philosophy. Although they grew up in a society still smarting from defeat in the Civil War, and although the family witnessed disease, death, poverty, and class and racial animosity, they were believers in progress. They accepted a role in making God's kingdom on earth a reality. They wanted their lives to witness to and promote the idea of progress. Susie's did. She marched through life, never thinking that it was anything but good. She was no stranger to sadness and she would weep profusely on occasion — she lost a grandson in the Vietnam War — but girded up when necessary and moved on. At spreading good cheer and having a good influence on us, she could not be excelled.

Edith "Weenie" Lofton

My mother, Lillian Edith Lofton, was given her nickname "Weenie" because she was small and energetic, like her mother, and because she shared her mother's name. From her mother and from Aunt Hattie, she learned to be industrious and in-

*Edith Lofton
riding sidesaddle
in 1921.*

quisitive. When, at age thirteen, she should have entered the
ninth grade at McClellanville High School, she found there
were not enough students to make up a class and went to
Winthrop College instead. Susie was taking Winthrop's pre-
entrance examination, so Weenie took the test on a dare. She
did so well that she was offered a full academic scholarship.

Throughout life, Miss Weenie was a voracious reader of
the Bible and general literature, and she often copied exhor-
tations to goodness and the pursuit of knowledge on notepaper
or scraps. Only a few weeks before her death at age eighty-
nine, she filled me in on the identity of the Assyrian king,
Sennacharib. When I expressed doubt about who he was, she
said, "Don't you remember Byron's poem?" She proceeded
to quote a long section from "The Destruction of Sennacharib" and told the Biblical story of the king's failure to
capture Jerusalem.

Mother liked to try new things. When she was young, a
barnstorming airplane pilot needing money and fuel stopped
in The Village and offered rides for a fee. She did not hesitate
and, thus, became the first McClellanvillian to ride in a flying
machine. Just a few years before she died, I visited her one

cold and wet winter day. She was studying the Parks Seed Company catalogue and was interested in the first-ever advertisement for snap peas. She told me she was ordering some and hoped someone would plant them for her. Her cousin Ernest Leland did plant them, and mother was one of the first to enjoy the "Vegetable of the Century."

She stayed on the move. The only time I saw her upset about her health was when, at about age seventy-five, she had a spell of abdominal pain. She feared cancer but was relieved to find she had diverticulitis. The Stroman family curse, nerve deafness, was her only impairment, and she managed to get along, even though she never learned to manage her hearing aid. One would hear the device whining or squalling while she was paying no attention to it. We found that she had let the battery die down and that she could hear better when new batteries were inserted. She was showing another family trait in being unable or unwilling to deal with mechanical or technical things. Stoic about her own hearing loss, she campaigned for compassion and understanding of others with the problem, often ending conversations or letters with the appeal, "Be kind to the deaf."

After our father died, Mother insisted she would live alone in her home on Jeremy Creek in The Village. She was determinedly self-sufficient, depending only on her sister Caroline to relay telephone messages or to drive her out of town. Having taught herself how to drive following my father's stroke, she applied for and was granted a beginner's permit. This allowed her to drive to church and to the post office. She could tell the car had started only by feeling its vibrations when she raced the engine. Tommy Graham (T. W. Graham, IV), a neighbor, said, "Walter, when I hear Miss Weenie cranking up, I call my two girls inside." So small she could hardly see over the dash, plus frail and deaf, she was rightly perceived to be a threat. We worried, too, but she gave up driving only a year or so before her death.

At home, she lived frugally. She burned as few lights as possible and, in winter, cut off all heaters at night, using only an electric blanket to warm her bed. In the morning, she would open the door to let sunshine and warmer air in. I spent the hottest and coldest nights of my life in that house but loved it. It was a beautiful place in a beautiful setting. Mother kept the yard and waterfront clean and, like her mother and her sister Margie, treated shrubs and flowers as if they were family members. Inside she kept a neat house, but she was not one to make it ornate. She never decorated for special occasions, and she never set up a Christmas tree. Neither did she pay much attention to Christmas gifts. She kept them in circulation: you might get back the object you gave her the year before. She did not wrap presents artistically but simply bundled them loosely in paper and handed them over. In truth, Mother had no time for these formalities. Every visitor was given cookies or date bread as well as a small painting or decorated seashell.

Mother was somewhat of a pyromaniac. She kept her neighbors and her sister Caroline on edge by her practice of burning trash wherever she found it. Miss Weenie set some dangerous fires in her yard and at "Around the Beach."

I did not always appreciate my mother. As a child, I found some of her policies and methods irritating. She would send me out to do a chore, saying, "Go out and get a scuttle of coal," and add, "then come back and I'll tell you what else to do." There would be three or four more things to do, and I would learn of them one at a time. Especially exasperating was her practice of making me go, all too often, to the cherry tree to select the switch with which I would be punished.

More to the point, I must say that while I was young, I thought of her as a bit corny, old-fashioned in her sentiments, and not up with the times. That was before I realized how tough, but also how wonderful, she was.

Frances Lofton

The next of the girls was Frances Havergal Lofton, born at "Around the Beach" on March 6, 1894. Richard and Edith named her for the English hymn-writer Frances Ridley Havergal, whose "Take My Life And Let It Be Consecrated" expressed her parents' religious intentions.

After schooling under Aunt Hattie and in the public school, Frances made the family proud by graduating from Winthrop College at the top of her class. The whole family journeyed to Rock Hill to hear her give her valedictory address. Frances taught high school English, and it came to pass that she brought her high standards to bear on some of her relatives. After marrying rather late and having her one child, she returned to McClellanville to live in the family home. She taught at McClellanville High School while Uncle Bob went on the road to sell lumber products. Her cousin Harry Mikell Lofton and two of Margie's children, my cousins Richard and Edith, had the benefit of her instruction. So did Jack Leland, who would become a journalist and would write of his appreciation of her insistence on good performance. Others, I have heard, did not enjoy the course.

Bob and Frances Kennon were not wealthy by any means but, being older and having worked for a number of years, they were not as strapped as some of her family members and other Village residents. They were a two-car family. Frances' car was an old, green sedan that had shades in the rear windows. Children who rode in the back came to realize that she had more on her mind than cleaning out a car; there were often cobwebs in the back recesses of the vehicle. Boys at school called Frances' automobile "The Green Barnacle."

Frances Kennon was a winemaker, which led to interesting developments, including the mild intoxication of her non-drinking mother. The Loftons, of all generations we know of, had ambivalent ideas regarding alcohol. Puritan ideals led each and every one to speak and vote against its consumption, but some who voted dry were heavy drinkers. Richard and Edith Lofton were teetotalers, but two of his brothers were alcoholics. It was the same in other family units. Some members warned against drinking; some drank. In Frances' own home, Frances drank socially and in moderation, but husband Bob was an alcoholic. On one occasion, recalled with great relish by some of my older cousins, Frances slipped her homemade wine into Ma Edith's punch. Ma, they observed, "traipsed around the house chattering happily," never realizing what made her feel so bright.

Frances lavished attention on her one child. Mary Frances, my cousin, was born when Bob Kennon was in his 40s and Frances in her 30s. Mary Frances was pretty, bright, and poised. She had books and toys in abundance. Her cousins held her in high esteem. Edith Dawsey remembers Mary Frances as "one sweet child," and Lloyd Johnson, who lived with Mary Frances in the old family home and was two years younger, regarded her as a "princess."

Frances did not get the opportunity to see Mary Frances grow up. At age 46, Frances died of rheumatic heart disease complicated by bacterial endocarditis. Her sisters would remember that she never complained. The day before she died, she had herself propped up for a game of Bridge. I was old enough to be ushered up to see her in the casket. Lloyd Johnson, a year older than I, was collared by our hardbitten Aunt Teen and led up to see the body. Our displeasure did not last long. After the funeral, Lloyd and I enjoyed food and outside play at the first of many family reunions we would attend.

Augusta Lofton, "My sister, the pianist"

When people see the formal portrait of the Richard Lofton family made in about 1904, they remark that Louise Augusta Lofton looks different from the other girls — "ethnic," "funny," "more like the Stromans, perhaps." She grew up to be a handsome woman and learned sophisticated, gracious ways. She was affable to everyone. Augusta was entertaining and humorous, an irrepressible person.

Aunt Hattie taught Augusta piano and, realizing that this daughter was especially talented, directed her to a career in music. After getting a degree in music at Lander College, Augusta taught music in public schools at Denmark, South Carolina, and at Andrew College in Georgia, before settling for a while in Columbia. She lived with Susie and Luther Bagnal while she worked as music director at the Baptist church that the Bagnals attended. In Columbia during World War I, she met Maurice Matteson, leader of the Camp Jackson band. In private life, Uncle Mattie played the dulcimer and sang. He was a collector and performer of folk music. Augusta became an accompanist for Mattie.

Like the other Lofton girls, Augusta was in no hurry to marry. It was not until 1924 that she and Mattie married in a service at "Around the Beach." She played her own preliminary music, and her sister Caroline rendered the wedding march.

Maurice Matteson became the first chairman of the voice department at the University of South Carolina. Augusta worked at the church and taught in private studios. The two Matteson boys were born in Columbia. The family then moved far away to Frostburg, Maryland, where Mattie would head the music department at Frostburg State Teacher's College. There, Augusta continued to teach private students and was regularly involved in musical events at the college. She played with a community orchestra, thus achieving the status of "concert pianist," as my mother would proudly say. The draw of the Carolina Lowcountry pulled the Mattesons back for frequent visits. As our cousin Richard Matteson says, they made regular "hegiras" to McClellanville. In between, they were reminded of the place by the receipt of fig preserves sent by those who remained.

The Mattesons retired and moved to Beaufort, South Carolina in 1964, choosing that site because it was close to home and because her sister Teen was living there. They stayed busy for many years, directing the choir at St. Helena's Episcopal Church, organizing a choral society, teaching, and performing. Augusta and Mattie considered themselves professional musicians to the end.

After Mattie's death, Augusta worked on, but Teen had to take charge of her financial affairs. Teen went so far as to organize the purchase of groceries and home supplies for her sister. It was an arrangement that suited both personalities. Augusta, like most Loftons, did not have time to waste on routine matters.

Caroline Lofton

Caroline Juliet Lofton was the sweetest, kindest, gentlest person this writer has known. Tears come into my eyes when I think how nice she was. I know, however, that for her sweetness and gentleness, she paid a price.

Caroline received instruction at home from Aunt Hattie. After attending the public school in McClellanville, and after graduating from Lander College, she taught school. Employed at Mt. Pleasant and Sullivans Island, she supplemented her income by playing piano at the local movie house. She went home almost every weekend. Before she married, Caroline wrote poetry expressing poignant ideas about love, nature, and faith. A decade later, her sister Susie collected Caroline's verses and published them with the title *A Rainbow Tinted Garland of Verse*. Here are samples, including the poem from which the collection's title is taken.

COMPENSATION
Though dark clouds lower and the sun is hid,
And raindrops falling on the shrinking leaves
Beat an insistent melody that wails

With sadness, and it seems the whole world grieves;
Though all the glamour of the sunlit gold
Is swathed from view in mists of gauzy rain,
And little gusts of wind left here by March
Sigh humanly in passing as in pain;
The laughing sunbeams presently will gather
 The tears of April, in their varied hue,
And make of them a rainbow tinted garland
 To fly across the sky of cloud-tossed blue;
And life, which seemed dull for a passing hour,
Will glow again, as lovely as a flower.

PRAYER

Now that I have come at last to the very narrow way
Now that my heart keeps crying what my lips dare not
 say,
Now that thorns tear my flesh and life has lost its charm,
Give me Thy love again, O Lord, to fill my empty arms.

1927 December

SUNLIGHT

Sunlight on a tossing wave, sunlight on a tree,
Sunlight is a lovely thing it seems to me.
Sunlight on a saddened heart, bright and clear and
 free,
Turns the dark to loveliness — it did for me.

At Sullivans Island, Caroline met Sergeant Dewey Johnson of Elberton, Georgia. A career military man, he was a decade older than she and was of a different temperament. "Johnny" was a boxer, a baseball player, and a hard drinker. They married in a double wedding ceremony with Frances and Bob Kennon on December 27, 1927. In view of the content and date of the above *Prayer*, one wonders if Caroline did not marry "on the rebound." Caroline never suggested this but did later tell her daughter, Lloyd, that a "sometime" romance had broken up.

Harriet and Lloyd Johnson were born at "Around the Beach" in 1929 and 1930, even though the Johnsons were maintaining another residence on Sullivans Island. A few years later, Caroline and the girls moved home full time. Their father continued serving at Fort Moultrie and commuted to The Village on weekends. "Uncle Johnny," as everybody called him, was a vigorous man in the pre-World War II years. He was a friendly, outgoing, exciting person, a favorite of many in the family and of others in the community. Once, at the farm, he tried to show us how to follow a .22 bullet shot from a rifle. We could not, and we doubted he could. Another time, we watched as he stripped down to shorts and dived into ten feet of water to retrieve an outboard motor that had fallen from an oyster bateau.

Johnny effectively disappeared into foreign service in 1942. He fought in Italy, France, and Germany with the Fifth Army. He rarely contacted home, and for a long time, he sent his family no money. Word came that he had been captured, but soon after, we heard that he had escaped. Some relatives were convinced he would not come back to The Village. He did come back, but he was a changed man, exhibiting little of the bravado and vigor that had been his trademarks. He did some hunting and fishing but more drinking.

Like the males of the family he married into, Johnny did little to keep up his own homestead but was quick to help neighbors and friends when they needed mechanical or electrical repairs. He did enjoy his grandchildren and was of great help to his daughters as he took care of the little ones. When he died of cancer in 1958, he was buried with the three Purple Hearts and the seven Bronze Stars he had accumulated in two World Wars and in one action on the Mexican border.

Caroline taught school. Through most of her career, she worked in The Village, but she did short tours of duty in Georgetown, in Moncks Corner, and in Awendaw when the McClellanville school board wars made abandonment necessary. The years after retirement were Caroline's happiest. She rarely left The Village. She rode about, providing transportation for many of the old-timers, including my mother. Grandchildren and great-grandchildren lived with her. Together, they watched the old Lofton home ripen. The rear apartment fell away, the dining room addition was removed, and the left wing added had to be abandoned. At this time, only the original center section of the house was occupied, and Caroline slept in the bedroom she had shared with Hattie Millar.

Caroline was, to us, a rather saintly figure to whom we made pilgrimage so we might feel her love and good will.

"Teen" Lofton

The youngest Lofton girl was a different kind of Lofton: positive, firm, direct, particular, precise in her dealing with others. This was Mary Evelyn Lofton, called "Teen." My cousins say, "Everything had to be just right around Aunt Teen." Appalled by what she saw as lax permissiveness by her sisters and brother, she felt obliged to look out for and correct those of us in the next generation. Though not a mother herself, she was the final authority on the raising of children. My thoughts of her will always be colored by my first memory of her: her releasing blood from under my toenail after I stubbed it on an oak root. She enjoyed doing it, I thought at the time. I gave her a wide berth after that and did not warm up to her for many decades.

At first called "Teenie" because she was as small as her sister "Weenie," she was spared that burden and given the nickname "Teen." Teen was as active and as energetic as Weenie. She was girlish but would never warm up to a man. Late in her life, she said to me: "There are some women, you know, who just don't want to marry. I don't believe I could have put up with a man." I replied, "Yes, ma'am."

At her place in Beaufort, where she lived with her friends Dixie and Lois, Teen was the gardener and outside caretaker.

The others had inside-the-house duties. Even after Teen had a myocardial infarction at age eighty-seven, she insisted on cutting the lawn with a riding lawn mower.

Teen was not the scholar or the musician her siblings were, asserting that she was not as talented as they. She said so respectfully, for she loved her brother and her sisters. On the contrary, high school records reveal that Teen was an "A" student. She just did not have the temperament or the will to concentrate on those skills. Teen enrolled at Lander College but left within a few months. She tried the University of South Carolina with the same result. Later, she excelled as a nursing student and an industrial nurse practitioner.

Teen experienced wider mood swings than did others of her immediate family. She clearly had a specific intolerance of alcohol, as she was unable to metabolize it as rapidly as one should. Small amounts did more than intoxicate her; a drink would lay her low. Through her early life, she partook of the fruit of the vine during spells of depression. In her maturity, she abstained from it and warned of it. Very late in her life, in her 80s, she visited The Village and had a brief reunion with her old friend Helen DuPre Satterly. Helen, as was her custom, offered a small glass of sherry. Teen was impaired within minutes, fell, and had to be helped into a car to go home to bed.

Teen was prone to fear, a surprising side to her vigorous nature. As a young woman she led a Girl Guides troop on a camping trip to Lofton Landing. When dark fell, strange sounds convinced her she should have the troop break camp and set up near the farm house instead. In Beaufort, she insisted on having a complicated system of locks and bars attached to the windows and doors of her home. It was a beautiful marshfront residence but looked rather like a fort.

Like other Loftons, Teen was not skilled at the management of resources. She often gave money to relatives. Impulsively and abruptly, she deeded properties to nieces and nephews, then spent years fretting over having let ownership pass out of her hands. When any recipient of her favor did something that irritated or disappointed her, she would threaten to leave the malefactor out of her will. That turned out to be a moot point, of course, for there was not much left for her to will.

The last two decades of Teen's life were marked by transformation into a person who was comfortable and satisfied to be who she was. She was a handsome, proud woman who was well-read and a good conversationalist. Her company was much enjoyed by a wide circle of friends. Dr. Louis Roempke, forty years younger than the three friends, was their family physician and their coffee-maker. He regularly visited the ladies on his afternoons off. They tried to teach him to play the piano but gave up and played cards or talked of books instead. Dr. Lou says that his method of handling their health care was to "do what Teen said to do."

Dick Lofton

At Richard Morrison Lofton, Jr.'s, birth on March 23, 1908, his father was forty-eight years old and his mother was thirty-nine. The oldest of his seven sisters, Margie, was twenty-three years old. Susie was nineteen, Edith was seventeen, Frances was fourteen, Augusta ten, Caroline six, and Teen four. He had abundant first cousins from our Henry Michael Lofton side of the family plus second cousins from the John Marion Lofton side. Soon, he also had nieces and nephews of our cousinhood. Watus Woodson Dawsey, Jr. ("June"), was born in February 1911. Richard Francis Dawsey was born a year later, and Lillian Edith Dawsey came in 1914. Because of his age, Dick Lofton was something of a transitional figure between one generation and the next. He differed from the members of his and the older generation in one important respect. He had not the intensity and busyness that marked the other members of his nuclear family. His pleasant, relaxed attitude was much appreciated by relatives and friends.

Dick was a nice-looking boy. He grew up among the many women in his home but had male companionship from among numerous cousins and friends of the family. He and Binks DuPre did a lot of fishing together. They collected terrapins ("Cooters") for sale but found no buyers. Dick designed and built a racing boat powered by an outboard motor.

Aunt Hattie found that he was not receptive to instruction in music but that he had an interest in art, which was another area in which she worked. By the time he entered The Citadel, he was doing woodcuts and oil paintings. At the military college, he made spending money by doing portraits of other students' girlfriends. He did a portrait of his mother, entered it in a contest at the South Carolina State Fair, and won an award. The success pointed him to a career in art at the very time the demise of cotton-planting convinced him to look away from farming.

The artist's graduation from The Citadel in 1928 was saddened by the death of his father four weeks earlier. He turned the farm over to Watus Dawsey and used the money from his State Fair award to study art in New York City.

A stint as an art teacher and portrait painter in Columbia, where he lived with the Mattesons, was followed by a long residence in the Bagnals' basement apartment in Winston-Salem, North Carolina, where he worked as director of an art center. In the course of that work, he supervised a student laboring over the portrait of young Nancy Schallert.

Nancy, a sophomore at Salem College, had played the role of Anna Pavlova in a tragic one-act play by Walter Spearman of the University of North Carolina and consented to pose in her costume for the student. Nancy recalls that "the handsome Richard Lofton" observed and made suggestions and that he "looked on me with a certain amount of disdain, perhaps because I was dressed in flowing robes and a wide-brimmed hat, which I suspect was just plain corny. But he did soon ask me out to a movie."

Nancy soon accompanied Dick to McClellanville. She was enchanted by the beautiful old family home, and she enjoyed the leisurely gatherings at which the family played bridge, drank endless cups of black coffee, and entertained friends. She, Dick, and Dick's friend Trapier Prentiss went out casting for shrimp at night. She remembers, "Red shrimp eyes shone in the dark. Occasionally, a mullet would jump onto the boat. The sounds of the night were many and varied. A night heron coughed or some mysterious creature rustled in the marsh grass, which towered over our heads. The stars shone bright above us." Richard carried her to Lofton Landing, where they selected the site for the home they would build "as soon a possible."

They married and brought forth our two youngest cousins. Called into military service in 1941, Dick served first at Camp Tyson in Tennessee and then for the rest of World War II as an instructor at the Coast Artillery School, Fort Ord, Monterey, California. The Monterey Peninsula turned out to be something of an artists' colony, so when the war ended, the Loftons made Carmel their permanent residence. Dick was committed to art. He painted, and Nancy helped support the family by teaching school. Disdain for the acquisition of money was another of the artist's commitments. He had the capacity to serve art, not Mammon.

Dick and Nancy never built the house of their dreams at Loftons Landing. At long intervals, they made extended visits to his old home. We were fortunate to have Dick do a portrait of Beverly during his and Nancy's 1964 stay. Numerous other relatives took advantage of these opportunities.

Dick drank a lot of coffee and was a heavy smoker. He also took on a little too much alcohol at times. His sister, Teen, always the one to straighten people out, visited Carmel to direct his steps aright. He responded and was healthy, active, and productive until he developed lung cancer. He died, too early, in June 1966. His lament was that he was "just learning to paint."

10

Education

W hen South Carolina was ready to educate its children, the Loftons were ready with the schoolmarms. All of the children of Richard and Edith Lofton sought education and six of the Lofton girls took training to be educators. Margie stayed and taught in St. James Santee, where she met her husband. Five girls moved away to teach, and each one married a man that she met in South Carolina. They were lucky that jobs were available. South Carolina had dallied 250 years before making a commitment to public education.

Interest in education was high in the community that the Loftons grew up in. McClellanville's school was stronger than most. It was a center of community life and was a focus of interest and conflict. It came to pass that national urgencies and local concerns would culminate in the loss of the McClellanville school. Here is the background of that loss and an account of one family's experience in that school.

The first Carolinians admired the educated mind but did not feel obliged to make education available to all citizens.

Education, if they thought about it at all, was a means of propagation of their ideal: Lockean, or radical, individualism. This ideal held that people are on their own in the search for status and wealth and are not to be aided or hindered by government. Education was a private or parental responsibility, available to those who could get it. These early Carolinians also believed that education taught the classics rather than acquisition of skills that could promote personal capability and community progress. In short, Carolina's leaders endeavored to reproduce society as it existed in England.

From the beginning, a few citizens disagreed and called for universal education. Later, some others advocated a broad-based curriculum. Progress toward those goals was thwarted time after time by sluggish enactment or with the retraction of legislation by the state's political leaders. Some communities collected taxes to start public schools. By 1776, there were twenty-four schools in the twenty-two parishes. In addition, there were private academies, especially in the upper state where the Scotch-Irish added a school to each church they founded.

After the Revolution, Americans fell away from adherence to English or European cultural ideals. Schools everywhere but in the South proliferated and began to offer instruction in science and business. Southern education remained a private responsibility and classicism held out. The few free schools established managed to do some good, even though they often consisted of only one room, were ungraded, and had untrained teachers and few books. Private schools and academies grew in number and excellence in this time. In 1860, the state had 202 private schools and academies with 333 teachers and 7,467 students. At the same time there were 1,270 free schools with 1,395 teachers and 18,915 students. Combined, these schools were educating just under fifty percent of the state's eligible white students.

Carolinians of the pre-Civil War era put more emphasis

on higher education than did previous generations. The South Carolina College was founded in 1806, and church-related colleges began to appear in the upper state in the mid-1800s. At the onset of the war, South Carolina's youths had a level of literacy equal to that of youths in the midwestern states but not quite to the level of those in the northeast. At the same time, a higher percentage of southern youths went to college than did their peers in any other part of the country. At that time, a few black youths were educated in South Carolina, even though an 1836 law forbade it.

Immediately after the war, public education remained under the direction of the locals, and many schools closed for lack of funds. In 1866, only half of the state's school districts had an operating school, and by 1869, only 8,225 of 68,108 white children of school age were enrolled. An undetermined number of black children attended academies run by northern missionaries.

The 1868 reconstruction constitution started an effort to introduce northern educational ideals. The document called for a universal system of public schools with compulsory attendance and racial integration "as soon as possible," but these changes would not occur for a long time. Not even the Republicans pushed for integration. Over fifty years passed before the state embraced universal education, and one hundred years went by before racial integration took place.

The efforts of the northern reformers did some immediate good. The 1868 constitution set up the office of State Superintendent of Education, initiated the training of teachers, and created systems for the financial support of schools. Northern religious organizations supported schools for the blacks, who responded enthusiastically. By 1870, white students numbered 11,122 while there were 15,874 black children in public schools. This preponderance of black students continued for several decades. Ultimately, the effort to educate the blacks weakened as the missionary ardor of the reformers died out and was replaced by corruption. The state's poor financial position and the resistance of whites contributed to the rollback, and by the 1890s, the education of blacks was in decline.

The Democratic Party under Wade Hampton took control of the state government in 1877. The Democrats had a mixed influence on public education. State Superintendent of Education Hugh Thompson tried hard to establish a state school system, but the resurgent Bourbons frustrated him. True to their ideals of individuality, personal responsibility, and frugality in government, the Bourbons reduced state appropriations from $300,000 to $100,000 and forbade school districts from raising taxes to better fund their schools. The Bourbon school policy was not popular. Solo voices and groups around the state called for strengthening of education, and many school districts did raise funds without permission. In 1888, during the Bourbon's last term in office, a state law gave the districts the right to collect taxes for support of schools.

In the last two decades of the nineteenth century and the first two decades of the twentieth century, much of the United States was under the influence of a crusading and progressive spirit in education. With the infusion of private funds and legislative and constitutional changes, there was advancement in education at the primary, secondary, and college levels. There were increased revenues, longer school terms, better teacher salaries and training, and consolidation of school districts. South Carolina fell further behind during these decades. Poverty and the loss of leadership occasioned by the Civil War had a lot to do with the state's failure to keep up, but the social ideals of the people and the policies of their elected officials hurt more than anything else.

Richard Morrison Lofton served in the legislature during the time that South Carolina was making up its mind to see that its citizens were educated. He was a member of the House

Students and principal in front of McClellanville school, 1908. This building burned down in 1917.

of Representatives from 1894 through 1906, in 1915 and 1916, and from 1927 until his death in 1928. The records of the legislature show that he favored the moves made to support public education. In 1897, the legislature sent school funds to poor counties. In 1903, Richard Lofton supported a bill that would have given the state its first compulsory education law, which would have required that children ages seven through twelve attend school a scant eighty days a year. The measure did not pass. That year, the lawmakers did agree to finance school libraries. The legislature added high schools throughout the state system in 1907, and in 1910, the state school system was reorganized.

The state's first compulsory school attendance law passed in 1915. A local option law, it allowed districts to require children eight through fourteen to attend school just eighty days a year.

In 1921, school attendance was made compulsory for

High school students and their principal, about 1915.

The McClellanville Public School soon after its construction in 1921.

children through high school. Introduced in 1924, the so-called "6-0-1" law, equalized spending in the state's school districts by setting statewide standards and giving financial support to districts in poor areas. Throughout that decade, school appropriations increased, as it was clear that the state would have to break from its agrarian past and diversify its economy. Larger shares of scant state funds were given to the schools. By 1930, South Carolina led the nation in the percentage of funds given for public education. Even so, South Carolina and the rest of the South still trailed the rest of the nation in per-student dollars for education.

The 1920s, '30s, and '40s saw tremendous changes in South Carolina's public schools: consolidation of school districts, multiplication of high schools, improved school buildings, transportation of students, longer school terms, smaller classes, improved teacher standards and salaries, broader curricula, and extracurricular activities. Four of Richard and Edith Lofton's girls taught in the state's schools during those decades. Thirteen of my first cousins, my sister, my brother, and I attended the schools of South Carolina during those years.

Education in St. James Santee

David Doar's 1905 history tells us that there were public schools in St. James Santee Parish as early as 1814. One was at Halfway Creek in the upper parish, on the inland side of Wambaw Swamp, and the other was at a site that would be on the outskirts of present-day McClellanville. In 1815, this school moved to the Kings Highway at the Thirty-two. It returned to the area of McClellanville in 1824 and, renamed the "Seashore School," remained there to be the predecessor of latter-day McClellanville schools.

Like other public or free schools, the Seashore School was overseen by commissioners appointed by the general assembly. The schoolmaster, usually a male and the school's only teacher, was paid $37.50-$75.00 per quarter and took in $3.00 or $4.00 from each student who could pay.

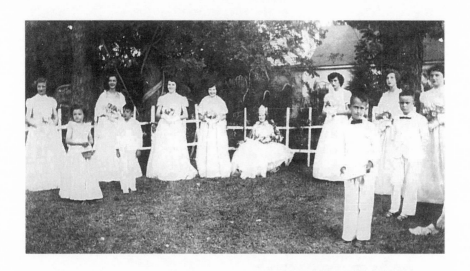

The May Queen with her attendants, 1951.

Maypole dancers, 1951.

The school closed during the last two years of the Civil War. It reopened in 1866 under leadership of the old regime but had its charter altered by the reconstruction constitution of 1868. The three new trustees included James C. Doar, L. P. McClellan, and Paul Drayton, the only black trustee. The new regime provided separate schools for black children. In St. James Santee and throughout South Carolina, multiple school districts were created, and each usually contained a

*Early Girl Scouts,
then known as Girl
Guides, in front of
the new school,
about 1922.*

*An early girls' basketball
team, 1921. The girls wore
dresses and bows, and the
game was played out-
doors on a dirt court.*

*Basketball coach
David Watson and
his state champion-
ship team receiving
a trophy.
McClellanville's
boys won state
championships in
1949, 1950, and
1955.*

one-room school for whites and a one-room school for blacks.

McClellanville grew slowly but steadily after the Civil War, and the McClellanville school grew proportionately. By the turn of the century, the people of The Village wanted a high school for their youths. McClellanville High School was created in time for Richard and Edith Lofton's daughter, Margaret Caroline Lofton, my Aunt Margie, to be a member of the first graduating class — the class of 1905.

By 1920, the rural, one-room schools for whites merged into McClellanville Elementary, the only elementary school for whites in old "lower" St. James Santee. An elementary school remained in Awendaw (Christ Church Parish) until 1951, when its students began to be bused to McClellanville. In spite of these additions, the McClellanville schools lost students during the 1920s and 1930s as people moved out of the depressed parish to find work elsewhere.

W. M. Bonner, Richard's son-in-law, became superintendent of schools in McClellanville in 1920. A native of Due West, South Carolina, the spiritual mecca of the Associate Reformed Presbyterian Church, he was a Presbyterian of the Covenanter tradition, steeped in the language and ideals of the Westminster Confession of Faith and of the Westminster Greater and Lesser Catechisms. He was serious and busy, not given to idleness. He had, however, been in the Lowcountry ten years, long enough to have warmed up to some of its charms and to be comfortable in it. He liked fishing and quail and dove hunting. His two bird dogs were named "Soc" and "Tip," for Socrates and Xantippe. Our father liked barbecues and fish fries. And he was recruited to The Village by his bride, Lillian Edith Lofton.

He graduated from Erskine College in 1910, and she finished at Winthrop College the same year. They taught at various towns around the state, first coming together at Greeleyville in 1915. Altogether, they taught or served as school administrator for 81 years.

EDITH BONNER

SCHOOL	YEARS EMPLOYED	ANNUAL SALARY
Mt. Pleasant	1910 – 1911	?
Tibwin	1911 – 1912	?
Johnsonville	1912 – 1913	?
Union	1913 – 1914	?
Kirkley (Near Greenwood)	1914 – 1915	?
Greeleyville High School	1916 – 1917	?
McClellanville High School	1923 – 1924	?
Berkeley Elementary School	1947 – 1965	$2,318
	(1948 – 49)	$6,792
	(1964 – 65)	?

WALTER BONNER

SCHOOL	YEARS EMPLOYED	ANNUAL SALARY
Greeleyville High School	1910 – 1915	$ 600 – 1,200
Plum Branch High School	1915 – 1916	$1,500
Greeleyville High School	1916 – 1918	$1,500
Porter Military Academy	1919 – 1920	?
McClellanville	1920 – 1927	$2,400
Moncks Corner (District Superintendent)	1927 – 1965	
	1927 – 1931	$2,000
	1931 – 1932	$1,440
	1932 – 1950	$?
	1950 – 1951	$6,186
	1955 – 1956	$7,500
	1962 – 1963	$8,600
	1964 – 1965	$9,044

After a courtship interrupted by World War I, Walter and Edith married in December 1920. He was thirty-one, she twenty-eight. When the school term ended they moved to McClellanville and purchased Henry Michael Lofton's summer house on Jeremy Creek from the estate. He was called "Professor Bonner" by everyone, on and off the school grounds, and that moniker remained with him the rest of his life. At McClellanville, Mother taught in the elementary school and filled in as a high school English teacher at times.

The journal my father kept during his seven years at McClellanville reveals that only 101 students attended the high school during those years. Some of those stayed only a year or two. Most of my kin were apt students, with the exception of one cousin who barely got by. Seventy years after graduation from McClellanville High, a retired circuit court judge who was a distant relative of mine told me that my father made him repeat his senior year. "Now — now I say — I respect him for it," the judge said.

In McClellanville, as he would later do in Moncks Corner, my father helped arrange the building of a new school. It opened in 1923. It still is an attractive, two-story building with prominent columns. Across the front, above the columns, is its name — MCCLELLANVILLE PVBLIC SCHOOL, the "V" rather than a "U" probably reflecting his training in Latin. He built a tennis court and coached a tennis team. The social life of the community revolved around the school. Movies were shown every Friday.

Not all was fun and games. School politics were intense. The factionalism prevailing in the community focused on school affairs, and my father caught some criticism from rivals of the Lofton clan. He departed in 1927 to direct the larger school system in Moncks Corner. No one in our family heard him say so, but we believe he jumped at the chance.

My father's departure was no reflection on the McClellanville schools. The elementary and high schools were strong. The people appreciated scholarship and sent a high percentage of graduates to college. The schools were, however, small and getting even smaller. Meanwhile, there was no high school for black children, whose families sent their children out of the parish to get a secondary education. Elizabeth Simmons Colleton, whose father ran the Lofton lumberyard and turpentine mill, moved from Buck Hall to Tibwin so she could attend the "Little Red School House," an elementary school.

Her father provided transportation to Lincoln School in The
Village for study in the higher elementary grades. She lived
with relatives in Georgetown while attending Howard High
School.

Education in Moncks Corner

When my father took the job of superintendent of schools
in Moncks Corner in 1927, he knew he was to direct a con-
solidated school system. Neither he nor anyone else foresaw
how large the system would grow. Small elementary schools
were closing, and students were being bused into town. Construction on the new Berkeley High School began under his
direction in 1928. During the last half of the 1930s, the county
began to change from a depressed, sparsely populated, rural
area to a growing and busy place. The Santee-Cooper Power
Project brought an influx of people who built the facility and
then stayed to manage it. During and after World War II,
population surged as families moved in and around the military bases on the Cooper River. The county lost an opportunity to land a major industry when property owners would
not sell land on the Tailrace Canal to the DuPont Company.
Berkeley County then mounted a determined effort to lure
industries, creating an industrial park on the Cooper River.
By the time W. M. Bonner retired in 1965, he had to build a
larger high school and convert the 1928 school into an elementary school. Whereas my 1949 high school class had
only thirty-one graduates, the Berkeley Stags now compete
with the athletic teams of the state's largest schools.

My parents never owned a home in Moncks Corner. We
lived in the girls' dormitory. Berkeley High School was one
of the few public schools in the country that had dormitories,
a necessity because the county was large, and rural roads were
impassable in bad weather. Buses brought students in from
remote areas on Monday morning and took them home after
school on Friday. From my infancy through my completion

of the sixth grade, there were 15 to 16 high school girls living in the second story of our home. Similarly, Jim Bradley and his family resided in the boys' dormitory. Mr. Bradley was the high school principal and coach of all the boys' athletic teams. Between the dorms was the mess hall, presided over by the affable Mrs. Moore. We called her the Wicked Witch of the East, or of the West, depending upon the dormitory we lived in.

At Berkeley, the elementary and the high schools were on the same campus. The rear of our residence looked out over the playgrounds and the athletic fields. A pop fly deep behind first base would land on our kitchen roof. Even before I entered the first grade, I would run out to take part in activities at recess time. I thought it was all there for my entertainment.

The dorms closed in 1946 because the roads were modernized and because the students were allowed to transfer to Charleston County schools in North Charleston and Mt. Pleasant. I lost some good friends, and Mr. Bradley lost some football players. For several years, the upstairs rooms served as a residence hall for single teachers. Later, however, growth of the student bodies necessitated conversion into classrooms. The dormitories and the mess hall were demolished in 1957 to make way for an entirely new elementary school. My parents rented a small home across the street from the school. It was the most comfortable home they ever lived in.

My father struggled annually to recruit skilled teachers. It was hard to find instructors for the sciences and foreign languages. He and Mr. Bradley had to substitute for long periods of time — he to teach English or Latin and Jim Bradley to teach biology. Elementary teachers were more stable or more durable, it seemed. The ones we studied under were old pros who had taught in the same homerooms for years. We went to high school well-prepared.

Discipline was not a problem in our day. Before we even

started first grade, we heard that Miss Harvey would jump over a row of desks to get anyone who misbehaved, and consequently, we behaved. Mrs. McCants, principal of the elementary school and sixth grade teacher, kept order at all levels. Mr. Bradley kept a paddle in his high school office, and he and my father would use it whenever necessary. Yes, they were *in loco parentis* and in that role had the support of mothers and fathers. Even now, around the Lowcountry, I meet men who say, "Your father cut my — good, but I respect him for it."

At Berkeley High, the first yearbook was published in 1939, and the first school paper circulated in 1941. In the earliest years, these were mimeographed. The annual had group pictures pasted on most pages and was covered with a binder. Beginning in 1946, the yearbook was published professionally. The school paper was printed by the local weekly newspaper, *The Berkeley Democrat*. Berkeley had its first football team in 1926, and it is thought that baseball started even earlier. Boys and girls played basketball on an outside dirt court until a wooden gymnasium was constructed in 1940. Barnlike and frigid in winter, it served until the present school facilities opened in the 1960s. Before World War II, there was a debating team, and the Future Farmers of America and the Junior Homemakers of America were favorite clubs. An orchestra formed in 1943. The first marching band, a glee club, and a drama club organized in 1946. The school auditorium hosted locally produced minstrel shows, beauty contests, dance and piano recitals, and concerts by country musicians and military bands. Magic shows were also popular. The first movies shown in Berkeley County premiered in the auditorium. There was always something going on around the school.

My mother did not teach from my birth to the time I departed for college, but she was an unpaid member of the school staff. She was counselor and tutor for the dormitory girls. She also played piano for school functions, decorated for junior-senior parties, and helped in the summertime cannery. For a couple of years during World War II, she ran the snack bar. Mother resumed teaching in 1948 and carried on until she and my father retired in 1965.

In Moncks Corner, W. M. Bonner was the superintendent of schools for white and black children. For some decades, he oversaw the schools in Cainhoy and in Hanahan. Cainhoy was a sparsely settled, almost completely black area. Hanahan was in the rapidly growing district near the military bases and the industries of North Charleston. Hanahan was a solidly white community. My father served his black constituents in Moncks Corner and Cainhoy faithfully, I am sure, but with some frustration. They were pushing for better facilities and instruction, and he could not provide them. He did, however, make some positive moves toward the black community. He attended functions at the schools for blacks. He permitted the town's black baseball team to use Berkeley's athletic facilities for its home games in the summer. He and my mother tutored several black students in our front parlor.

In 1965, at the end of Professor Bonner's fifty-three-year career in education, the schools he superintended included Howe Hall Elementary School in Goose Creek. Many military families resided in Goose Creek, and one black family entered a child in Howe Hall School. It can be said that my father's career extended to integration. When Dad retired, his superior, the county superintendent, was his own son, my older brother Henry. The best thing my father did for education in Berkeley County was to inspire and prepare Henry to ease the county schools through the rocky shoals of integration.

The years my parents worked in Moncks Corner were characterized by peaceful progress in education in most South Carolina communities. I believe that South Carolina's schools had a lot to do with pulling the state's citizenry through the tough twenty years of agricultural loss and great depression. We did not think we were as poor as we were. The state's escape from poverty during the prosperous 1940s seemed a natural occurrence. Further expansion of the schools in the 1950s and 1960s made it possible for communities like Moncks Corner to survive the storm — integration — that would follow. But integration, or the threat of it, dealt a fatal blow to McClellanville High School.

How They Dealt With Integration

In 1951, South Carolina made a move to protect the racial homogeneity of its public schools. It tried the separate-but-equal policy, intending to provide good schools for black students. To achieve this goal, it would be necessary to reduce the number of school districts so that each would be large enough to support at least one high school for whites and one high school for blacks. Across the state 1,265 districts dissolved into 108. The schools at Awendaw combined with those in McClellanville. Lincoln Elementary School added a high school for black youths. As a result, there was one black high school and one white high school in a large district extending from Wando Neck to the Santee River. Both were located in The Village. In the same district, there was one elementary school for whites and three for blacks — at South Santee, McClellanville, and Awendaw.

The separate-but-equal policy led to expansion of facilities and the schooling of more black youths, but it did not stop integration. On May 17, 1954, the United States Supreme Court ruled that public schooling must be integrated. When integration became the law of the state in 1970, a negative effect of the separate-but-equal policy became apparent. Most of the new schools for blacks had been constructed in less-than-ideal locations — cramped or unattractive places where white parents were reluctant to send their children.

In the growing Moncks Corner area, people were willing

to let the great experiment proceed, and the schools integrated. Paula Bonner, a senior at Berkeley High, served on an interracial committee to smooth the transition. On the periphery of Berkeley County — at Cross, St. Stephen, and Cainhoy — there were great black majorities. In those areas, private academies appeared to serve white students, and the student bodies of public schools became, or in the case of Cainhoy remained, solidly black.

A large black majority existed in the McClellanville school district. Lincoln High School and McClellanville High School were only a half mile apart. It was impossible to carve out a predominantly white district. The townspeople hoped that separate schools might be allowed to function, but county school officials made it clear they could not. McClellanville Elementary School and McClellanville High School closed with the graduation ceremonies of May 1969. Watus Woodson Dawsey, Jr., oldest of our cousinhood, presented a diploma to his daughter, Junie. It was an appropriate gesture. June's mother, my aunt Margie, was a member of the high school's first graduating class, 1905. With that ceremony, the building was closed down.

The white community banded together to found a private school: the Archibald Rutledge Academy, which exists to this day. Lincoln Elementary and Lincoln High Schools integrated — or, at least, the faculty integrated. Over the 30 years since the McClellanville schools closed, only a handful of white children have chosen to attend Lincoln High. Likewise, few white students went to Lincoln Elementary as long as it existed. White children either attended Archibald Rutledge Academy or moved out of the parish.

In November 1983, public education returned to Lofton — that is, to the place that once was the Lofton Community. A new, modern elementary school appeared at the intersection of the Landing Road (renamed Lofton Road) with Highway 17. It is called the St. James Santee Elementary School,

*McClellanville Public School, now McClellanville Middle
School, showing wings added. Photographed in 1996.*

even though it also serves students who live in the fragment of
Christ Church between Wando Neck and Awendaw Creek.

The McClellanville Public School, which we know existed
from 1815 to 1969, for which my grandfather had secured
funds and at which parents and cousins had taught or studied, was defunct. Young men of the town got permission to
play basketball in the old gymnasium but ceased using it when
the academy added its gym. The McClellanville Arts Council
used the former cafeteria for a few years, then found its own
home in the vacated telephone company building. A devel-
oper wanted to buy the school building and convert it into a
bed and breakfast but could not. The town had no sewer
system, and there was no way to dispose of waste. The lonely
building seemed symbolic of the depressed village.

Then the old school got new life as a middle school. The
idea that the school could be revitalized and play a new role
in public education caused a great stir in the community. The

townspeople objected. They preferred to keep traffic down and pointed to the unresolved sewage problem. They suggested it would be better to start an entirely new middle school and that it should be placed out of town, where there would be more room for a good campus. The opponents of the renovation plan were accused of racism, and they made countercharges of slander. In the end, the need of a middle school prevailed over the sentiments of The Villagers. Sewage was pumped to the Lincoln High School campus. The old buildings were renovated and expanded and ended up looking quite nice. In front of the main entrance, at ground level, the name McClellanville Middle School is set in concrete. High above, the lettering still reads: "McClellanville Pvblic School."

11

Getting Back To The Village

There were twenty-two in my generation, and for a long time, I thought I was the youngest. Nineteen first cousins had been born before me at a rate of almost one per year. Not until I was about 35 years old did I fully realize, with satisfaction, that there were two younger than I. Nana and Melissa Lofton lived in California. Their identity as first cousins escaped me, not just because they lived elsewhere but because generations of Loftons overlapped and because my mother and other people of McClellanville called one another "cousin," or "aunt," or "uncle" without true reference to relationship. The two girls were daughters of Uncle Dick, the youngest member of my mother's generation. Nana and Melissa were the only ones of us who bore the Lofton name, but we hardly knew them.

The twenty of us who lived on this side of the country lived in or near McClellanville, or got here as often as possible.

Lofton family reunion at McClellanville, 1963. Front: Susie Bagnal, Margie Dawsey, Edith Bonner. Rear: "Teen" Lofton, Richard Lofton, Augusta Matteson. Not shown: Caroline Johnson.

The Dawseys

By 1930 Margie ("Monnie") Lofton Dawsey and her family had adjusted as much as possible to the lack of cash flow that followed the cataclysmic loss of cotton. They produced, or gleaned from the forest and the creeks, nearly everything they consumed — their own vegetables and fruit and their own eggs, milk, and meats. Margie bought flour, coffee, and pepper; her husband, Watus, rolled his own cigarettes; and they had enough money to make a contribution to the church every Sunday. They were a closeknit, stay-at-home group and remained so for an exceptionally long time.

The two oldest boys married before World War II began.

Watus, Jr., called "June," lived in Winston-Salem, North Carolina, with the Bagnals for a few months. He returned with his bride, Mary Reddick, and built a small home about 300 yards away from Margie's. He was called into the Army. Richard, the second son, went to work at the Charleston Naval Shipyard, married Nellie, and resided in The Village. Because he was employed in a vital industry, Richard was exempt from military service. After World War II, Richard and Nellie moved to Sullivans Island, thirty miles away.

Margie's oldest girl, Edith, studied nursing in Winston-Salem and later did service as an Army nurse. Harley, John, Ellis, and James stayed home until Uncle Sam called during World War II. Margaret Caroline never left the Lofton community. She married her second cousin, Thomas Legare "Nunk" Lofton, and lived in a house 100 yards from Monnie's on the opposite side from June's.

The six Dawseys who did military service got close to home as quickly as possible at the end of the war. June and Reddick raised their four girls at their place on the farm. Edith, married while in the Army to the veterinary surgeon Dr. Clyde Moses, induced him to open his practice in Georgetown and live in the Maryville section, just twenty miles from McClellanville. The four younger boys (Harley, John, Ellis, and James), whom everyone around McClellanville spoke of as the "Dawsey Boys," came back to the farm home and stayed there for nearly two decades. Harley commuted to work at the Naval shipyard. John farmed until called to the military again during the Korean War, after which he commuted to the College of Charleston to get a degree in education. Likewise, Ellis farmed until he used GI Bill funds to finance study at the University of South Carolina and its school of law. James helped on the farm while becoming a master netmaker for the shrimp fleet.

Monnie made a lot of cookies and cooked a lot of venison, and the family circle was not broken until it came to pass

that the four boys married within a few months of one another in 1961 and 1962. The concurrence of these weddings
led Monnie's contemporary, Harrington Morrison, to say:
"This will be known as the year that the Dawsey boys got
married." Edith Dawsey Moses was the broker of all four late
marriages, finding the brides among her acquaintances at the
Georgetown Memorial Hospital.

So it was that the children of Margie Dawsey lived with
her, in her home, for fifty-one years. There was some coming
and going occasioned by military service and education or by
temporary work elsewhere, but, with four boys living in the
farm home through more than five decades, hers was a nuclear
family that stayed in place a long time. When her children
married, they did not move far away. Richard, having moved
to Sullivans Island, was furthest from home and hearth, living thirty miles away. Two married children and five grandchildren lived within three hundred yards of their Monnie.
With such an abundance of descendants around the homestead, it is a marvel that the grand matriarch was glad to see
the rest of the Lofton clan descend on her. Indeed, I wonder.
Was she always so happy to see us drive up?

The solidarity, cohesiveness, and interdependence that the
Dawseys exhibited did not derive from any uniformity of personality traits. They varied wonderfully. June was a casual student, which must have been a surprise to his studious and
performance-oriented forebears. As a farmer, June had ways
of getting others to do the work while he made rounds to
many kitchens to drink coffee. Reddick could never be sure
he would meet her at the bus stop when she returned from
work at the hospital in Georgetown. But June was always
ready to help neighbors and friends. His brothers complained
about him among themselves, but covered for him, and June
was one of the best-liked citizens in old St. James Santee.

Richard and Edith were more reliable and dependable than
June. Both were called on to live with and help our grand-

mother after she was widowed, and both are immensely proud they did so.

Harley was, perhaps, the best looking of all the male cousins and exhibited a quiet confidence and self-sufficiency that made him easy to meet and talk to. Richard Matteson, son of Augusta and from a more effusive family, thought of the Dawseys as the "quiet" people. Harley was one who gave that impression.

Margaret Caroline was small, attractive, cheerful, and outgoing – as unfailingly positive as were members of the previous generation. Margaret Caroline seemed to function as her mother's symbol and bearer of good cheer. She grew up under a great deal of teasing. Her brothers never let her live down the fact that her mother-in-law (Mame Leland, the avenging angel of the poker episode) expected Margaret Caroline to stir the butter into her husband's grits.

There was a three-year gap between Margaret Caroline and the next child, John, a transitional figure in his own family and among the cousinhood. John was the oldest of a trio of Dawsey boys (John, Ellis, and James) and oldest of a tight group of cousins from our other Lofton families. John was in charge on our walks to the landing to play and swim. The experience made him well-prepared for a career as an elementary school principal. John was a strong supporter and worker for his Dawsey family but was independent enough to criticize his father for what he perceived to be complacency and inaction. He urged a return to Horry County. His mother held them in place in old St. James Santee. She knew that the family had no better prospects elsewhere and would not leave.

Ellis was quiet and studious. He could seem to be solemn or brooding. He endured financial disaster and a divorce but made a strong recovery in a second marriage and a new life of shrimping and clamming back in St. James Santee. Ellis did smoke too much and was one of three cousins who died of lung cancer. At his death, he displayed the stoicism he learned from his forebears.

The youngest Dawsey, James, was a most comfortable person on this earth. He exhibited a gentle and calm personality and a far-reaching competence. "James can do it," was the word around the farm and amongst his Lofton relatives. He was, I believe, the best of us all.

The Dawseys, of the Lofton family groups, endured the most deprivation during the difficult and discouraging 1920s and 1930s. Because there was a large number of them, each of the rest of the cousins had at least one Dawsey close in age. The toughness of the Dawseys was exemplary. Their willingness, in their situation, to play host to us made possible our enjoyment of the farm, the landing, and The Village.

The Bagnals

The second and the third children of Richard and Edith Lofton were close. Susie was three years older than Edith, but the two went off to college at the same time and, together, moved about South Carolina for six years, teaching in various communities. After marriage, the two girls lived much of their adult lives apart from one another and away from McClellanville, but they and their children were attached to the old home ground, visiting McClellanville as often as possible and finally living there permanently. The Bagnal and Bonner families have kept close family ties.

We thought Susie Lofton's husband, Uncle Luther Bagnal, was our rich uncle. Everybody was supposed to have a rich uncle, and no other man of the family qualified. He was a successful businessman, a salesman. He drove an Oldsmobile 98, dressed ready for business (walked on the beach in coat and tie), and had a cheerful, outgoing manner. He greeted us happily, and you could tell that he enjoyed talking to us. He would often slip a quarter into your pocket when you were not looking.

Luther was no taller than Susie, and he looked small and rounded in her presence. He was two years younger than his wife and liked to make the point that marriages in which the husband is the younger of the pair are known to be the most lasting and the happiest. He was a devout Baptist, the first of that denomination in the Lofton clan since there had been no Baptist congregation in St. James Santee. He sowed Baptist seed wherever he went, offering financial support to churches and teaching Sunday school. If one spent the weekend with the Bagnals, one went to Sunday school and to church services.

Luke, Richard, Suzanne, and Harry Bagnal turned out to be as outgoing and friendly as their parents. There was much difference, however, in other aspects of the children's personality.

Luke was the dude, the sport, the playboy of our entire cousinhood, a snappy dresser and driver of fancy cars. Luke curtailed his college career by doing something that would these days be looked on as a harmless prank. At Washington and Lee, he found fraternity life to his liking and went on a joy ride in someone else's car. Although he had compiled a good academic record and ran on the track team, he was invited to leave the university. At the time, Luther and Susie were stunned; Susie told her sisters it was the shock of her life. Antisocial conduct was not the kind of behavior his parents had learned and not what they expected of him. A few years later, Luke gave the family another surprise when he and Billie eloped and married two days after they met as participants in his brother Richard's wedding.

Richard Bagnal proved to be the antithesis of his older brother. Richard is steady, cautious, and conservative but just as friendly as Luke. In his dress uniform at The Citadel, he bore a striking resemblance to his grandfather, Richard Morrison Lofton, whom he remembers and adores. At the college, Rich rose to the rank of captain and was a Southern Conference boxing champion.

Suzanne Bagnal says she is lucky to be here at all. She was

nearly given away. While delivering the clothes to the washerwoman, Uncle Luther heard a muffled cry from the basket. Luke and Rich had hidden Suzanne in the clothes to send her to a new home because they did not want a little sister. Thus rescued, she grew up to become, in the manner of her Aunt Frances Lofton Kennon, a feared, respected, and loved teacher of Latin. In the 1970s, Suzanne and Don Britt moved toward McClellanville. They built a cottage "Around The Beach." The cottage was destroyed by Hurricane Hugo, but the Britts rebuilt and in 1993, after retiring, became full time residents of The Village.

The Bagnal's fourth and last child, Harry, was the only one born in Winston-Salem, North Carolina. The others arrived while Luther and Susie resided in Columbia, South Carolina. His parents, it is suspected, saw echoes of brother Luke in Harry's demeanor. They enrolled him in The Citadel, not taking a chance on a college that had fraternities. There, Harry made sure he rose no further than about the rank of senior private, a position that guarantees a minimum of responsibility and an abundance of free time.

Harry is about three years older than I. He stayed single until age twenty-nine, and I did so until I was well into my twenty-fifth year. We spent a lot of time together, hanging out around Charleston, Winston-Salem, or Myrtle Beach. Our aim was to make out with girls, but we were totally unsuccessful. Inept, inhibited perhaps by a familial reticence in such quests, Harry and I ended up shooting pool or going to a movie. Finally, almost simultaneously, Anne saw the value in Harry, and Beverly took a chance on me. Their initiative saved the two of us from a lifetime of cruising.

Our families were among the largest derived from our cousinhood. Harry and Anne had five children, and Beverly and I had three: Walter III ("Rick"), James Michael, and David Sims. In all, our twenty-two-member cousinhood produced fifty-four children out of twenty-one marriages. The seven married members of the previous generation had the twenty-two of us, and our two grandparents had nine children. (One died shortly after birth.) Our generation has participated in the slowing of the birth rate, which has occurred as we have changed from rural to urban people.

The Bonners

Edith Lofton Bonner and her family lived in Moncks Corner for thirty-eight years. The professor's positive impact on education was recognized in his being allowed, by special action of the state legislature, to continue working until age seventy-eight. Edith Bonner was seventy-five when she retired at the same time. They liked Moncks Corner but always intended to return to McClellanville and the only home they ever owned, the one on Jeremy Creek.

From 1927 through the late 1930s, our family spent the summers in McClellanville. We would have the car packed for departure as soon as school closed on the last day of the spring term. It seemed to me that there was always some last-minute business to attend to. The obligatory waits were interminable. When, finally, we turned between the crepe myrtle trees at Rutledge Court in McClellanville, I felt the summer had started.

During the summer, our father would return to Moncks Corner for two or three days each week to attend to business or meet with the school board, but the rest of us stayed in The Village. Berkeley County's population expanded, and the schools grew larger, requiring the superintendent to be present all twelve months of the year. By 1940, we had to cease going to McClellanville for any extended time, and when World War II began, the Jeremy Creek home was rented to the Chanler Stroman family. In 1949, our folks ceased renting and began preparing the place as a permanent home, putting in natural gas heaters, and adding a modern stove and refrigerator. Their retirement was delayed nearly fifteen years, and during those years, our parents passed nearly every holiday and vacation in the home. Lillian, Henry, and I would bring our families to rendezvous there.

Professor and Mrs. Bonner wanted their children to grow up to be positive, productive members of society. They did not exhort us to excel, lead, or surpass, and in no way did they suggest we should be acquisitive or prideful. It was by their example that they admonished and directed us to live clean lives and to treat other people right. When I was nearly forty-five years old, my mother and I talked about an old friend who had gotten in trouble with alcohol and drugs, and had lost his job. She said she regretted hearing of his plight, and added, "I sure am glad that my children turned out as well as they did." My immediate impression was that she was proud of our accomplishments. It occurred to me, later, that she said this with a sense of relief. We had sometimes given them cause to wonder if we were heading in the wrong direction.

In truth, I do not remember that Lillian caused them any trouble other than demonstration of the usual, normal fussiness and petulance of youth. Lillian was pretty, a source of pride and relief for our mother, who always felt that she, herself, was not good-looking like our father was. Lillian was smart; as a high school senior she made the highest marks in South Carolina's scholastic aptitude tests. Lillian was also talented; her Berkeley High School annual lists her as "prettiest," "smartest," and "most likely to succeed." By contrast, Henry and I hacked our ways through school, misbehaved in church, and fought at home. We, I suspect, were the ones Mother and Father worried about.

Lillian went off to Erskine College, the college of the Associate Reformed Presbyterian Church, which our father had attended and with which the Bonner family had close connections. Our great-grandfather, John Irvin Bonner, was a founder and president of the Due West Female College, which merged with Erskine to make a coeducational liberal arts college. Lillian did well in college — so well that after graduating magna cum laude, she was asked to stay to teach mathematics to classes of soldiers getting pre-flight training. In taking that job, she met the man she would marry, William Jerome Jamieson. In making that choice she, I am sure, finally caused our parents some concern.

A central tenet of the faith of the mainline Protestants holds that religion is of the utmost significance, and, therefore, it is wrong to attack or belittle another person's belief, regardless of whether it is different from ours. We were taught at home that one should not criticize other religions or other Christian denominations. We might believe that ours is the best or the most correct belief, but we never attacked the other one. This respect for religious belief was the expressed ideal, even though our forebears in the Reformed Faith had been bitter opponents of Roman Catholicism and often had argued with the Anglicans. That Jerry was a Roman Catholic must have made our parents wonder why Lil could not have picked a man from the Reformed tradition.

I never heard them make a complaint, though. I believe they supported Lillian's decision to marry. Only later, when her second pregnancy followed soon after her first, did I hear my father lament, "Oh, Lord, she'll have to have eight or ten children." They had only three.

It was Jerry's Irish descent, not his Catholicism, that proved hard for the family to get used to. He would not eat rice — he had to have potatoes — nor would he eat collard greens or field peas. Seeing those peculiarities and knowing that he grew up in Washington, D.C., I figured he was a Yankee. Jerry assured me, however, that his sentiments were entirely Southern. His mother was from southern Virginia. Three of Jerry's great-uncles, brothers, died in Pickett's charge at Gettysburg. Jerry's most cherished connection with the Roman Church is his love of the Fighting Irish of Notre Dame.

In his pantheon, Knute Rockne, Pat Leahy, and Lou Holst are located not far behind the Trinity.

Lillian and Jerry married in November 1945, as soon as Jerry could get out of military service. They relocated to Detroit, where Jerry worked for a short while with the FBI. A job as a private detective with a trucking firm took them to Winston-Salem, North Carolina, where Jerry found himself in philosophical conflict with the Bagnal branch of the Lofton clan. He was a devoted and outspoken Democrat. They were Republicans. Harry Truman's victory over Thomas Dewey in the 1948 presidential election gave Jerry a chance to crow.

Lillian, Jerry, and their three children born in Winston-Salem moved on to Hyattsville, Maryland. He worked as a private detective and an accountant, and for one four-year term, was a sheriff of Prince George's County. Lillian raised her children and then went to work as a mathematician for the National Aeronautics and Space Administration (NASA). In the Washington, D.C., suburb of Hyattsville, the Jamiesons learned they were in proximity to another member of our cousinhood. Richard Matteson was teaching at the University of Maryland. Although Jerry found a like spirit in Richard, a liberal and a Democrat, he was confounded at not being able to escape the Lofton cousinhood. He protested, "Lillian, you never told me you have all these relatives."

Through four decades of life in the Washington suburbs, Lillian longed to return to South Carolina. We thought she would never make it, that Jerry would not agree to full-time existence in the land of field peas and collards, but she wore him down. First, she regularly brought her children (Kathy, Ellen, and Jimmy) to visit their grandparents in McClellanville. They loved the place and thought of it as their true home. As soon as Jimmy finished college, he took a job with an insurance company whose headquarters was in Charleston. Lillian had the opening she needed.

The explosion of the Challenger Space Shuttle convinced

Lillian she should retire from NASA. After doing so, she set out on her campaign to return to St. James Santee. She convinced Jerry that they should have homes in Maryland *and* in the Lowcountry of South Carolina. From the place in Maryland, they could visit the daughters who continued to live there; a residence in the Charleston area would permit visits to Jimmy and his family. Jerry consented, and Lillian purchased a patio home in Mt. Pleasant.

Kathy, Ellen, and their families visited Mt. Pleasant frequently. Two grandsons attended the College of Charleston. A granddaughter spent a summer on Kiawah Island. Jerry desired to stay in Maryland during football season because he was not confident that South Carolina's television stations would carry Notre Dame football, but the movement to South Carolina had progressed so far that its completion was inevitable.

In 1995, Lillian and Jerry began construction of a home in McClellanville. They built on Lot 3, one of the seven lots into which the "Around The Beach" property was divided after Edith Stroman Lofton's death. After a year or two, the Jamiesons sold their Mt. Pleasant home. Lil and Jerry are full-time residents of The Village; Jimmy lives at the other end of the county; Ellen has plans to build a home in the East Cooper area; and Kathy seems likely to move to McClellanville when she retires.

McClellanville exerted its pull. Lillian, like the Roman general Fabian, successfully used a strategy of gradual movement to get back home.

Henry Bonner finished high school in 1942, entered Erskine that fall, and lettered in basketball. But his schooling was interrupted by a call to military service. Securing a transfer from the infantry to the Army Air Corps, he spent his time overseas in England as part of the ground grew for a squadron of bombers. When he returned, I found him a much easier person to get along with.

Following the family path, Henry completed his college education in 1948 and secured a job as mathematics teacher and junior varsity coach at Concord, North Carolina. During the summers, supported by the GI Bill, he began work on a master's degree at the University of North Carolina. I, an undergraduate at Erskine by that time, spent the 1950 summer session in Chapel Hill. Harry Bagnal was doing graduate studies also, and the three of us roomed together. Mary Frances Kennon was on campus as well, getting her Ph.D. in library science, so four of the members of the cousinhood were connected again.

In 1951, Henry came back to South Carolina to fulfill his marital destiny. Signing on as teacher and coach at Greeleyville, he found matrimony waiting for him, just as our parents had. Betty Smith embarked on her teaching career at the same time. Henry came courting faster than our father did. By Christmas he and Betty were engaged, and in March 1952, they married.

The newlyweds moved to Berkeley County, where Henry began as an elementary principal in St. Stephen, then became an area superintendent at Macedonia (the vast rural area between Moncks Corner and the Wambaw Swamp, including Hell Hole), and finally was given the position of county superintendent of education. Betty taught home economics for many years before becoming a pioneer in the field of guidance counseling. As county superintendent, Henry was our father's boss during the last three years the professor was area superintendent at Moncks Corner. I noticed, however, that at our family gatherings Henry spent a lot of time consulting with our father. It was time well spent. Walter and Edith Bonner's commitment to education inspired the younger administrator as he faced the challenge of a lifetime: the integration of public schools in a poor county.

Henry saw the change through peacefully. It helped that the county enjoyed a population boom and an economic expansion before and during his long term in office, but many people believe that Henry's good will and dedication had much to do with the good result. During his tenure, he remained a loyal Democrat. An influx of white citizens and their wholesale removal to the Republican Party left Henry as the last Democrat to be elected to a county-wide post. He was never seriously challenged.

In other efforts, Henry has been impaired by the Lofton in him. Mechanical devices are an abomination to him. Lawnmower engines and fishing reels have short lifespans under his management. He loses parts of his hearing aids. Part of the problem is a lack of caution. On one outing to Cape Romain, he ran onto shell banks three times, losing three propellers. We knew of his prop-busting capacity and kept spare ones available, but he succeeded in marooning his guests in spite of our efforts. Those World War II flight crews were lucky they survived Henry's work on the ground.

Henry remembers that he was playing on Uncle Jimmy's joggling board when he heard of my birth. He was not inclined to rush to "Around the Beach" to see his new sibling. Lillian was more curious but was not favorably impressed by the red-faced little one she saw. Indeed, I suspect that my coming was something of a shock and a disappointment to my folks. Times were hard in 1931, and my parents had passed the usual childbearing age limit: he was forty-two and she was forty. Realizing now that my advent must have been something of a surprise, I salute my parents and my siblings for never having made me feel unwanted. My siblings, all my cousins, and I received the blessings of acceptance and appreciation by our parents. To be welcomed into this world and to live amongst supportive relatives does not guarantee that one will live successfully, but it does give a youngster a fair start.

In Moncks Corner, we attended the Methodist Church. There was no air-conditioning in that time, and I remember that worshippers kept themselves cool by using fans. Some fans were made of palm branches, while others had wooden handles and stiff paper faces with a religious figure or painting on the front and advertisements for an automobile dealership or store on the reverse. That we would attend Sunday school was taken for granted. In the public school, there was no religious education nor even any religious exercise, such as morning devotions or prayer. Both in school and in community affairs, however, special events or meetings were opened with prayer. We lived in a society imbued with the ideals of the Theodemocrats.

At home, our religious observances included saying the traditional blessing before meals and bedtime prayers uttered under the supervision of our parents. Religious books, magazines, and newsletters were all around. I liked *Hurlbutt's Stories of the Bible*, especially the great tales of the patriarchs of the Old Testament; recently I purchased one, still in good condition, at a book sale. We were surrounded by the trappings of our religion but were not actually instructed in the faith. Religious observance was so pervasive, so readily available to us, that it was assumed our beliefs would be shaped by it.

When I was six or seven years old, and Henry thirteen or fourteen and old enough to know better, he got me in trouble at church. We talked so much one day that we disturbed our fellow worshippers. Our father sent us out, making it clear he would straighten us out later. We congratulated ourselves on getting out of the boring service, but as the time neared for the folks to come home, we worried. Henry thought it might help to treat our backsides with ice packs. We applied them, but the professor had years of experience paddling boys who misbehaved. Needless to say, it hurt.

The Moncks Corner Presbyterian Church was founded in time for me to be confirmed as a communing member after my twelfth birthday. Our parents helped draw the congregation together. Dad served as Clerk of Session for many years, and Mother dutifully banged out hymn music on the piano when the music director was absent. Although I attended Sunday school classes and worship services, I found myself increasingly confused by the concept of faith. We were told we must have it, but I had doubts. It was not that the concept of God seemed entirely wrong, or alien, or that I thought religious people were stupid. I simply saw no indication that He was at work in this world.

I attended a church-sponsored college and took the obligatory course in religion but, otherwise, took no part in religious activities. While in medical school and in postgraduate training, I absented myself from church. It was marriage to a quietly determined believer that brought me back into the fold. My wife, Beverly, saw to it that we joined and began to participate in the life of the Presbyterian Church. Her Baptist upbringing provided the same value system and beliefs as we had grown up in. They baptize by immersion and their worship services are less formal but, otherwise, in and away from church, one cannot tell a Baptist from a Presbyterian or from a Methodist.

Later, I was greatly discouraged by my father's long illness and death. It was good for me that I had the means to indulge myself in the study of the works of the religious and secular philosophers. Energetic discussions at a Sunday school class, which I listened to even if I made little contribution, always seemed to focus on the question of whether Jesus is or is not divine. What caught my attention was the realization that I was not the only person wondering about the meaning of life. I began to suspect that religion touches on important matters and that the church has much to offer those who are perplexed.

With the further passage of time, I have gone from being something of a deist to becoming more of a Calvinist. That is a big change. Both traditions have an exalted conception of

God, but the deists believe that God created the universe, set its immutable laws, and then let it run on its own, while the Calvinists suppose that He pays attention to everything and has a master plan under which all things operate. I expect that this dichotomy of belief will not be fully resolved in my mind in this lifetime, but the older I grow, the more I concede to God the power and the will to do whatever He wants to. This Augustinian appreciation of God is, like a slow gene, becoming evident or manifest as I mature. This idea is in my bones, and I feel that the changing of my thinking is not a retreat from rationality but an advance toward recognition of the truth: God is glorious, separate from me, unlimited in power, and able to have things turn out as He wills.

Now, Lillian and I live in McClellanville full time. Henry has mother's house (the Seabrook House) on Jeremy Creek, and spends as much time here as he can. The Village and St. James Santee drew us home.

The Kennons

Our cousins who grew up in McClellanville had to survive Aunt Frances' literature class. She had high expectations of all of her students and demanded even more of her nieces and nephews. Richard Dawsey still recites sections of poems that Frances Lofton Kennon wanted her students to not only memorize but also to learn the meanings of: William Cullen Bryant's "Thanatopsis" and Thomas Gray's "Elegy Written in a Country Churchyard." These works are replete with the philosophy of the Theodemocrats: the inherent nobility of the person, the value of a satisfied mind over money or fame, acceptance of one's place in the great scheme of things, preference for the quiet life, and the love of nature.

Frances told her sisters she was inclined to get a divorce. Her marriage to Robert Kennon was not a happy one. He was a heavy drinker and smoker. He was a rather solemn fellow, who spent a lot of time on the road and, it was believed, had a girlfriend in Columbia. Frances never got around to divorcing him. I suspect that she was inhibited by the prevailing belief in the sanctity of marriage and by earnest feelings of loyalty. Besides, I doubt Frances expected joy in marriage anyway. I suspect she wanted children.

Frances' early death left my cousin, Mary Frances, a virtual orphan. Robert Kennon was incapable of providing a home life for his daughter. Mary Frances moved back to "Around the Beach" with Caroline, Harriet, and Lloyd Johnson. She spent one year with us in Moncks Corner, then returned to The Village to board with Jennie Hamp Graham and graduate from McClellanville High School. As intellectually proficient as her mother, she studied at Wesleyan College, at the University of South Carolina, and at the University of North Carolina.

Mary Frances completed work toward her doctorate in library science. Teaching was in her bones; she joined the faculty at the University of North Carolina-Greensboro and rose to become the head of the library science program. Mary Frances married Leonard Johnson, also a librarian, and they visited McClellanville frequently. To our sorrow, however, Mary Frances followed in her mother's footsteps again; she died young. She was a smoker.

The Mattesons

Music played a large role in the early lives of the Lofton girls, but only the Matteson family kept musical performance alive. Augusta Lofton Matteson's children, Mattie, Jr., and Richard, became educators and not professional musicians, but they did stay active as choir members and stage performers. What is amazing is that the rest of us have scant involvement in music. We may enjoy having music provided for us, but we hardly even sing in the shower.

Augusta Matteson herself stayed active in music to an advanced age. She continued teaching even after she was unable to keep house or go shopping. If someone asked her to play, she played. "If they really didn't mean it, they won't ask again," she would say with a firm nod of the head. She wanted to be considered a professional. If asked to provide music for some public occasion, she assented with the expectation of receiving a payment, however small.

Augusta spent the last years of her life with Richard and Anne Matteson, in College Park, Maryland. She was cheerful and upbeat to the end, and the music continued at her funeral. At a graveside service back in Beaufort, South Carolina, the mourners sang a few hymns. Six of us cousins were present, and led by her musical grandchildren, droned along as best we could.

The Johnsons

Caroline Lofton Johnson was one of the last residents of The Village to be called "Aunt" by everyone in town. She spent almost her entire life in the old family home. It was to her place — "Around the Beach" — that we went on visits to The Village, just as it was to Margie's when we went to the farm. To all of us cousins, she was a symbol of McClellanville.

Caroline's daughters, Harriet and Lloyd, were the cousins closest to me in age and space. In our early years, we were playmates. They grew up in McClellanville and spent two school terms in our Moncks Corner home. From Lloyd, I learned who Santa Claus is. Harriet married and moved away, but Lloyd has always kept a residence in The Village. Lloyd keeps track of all the Lofton people. She has their addresses and telephone numbers and keeps pictures of them on the wall of her den. She is the Aunt Caroline of our generation in that she is the person we contact in McClellanville.

Both girls married early. In doing so, they differed from the females of the previous generation, who left the homestead at equally early ages but went to college and to work. First, like her Aunt Teen, Harriet had a short college career.

She graduated from McClellanville High School and entered the University of South Carolina. In a few weeks, she was back in The Village. At home, she met and showed interest in a young shrimp boat captain from North Carolina. Knowing of the reputation of shrimpers as being mobile and unreliable, Caroline arranged for her daughter to spend some time in Susie's home. She sent Harriet to Winston-Salem, but it did not work out. Harriet found a way to get back to McClellanville, eloped with Jack Lewis, and soon had four children.

Harriet differed from all of us in one distinct way. She had brilliant red hair, a feature unique in the Lofton family. We boys loved to put hermit crabs in her hair and then laugh wildly as she screamed in horror. On the other hand, she exhibited the quintessence of Lofton behavior. Harriet was restless and would never sit down and join a group. Harriet had a certain disdain for or lack of interest in money. Sent to Georgetown to cash a check for her mother, she laid the bills on the back seat and discovered, on returning to "Around the Beach," that some had blown out the window.

Harriet was talented. She was a skilled seamstress who could analyze a pattern and could cut the fabrics to size in minutes. She was also an artist. Her drawing of the "Around the Beach" house, done while she was in high school, is my favorite portrayal of the place. But Harriet did not follow through with or make use of either talent. She made no clothes during her adult life, and she drew or painted no other thing until I prevailed upon her to duplicate the house drawing when she was sixty-three years old.

Harriet, like others of the Lofton clan, was given to profound or all-encompassing enthusiasms. She would pour all her effort and interest into her passion of the month or year or decade. The most long-lasting was nursing. Captivated by the subject matter in several contacts with the profession as a patient, she decided to join it. She started work as an aide, before taking training as licensed practical nurse, then became a registered nurse. In her last endeavor, she graduated at the head of her class when she was over fifty years old. When hypertension and heart disease made nursing impossible for her, she seized upon accounting, becoming bookkeeper for her son's auto repair business. She had wide-ranging capabilities but took on one thing at a time.

Jack Lewis turned out to be a reliable, supportive, and protective husband. He turned from shrimping and became captain of a head boat working out of Morehead City, North Carolina. Jack took care of the house and yard, minded children and grandchildren, and did most of the cooking, giving Harriet the freedom to direct her attention to her current interest. When Jack died of heart disease, Harriet did not survive for long.

Lloyd's path to marriage was even shorter than Harriet's. She did well in school, accumulating good grades even though she was, and still is, an atrocious speller. Having a smiling countenance and a happy disposition, Lloyd was a favorite of her schoolmates. She fell in love and began raising a family of six children.

Her husband, James McClellan, was the youngest of eight children. He was a descendant of the man for whom The Village is named, and his mother was a Whilden, a descendant of the first owner of the property on which The Village stands. Like other returning servicemen, James tried shrimping and farming but turned to electrical construction as a career. He did well, becoming a supervisor for a large firm, and the family enjoyed a good income. The work did require the family to sometimes reside out of town for months at a time. Living out of town and being crowded into a trailer or a small residence was a strain on the group. They tried to get back to their McClellanville home every weekend, but the trips were stressful rather than satisfying.

James' health faded. Diabetes and varicose veins with leg

ulcers contributed, but progressive visual loss due to glaucoma was his main problem. When he retired, he needed full-time service at home. He was able to get out and about for a few years but soon adapted to a "bed-and-chair" existence. Lloyd's duties were increased when her mother had to move in. Caroline had a series of convulsions that caused compression fractures of her spine, necessitating bed rest. In a later fall from the bed, she fractured a femur. She was cheerful, a delight to visit. No cousin came to town without stopping at Lloyd's to see Caroline, but her arrival meant that Lloyd had two patients in her nursing home. It was not until James died in September 1999 that was Lloyd relieved from duties as a primary caregiver.

Teen

Aunt Teen had a heart attack, a brief inconvenience, when she was eighty-five years old. She tried to pay no attention to it. When I called to get more clinical details from Dr. Lou Roempke, he declared he had not dealt with such an obstinate person. She would not stay in the hospital over seventy-two hours, even though she needed to remain longer. "She *went* home. Understand? I could not hold that tiger any longer," remarked the doctor. At home, she did not curtail her activities.

Teen idolized her parents and adored her sisters and her brother. As they passed away, she transferred all of that devotion to her nephews, nieces, grandnephews, and grandnieces, including those she had never met. She knew our names, knew where we were, and what we did. She praised our virtues and accomplishments whenever possible. When we slipped, she felt obliged to let us know we had done wrong, but she defended us against criticism by others. Lofton genes and Lofton nurture could not account, she thought, for any failings or misadventures. Those deviations happened because of contamination by outsiders. Her expectations of us were such that we were careful to do right and not let her down. Teen was not a mother, but she was a powerful aunt.

The Loftons

In August 1998, Dick Lofton's daughters, Nana and Melissa, flew home to The Village. It was their first visit since their youth, when they made the cross-country trip with Dick, Nancy, and the family dog in a Volkswagen. They had not liked the heat and the mosquitoes encountered on the first venture to their father's hometown, but now they were drawn by curiosity. They wanted to learn about his family and about his upbringing, why he was the way he was, and why they are the way they are. Dick's early death, when they were ages at which they had not been receptive to much family history, deprived them of knowledge of his background. Besides, he had not been much of a talker and rarely told tales of the family or of the region he grew up in. They knew that Dick had loved his family, but they knew little about their relatives.

In McClellanville, Nana and Melissa visited relatives and talked with some of Dick's contemporaries. They drove to Sullivans Island to hear Richard Dawsey tell about Dick's youth. They looked at pictures and read accounts of the family, and they toured some of the old family properties. All of us here in McClellanville and the Lowcountry enjoyed the contact with our cousins from California. Nana Dee and Melissa felt reconnected to the family. Their journey to McClellanville seemed to close the family circle.

Family Loyalty

Our grandparents and our parents were products of their culture and their particular home environment. They participated in a society that, though isolated geographically, was the norm throughout the region. Their upbringing was like that of the great majority of people in our region. The generations that preceded them were immigrants, proud of finding identity as a people, proud of getting educated, proud of having their own churches. They were poor dwellers in small towns, perpetual underdogs, losers of the Civil War.

Our grandparents and parents were not unique people. They had no extraordinary qualities or abilities. They had strengths and weaknesses, good points and bad. They had little impact on people outside their geographic region. We think they were special because they bequeathed to us a few ideas and ideals that have made life enjoyable and comfortable.

Most important, our parents left us with an intense family loyalty. They showed us how individuals in a family can enjoy and support one another. So far, we can see this ideal being retained by our descendants. Our nuclear family groups are disseminated — far apart — but from all accounts, we understand that they pay attention to one another. They will set up smaller cousinhoods similar to the one that has worked so well for us.

Why was family so important to our parents? Why were they successful in passing the idea on? They had some things working for them, things which are not so readily available to us these days and which we may need to recapture. They grew up in a community that supported and depended on family life. They grew up in a loving home environment in which they were secure. They were safe, free to roam, and enjoy childhood in a supportive neighborhood. Lacking television, computers, and easy travel they used their own wiles to have fun. They learned to entertain themselves with hobbies and crafts. They played with their peers. They learned to entertain and appreciate guests in the home. In their home, and throughout the community, morality was stressed. Good behavior was expected. They were surrounded by beauty and were deeply affected by it, falling under the influence of the spirits of the place.

12

The Spirits of the Place

After the agricultural depression of the 1920s, the area lost population; black people, especially, left St. James Santee to find employment in the Northeast. The population of The Village fell from 500 to 350 persons. Stores closed. Pinckney Street had been crowded with twenty stores or shops in World War I years; now four or five survived. School enrollment declined.

We heard our folks talk about hard times but never got from them a feeling that The Village, the region, and the country would be overcome by the troubles. Being patient and optimistic was all part of the value system, the religion, of our people. Their attitude was a source of our contentment. Other sources were the spirits of the place: the rise and fall of the tides in the creeks, sunrise over foggy marshes and the golden glow of marsh at sunset, the stately lighthouses far across the marsh, palmetto branches rustling in the wind, ancient oak trees, cypress swamps, stands of pine trees.

In the 1950s and '60s, the town remained dormant but peaceful. The Village in these years looked mature, rustic, and tranquil. Long-time residents accepted its inconveniences and felt comfortable in it. Outsiders, though they would not come there to live, were expressive about the attractiveness of the place. Here is a poem written by a one-time visitor, a young man. Trevor Shanklin gave this to my mother, who inscribed the words on one of her watercolors.

JEREMY CREEK AT THE VILLAGE

The sun sets on the marsh,
And the moon lights up the sea,
A seagull glides, then sways, and dives,
And for a moment disturbs the tranquility.
A shrimp boat rides back into dock,
And its waves ripple gently on the shore.

    A yelping dog is heard,
    As it runs along the creek,

A girl's carefree laugh takes off,
And glides through the freshness of the air,
While a gentle breeze comes and carries,
A sailboat on its way.

The beauty of the scene
 Is there for all to behold,
The diving of the seagull,
The shadow of a tree,
The freshness of the liquid air,
And the lapping of the creek.

There is no painting that could express
The beauty of its charm.
No poem could say — no song could sing,
The loveliness of this place.
I only hope that all who see the rippling marsh
Will know how blessed they are.
                  M. Trevor Shanklin

The fuel crisis of the 1970s following the Arab-Israeli war made The Village seem far from town (Charleston). The McClellanville schools closed. Houses and rural properties were for sale at bargain prices, but no one was buying. The town, at this point, might have shut down.

It bottomed out, and the 1980s marked the beginning of metamorphosis and growth in The Village, which gained speed in the last years of the millennium. Young people — children of the sixties, free spirits, hippies — found the natural environment of old St. James Santee and the charm of The Village appealing. Some resided temporarily, some stayed permanently. Other families, descendants of long-time residents, insisted on taking their stand in and around McClellanville. These people found employment in the seafood industry and with the United State Forest or Fish and Wildlife Services or were willing to commute to work elsewhere. The Archibald Rutledge Academy educated their children. The Academy ini-

Pinckney Street in 1991, looking north. The building behind the second truck was a false front, set up for the filming of the movie Paradise.

tiated the South Carolina Shrimp Festival, which continues to crowd The Village for one day every May. People involved in the arts settled in the area, and an arts council was created. Retirees, people who had grown up in the area, moved back to town. McClellanville began to grow so much that a housing shortage developed.

House trailers appeared in The Village. They looked quite aberrant amongst the mature Victorian homes, and the town council forbade the addition of more of them. McClellanville added a subdivision. Silver Hill, located across upper Jeremy Creek and almost equal in size to The Village, was annexed. Homes smaller than those in the original village were constructed in abundance. In the old Village, just a few dwellings were put up. Beverly and I built our home, "Short Straw," on lot 7 of the Lofton place. Ours was the first Village home to be built on pilings, a requirement if it was to be covered by flood insurance. We became part-time villagers when we took occupancy in June 1989. Not long afterward, at midnight on September 29-30, 1989, the moving hand of Hurricane Hugo wrote a new plan for the old Lofton property and for McClellanville.

Hurricane Hugo

The eye of the great tropical storm passed directly over Charleston. The highest winds and greatest storm surge, a 20-foot flood, moved in at Awendaw, which had the misfortune to be at the most violent edge of the eye, the northern edge, and was attacked by the highest winds and the greatest storm surge. McClellanville, fifteen miles further to the northeast, was hit by winds of at least one hundred miles per hour and a flood of sixteen feet. Every home facing the Inland Waterway, from Awendaw nearly to McClellanville, was devastated. One home located two miles southwest of The Village was still standing but was uninhabitable for months. Our new home was the first marshfront home that could be lived in as soon as electrical service was restored.

By the arrival of Hugo, things were greatly changed for the Loftons. Indeed, the Loftons, by that name, were extinct in The Village. Both founding families, those of Henry Michael Lofton and John Marion Lofton, had "girled out," leaving plenty of cousins, second cousins, and cousins once-removed, but not one retaining the family name. Now Lionel Lofton, a grandson of Henry Michael Lofton, Jr. ("Uncle Harry"), has reestablished a residence in town and is the sole bearer of the old family name in The Village.

When Hugo came, the homestead of Richard and Edith Lofton looked quite different from the way it had in its prime. For one thing, it was no longer on the beach. The very beach was gone, filled in with spoil from the digging of the Intracoastal Waterway in the 1930s. Having been convinced that the presence of the waterway would help the economy of The Village, and in the expectation that valuable new land would be created, the family allowed the Corps of Engineers

Edith Lofton Bonner, 1955, with shells from the landfill formed by the cre- ation of the Intra- coastal Water- way, 1939.

to fill in the marsh in front of the homestead. It was an aes-
thetic disaster. A five-hundred-yard-wide mud bank, appro-
priately termed a spoil area, lay before the home. The fill grew
up in heavy grasses and shrubs, blocking the view of the marsh
and of the lighthouses, cutting off the sea breeze. Over the
last fifty years of its existence, the homestead was less frequently identified as "Around the Beach." It was usually called
"Aunt Caroline's Place."

Now, since real estate values have soared in the last two
decades of the twentieth century, we see that our parents were
correct in expecting that the filling of the marsh would produce valuable (if not so beautiful) land. Richard and Edith's
descendants own lots on deep water. The value of these lots
pleases and shocks us. When we receive our tax notices we,
like all good McClellanvillians, complain bitterly.

I was lucky. Lot 7, the one Edith Lofton Bonner pro-
cured by drawing the short straw when the property was divided, was at the low end of the pasture. It ended at Cooter
Pen Creek and, because that creek is a drainage conduit for a
portion of The Village, the marsh in front of Lot 7 was not
filled. "Short Straw" is the only place in McClellanville that
stands on the original high land to view the great marsh that
our grandparents enjoyed.

"Short Straw," constructed in 1989. In this photograph,
taken in the year 2000, the irregular tree line shows the
effects of Hurricane Hugo.

The "Around the Beach" house had, as related earlier, seemed to be on its last legs, never having gotten much up-keep. It still looked comfortable, pleasant, pleasing, and rest-ful. There had been talk amongst us as to who might acquire and restore the house. Hugo made sure that restoration was not an option or possibility. We have a picture of Aunt Teen viewing all that remained — a segment of the picket fence in front of the brick front steps. The rest of it was in a pile at the back of the lot. In the wreckage, there was nothing worth salvaging. Many months later, the remains were bulldozed to the edge of Lofton Court and hauled away.

The only children of Richard and Edith Lofton that were still alive when Hurricane Hugo struck "Around the Beach" were the youngest girls, Caroline and Teen. Caroline was con-fined to her bed by osteoporosis and multiple fractures in daughter Lloyd's home in the middle of The Village. Caroline lived almost exactly two years after the storm, to September 1991. Her mind was clear to the end, and we enjoyed visits to her bedside.

In January 1992, Teen was weakened by her second heart attack. Still alert and in control, she told of her sadness at

Mary "Teen" Lofton viewing the wreckage of the Lofton House, "Around the Beach," in October 1989, after Hurricane Hugo.

having spent the holidays as the only remaining member of her family. Undaunted, she resumed writing poetry. One seems especially appropriate:

> UNTITLED
> The day has passed,
> The quiet has come,
> The night closes around us,
> And we are at home.
>
> There is news of the tumult,
> Of sadness and woes,
> Yet this morning we picked
> A fresh blooming rose.
>
> Tomorrow there may be
> Much grief in this land,
> But today we still have
> A rose in our hand.
>   Mary (Teen) Lofton 1992

Teen's instructions regarding her final arrangements were absolute. She ordered graveside services only and burial beside her parents in the Methodist part of the cemetery across Jeremy Creek. She insisted that there be no maudlin commentary by the drunken minister who had presided at Caroline's funeral. Cousin Richard Matteson said, "Yes, Ma'am."

Teen lived bravely and stoically until September 13, 1992. Her funeral instructions were followed to the letter, and after the service, we adjourned to Henry Michael Lofton's summer home on Jeremy Creek for one more reunion of his descendants. Conversation naturally turned to tales about all those family members who preceded us. When the gathering ended, Lloyd McClellan returned to the cemetery to tidy things up. She moved flowers and pots around until she was satisfied that things looked good, got into her car, and got back out to return to the grave to make sure everything was centered correctly. It was expected of her.

Recovery

Reports reaching the outside world after Hurricane Hugo suggested that McClellanville had been utterly destroyed. Even the natives wondered for a few days if it was inhabitable. Jack Leland, a devotee of and a teller of tales about The Village, wrote in the *Post and Courier* that McClellanville was born of one storm (1822) and was destroyed by another (1989).

Amazingly, the town survived. The old Victorian homes could be lived in; families moved up to the second floors of these homes until the first levels could be cleared of mud and debris. The few ranch-style, brick veneer homes built over recent decades suffered extensive damage to their walls and several of them had to be torn down. The storm took care of clearing the town of house trailers.

A contingent of U. S. Marines used heavy equipment to clear the streets of broken trees and, with water tanks and hoses, cleared mud out of the houses. The marines were the vanguard of an avalanche of volunteers who came to the aid of the people of St. James Santee. Water, food, and money flowed into the area. Insurance companies were surprisingly generous, with several claims paid for what seemed to be flood damage when the property owner had insurance against only wind or fire. Black and white citizens worked together and were pleased at having done so. The shrimp boat fleet recovered and returned to action.

As restoration proceeded, the continual piling of drywall and other rubbish on the sides of streets and roads of the town and countryside made the place look even worse than it had immediately after the storm. Charleston County was having to conduct a massive clean-up campaign. Not until two years later did trucks haul McClellanville's refuse to a dump on the other side of Charleston. Suddenly, it all looked better. A lot of the old ramshackle outbuildings were gone; some small and ill-conceived dwellings had been replaced by more substantial ones; and most of the old homes tasted paint for the first time in seventy-five years. The most mature pine trees were gone, but there were plenty of young ones coming along. Best of all, the live oak trees, the glory of The Village and of St. James Santee, were still there. The storm revealed the secret of why the oaks reach hundreds of years in age in this storm-ridden area. They drop their leaves rather than let their limbs or trunks be snapped off. In time, new leaves appeared on the oaks. After about three years, with the broken and scarred streets repaired, the town looked better than it had in decades.

Enthusiasm for restoration did not stop at the limits of the town. Young volunteers stabilized and partially restored the Cape Romain lighthouse. In a major campaign, the Parish Church of St. James Santee saw its building and grounds protected and restored.

The preceding paragraphs tell only of the ultimately good effects the storm had on McClellanville and St. James Santee. There was much more to it. People were stunned and disheartened until they saw the recovery effort taking effect. They lost a lot of personal property, including valuable documents, photograph albums, paintings, clothes, tools, and vehicles. The cost of replacing these items far exceeded the seemingly generous insurance payments, which went to the restoration of the houses. No one made money on the storm, and many suffered heavy losses. Furthermore, families had to crowd in on one another as homes were put back into service. The schools could not be used. Through the rest of the 1989-1990 term, students of Lincoln Middle and Lincoln High Schools were bused to Mt. Pleasant to use Wando High School facilities in the afternoons.

The shrimp boat, Captain Huck, *in Lighthouse Hole off Cape Romain, 1996.*

Cape Romain lighthouses, 1996, after restoration of the 1857 light by local volunteers.

McClellanville became the darling of the state. In the years that followed, newspapers and television programs carried stories about The Village, and people came to see for themselves. Churches and towns in faraway places "adopted" McClellanville and sent money or volunteer workers. The community got a transfusion of people. Volunteers stayed for months or years, some even permanently.

Commercial developments appeared on Highway 17 and were so successful as to bear out the wisdom in the advice given by the 1973 planners. Most impressive was the swarm of activity around a new, large filling station at the intersection of Highway 17 with Highway 45, the road to Honey Hill. Open from 6:00 A.M. to 11:00 P.M. seven days a week, its multiple fuel pumps seemed constantly in use, and its convenience store sold a lot of snacks and fast food. This was a revelation to The Villagers. The town council, as soon as it could, hiked the business tax rate to extract revenue from the Christ Church Parish concern that had established this gold mine.

The one restaurant built on the highway prior to the storm did a lot of business, and Hathaway's gas station, at the edge of town, became a café that catered to the workers who came to the region. The hardware store on Pinckney Street was replaced by a much larger new hardware store at the intersection of Highway 17 and Highway 45, diagonally across from the big filling station. The hardware store had new owners, a couple who had recently moved to the area, and in 1998, it added gasoline pumps. The telephone company headquarters moved to a new site on Highway 45, across Highway 17. In the year 2000, the highway sported a third large filling station plus convenience store plus pharmacy. Each of the large filling stations serves fast food. Leisurely meals and relaxed conversation still take place in The Village, but Hugo taught its people that they can eat on the run.

On Pinckney Street, in the old business section of The

Village, the vacated hardware store became headquarters for an artist who designs and prints T-shirts. His wife put up a gift shop and a butterfly barn in an adjacent building. The couple lives nearby in what was once a pharmacy. The original telephone company building is a meeting place and exhibit hall for the arts council. The one automobile repair shop that had served the community, and which closed in the1940s, lay abandoned and neglected until 1998, when it was repaired and painted. The front of it is an artist's studio, and the remainder is a gift shop. The street's last grocery store evolved into a highly successful pub, and from that, it evolved into a restaurant. Whereas village elders like Henry Lofton, III, and Dunks McClellan had, in previous years, sat in the corner and watched Bob Graham take telephone orders from widows of the community, the T. W. Graham Company now draws diners from all around the Lowcountry. The Graham family is completely out of the mercantile business. The T. W. Graham Company building is leased by — and the restaurant is run by — a couple who moved into town before the storm. The restaurant is called "Buster's."

There is now vast growth in the entire East Cooper area, especially in the old Christ Church Parish, nearer Charleston. Mt. Pleasant is the fifth largest city in South Carolina. Expensive subdivisions are moving northeastward along the coast. Awendaw is a municipality, an eight-mile-long strip town along Highway 17. It extends on both sides of Awendaw Creek, so a smaller part of it is in old St. James Santee Parish. McClellanville is an exurb, that is, a settlement beyond the suburbs of a population center. Another term being used, here at the end of the twentieth century, for a place like St. James Santee is "amenity place," meaning an attractive or scenic place in which to live. With its forests, marshes, and waterways, St. James Santee qualifies.

During the 1980s and 1990s, a number of McClellanville's Victorian homes became the property of persons who had no previous relationship to The Village. This occupation of The Village by newcomers is gaining speed. After the St. James Santee Historical Society's home and plantation tour in February 1997, three village homes sold to nonresidents at prices that were unimaginable in the depressed 1960s. Some new owners are full-time residents, and some come on weekends or holidays. Most of these second homeowners are well-to-do.

Taken together, these new residents (the children of the 1960s, the working people who came before or after the storm, the artists and writers, the wealthy second home buyers) comprise the group we have called the Neos, the new arrivals. They bring new life, new blood, to The Village and to the parish. What is their identifying characteristic, their tag? What will be their impact? What will they do?

It is hard to say because, so far, they do not look or act differently from our Theos. They participate in the life of the community as members of the arts council and of the civic club, as supporters of the private school, and as customers of the restaurants and stores. They enjoy boating, fishing, and hunting. They are courteous to, and respectful of, black citizens but have little interaction with them, certainly less than whites did during the ascendancy of the Theodemocrats.

The new residents of McClellanville and people from the old families live their lives in accord with values held by the Judeo-Christian traditions, but they accept these as inherent and natural, rather than as products or manifestations of church membership. Occupants of the parish and The Village are not being identified as members of particular churches — "the Methodist women," or "a Presbyterian," or "one of the Baptists." Denominational differences never were critical in and around McClellanville and now are not considered to be important.

The white people of McClellanville and St. James Santee still live in a Theodemocratic atmosphere but are in position

New Wappetaw Presbyterian Church, 1996, showing the steeple replaced in the 1950s.

to take on a new identity. A new consensus will emerge. Another peaceful handoff of power and influence is in the making. Some day, we will be able to give this new society a proper name.

Preserving the appearance of the town is one thing that we worry about. Towns used to look like they fit their locales. The transition from countryside to town was gradual. Now, everywhere, on entering a town, one's eyes are insulted by garish commercial establishments, such as fast-food places and automobile dealerships. Moncks Corner already has a bad case of urban sprawl disease. McClellanville could be next.

Growth, we must believe, is good for The Village. It was too small for comfort during its dormancy. It cannot be expected to retain the individuality for which it has been loved, an isolated refuge for people of like minds. Will it be a living, working community where people are connected? Will it have its own identity and not be just another resort or another retirement community?

The Deerhead Oak, over 500 years old, is a symbol of The Village.

In November 1997, I conversed with a villager, T. W. ("Tommy") Graham, IV. He suggested what it may take to let McClellanville be McClellanville. He said, "We may need another outbreak of poverty to keep this town from changing utterly." I think we both know, however, that the change is already upon us and that we do not want to have poverty prevail for any reason.

In The Village, the Theodemocrats did strive mightily to create a community, a commonwealth. Their idea was that society should be based on, and reflect, their Judeo-Christian ideals and should be distinctly Protestant and Reformed in tone.

The Village on Jeremy Creek, 1996

They were tolerant, however, of other systems of belief, willing to let others have their way as long as the Theodemocratic majority ran things. They learned this managerial style from their predecessors, the Aristos.

Our people promoted education. They were civic minded. Our people had the feeling that they should create or participate in community. They produced and promoted a society that supported personal development for citizens. What they did not do, and left for us to do, was expand the range of our community, extend its benefits to all citizens in the area. Still, in general, our people have been most acceptant and inclusive.

I am proud to claim the creators of The Village as my people. I revere their courage, their determination, and their patience in hard times. I respect them for their adherence to their religious ideals. Such a rosy appraisal of their worth may be affected, I know, by my looking back at them through loving and sympathetic eyes. But even when I think objectively of them, recognizing their imperfections and inconsistencies, I cherish and salute their striving to be good people. They wanted, above all, to be good people.

Now, Beverly and I reside in The Village. We enjoy its natural beauty and the sense of belonging that the cordial people inspire. And I understand that we and other residents of this place have a job to do. We are beneficiaries of a sacred trust. We must keep this place looking good, and we are obliged to carry into the twenty-first century the best ideals of those who went before us — the Huguenots, the Aristos, and the Theodemocrats.

It is good to be here.

Bibliography

BOOKS

Baldwin, William. *The Hard To Catch Mercy.* Algonquin Books of Chapel Hill, Chapel Hill, North Carolina, 1993.

Baldwin, William P. *Lowcountry Daytrips: Plantations, Gardens, and a Natural History of the Charleston Region.* Legacy Publications, Greensboro, North Carolina, 1993.

Ball, William Watts. *The State That Forgot (South Carolina's Surrender To Democracy).* The Bobbs-Merrill Company, Indianapolis, 1932.

Bargar, B.D. *Royal South Carolina, 1719-1763.* University of South Carolina Press, Columbia, 1970.

Biographical Directory of the South Carolina House of Representatives. Volume I: Session Lists.1692-1973. University of South Carolina Press, Columbia, 1974

Boddie, William Willis. *History of Williamsburg.* The State Company, Columbia, South Carolina, 1923. Reprinted by The Reprint Company, Publishers, Spartanburg, South Carolina, 1992.

Boorstin, Daniel J. *The Americans: The Colonial Experience.* Random House, New York, 1958.

Bridges, Anne Baker Leland and Roy Williams, III. *St. James Santee, Plantation Parish.* The Reprint Company, Publishers, Spartanburg, South Carolina, 1997.

Brownlee, O.Y. *Bonner Family Record, 1753-1946.* O.Y. Brownlee, Greenville, South Carolina, 1946.

Burts, Robert Milton. *Richard Irvine Manning and the Progressive Movement in South Carolina.* University of South Carolina Press, Columbia, 1974.

Butler, Jon. *The Huguenots in America: A Refugee People in New World Society.* Harvard University Press, Cambridge, Massachusetts, 1983.

Cash, W. F. *The Mind of the South.* Alfred A. Knopf, New York, 1941.

Clarke, Erskine E. *Our Southern Zion: A History of Calvinism in the South Carolina Lowcountry, 1690-1990.* University of Alabama Press, Tuscaloosa, 1996.

Clowse, Covern D. *Economic Beginnings in Colonial South Carolina, 1670-1730.* University of South Carolina Press, Columbia, 1971.

Coclanis, Peter A. *Shadow of a Dream: Economic Life and Death in the South Carolina Lowcountry, 1670-1920.* Oxford University Press, New York, 1989.

Crane, Verner W. *The Southern Frontier, 1670-1732.* University of Michigan Press, Ann Arbor, 1926. Reissued 1956.

Cross, J. Russell. *Historic Ramblin's Through Berkeley.* R. L. Bryan Company, Columbia, South Carolina, 1985.

Davidson, Chalmers G. *The Last Foray: The South Carolina Planters of 1860.* University of South Carolina Press, Columbia, 1971.

Doar, David. *A Sketch of the Agricultural Society of St. James Santee, South Carolina, and an Address on the Traditions and Reminiscences of the Parish, Delivered Before Society July 4, 1907.* Reprinted by the St. James Santee Historical Society.

DuBose, Samuel and Frederick A. Porcher. *History of the Huguenots of South Carolina.* Knickerbocker Press, New York, 1887. Reprinted by R.L. Bryan Company, Columbia, South Carolina, 1972.

Edgar, Walter. *South Carolina, A History.* University of South Carolina Press, Columbia, 1998.

Fite, Gilbert C. *Cotton Fields No More — Southern Agriculture, 1865-1980.* University of Kentucky Press, Lexington, 1984.

Fraser, Walter J., Jr. *Charleston! Charleston! — The History of a Southern City.* University of South Carolina Press, Columbia, 1989.

Gregorie, Anne King. *Christ Church: 1706-1959*. The R. L. Bryan Company, Columbia, South Carolina, 1961.

Guest, William Francis. *South Carolina, Annals of Pride and Protest*. Harper and Brothers, New York, 1957.

Hirsch, Arthur Henry. *The Huguenots of Colonial South Carolina*. Duke University Press, Durham, North Carolina, 1928. Reprinted by Archives Books, London, 1962.

Iseley, N. Jane and, William P. Baldwin, Jr. *Plantations of the Lowcountry, South Carolina, 1697-1865*. Legacy Publications, Greensboro, North Carolina, 1985. Revised 1987.

Jones, Lewis P. *History of Public Education in South Carolina: Historical, Political, and Legal Perspectives*. Edited by Thomas R. McDaniel, 1984.

Joyner, Charles. *Down By the Riverside — A South Carolina Slave Community.* University of Illinois Press, Urbana, 1984.

Lander, Ernest M., Jr. and Robert K. Ackerman, eds. *Perspectives in South Carolina History, The First 300 Years*. University of South Carolina Press, Columbia, 1973.

Lander, Ernest McPherson. *A History of South Carolina, 1865-1960*. University of North Carolina Press, Chapel Hill, 1960.

Lawson, John. *A History of Carolina: Containing A Description and Natural History of That Country.* London, 1718.

Lesser, Charles H. *South Carolina Begins: The Records of a Proprietary Colony, 1663-1721*. South Carolina Department of Archives and History, Columbia, South Carolina, 1995.

Leyburn, James G. *The Scotch-Irish: A Social History.* University of North Carolina Press, Chapel Hill, 1962.

Libby, Charles H., ed. *Religion in South Carolina*. University of South Carolina Press, Columbia, 1993.

Lofton, John. *Denmark Vesey's Revolt*. The Kent University Press, Kent Ohio, 1983.

McClellan, J.O., Jr. *The McClellans of St. James Santee Parish*. The Gahagan Print Shop, Walterboro, 1988.

McCrady, Edward. *The History of South Carolina Under the Proprietary Government, 1670-1719*. Paladin Press, New York, 1897. Reprinted 1969.

McDonald, Jerry N. and Susan L. Woodward. *Indian Mounds of the Atlantic Coast*. The McDonald and Woodward Publishing Company, Newark, Ohio, 1987.

Miles, Suzannah Smith. *A Gazetteer Containing a Concise History of the People, Places, and Events of the Area Known as East of the Cooper.* Charleston, South Carolina, 1993.

Moynihan, Michael. *The Coming American Renaissance.* Simon and Schuster, New York, 1996.

Nash, Gary B. *Red, White, and Black: The Early Peoples of America.* Prentice-Hall, Inc., Englewood Cliffs, New Jersey, 1974.

Orvin, Maxwell Clayton. *Historic Berkeley County, South Carolina, 1671-1900.* Comprint, Charleston, South Carolina, 1973.

Petty, Julian J. *The Growth and Distribution of Population in South Carolina.* State Council for Defense, Columbia, South Carolina, 1943.

Quattlebaum, Paul. *The Land Called Chicora.* University of Florida Press, 1956. The Reprint Company, Spartanburg, South Carolina, 1973.

Robertson, Ben. *Red Hills and Cotton — An Upcountry Memory.* Alfred A. Knopf, New York, 1942.

Rogers, George C. *Charleston in the Age of the Pinckneys.* University of Oklahoma Press, 1969. Paperback Edition, University of South Carolina Press, Columbia, 1980.

Rogers, George C. and C. James Taylor. *A South Carolina Chronology, 1497-1992,* second edition. University of South Carolina Press, Columbia, 1994.

Rogers, George C., Jr. *The History of Georgetown County, South Carolina.* University of South Carolina Press, Columbia, 1970.

Rosen, Robert N. *A Short History of Charleston.* Lexicos, San Francisco, 1982.

Savage, Henry, Jr. *The Santee: River of the Carolinas.* University of North Carolina Press, Chapel Hill, 1968.

Simkins, Francis Butler. *Pitchfork Ben Tillman, South Carolinian.* Louisiana State University Press, 1967.

Sirmans, M. Eugene. *Colonial South Carolina, A Political History, 1663-1763.* University of North Carolina Press, Chapel Hill, 1966.

Sproat, John G. and Larry Schweikart. *Making Change: South Carolina Banking in the Twentieth Century.* South Carolina Bankers Association, Columbia, 1990.

Tower, R. Lockwood. *A Carolinian Goes To War: The Civil War Narrative of Arthur Middleton Manigault: Brigadier General CSA.* University of South Carolina Press, Columbia, 1983.

Towles, Louis P. *A World Turned Upside Down: The Palmers of South Santee, 1818-1881.* University of South Carolina Press, Columbia, 1996.

Waddell, Gene. *Indians of the South Carolina Lowcountry, 1562-1751.* South Carolina Reprint Company, Spartanburg, 1980.

Wallace, David Duncan. *South Carolina, A Short History, 1520-1948.* University of South Carolina Press, Columbia, 1951.

Wickwar, W. Hardy. *300 Years of Development Administration in South Carolina.* University of South Carolina Press, Columbia, 1970.

Wilson, Charles Reagan and William Ferris, eds. *Encyclopedia of Southern Culture.* University of North Carolina Press, Chapel Hill, 1989. Sections: "Naval Stores" by Percival Perry; "Cotton Culture" by Pete Daniel; "Crops" by Henry C. Dethloff.

Wood, Peter H. *Black Majority: Negroes in Colonial South Carolina from 1670 through the Stono Rebellion.* W. W. Norton and Company, New York, 1996.

Wood, Peter H. , Gregory A. Waselkov, and M. Thomas Haley. *Powhatan's Mantle: Indians in the Colonial Southeast.* University of Nebraska Press, 1989.

Writers of the Federal Writers Project. *South Carolina: The WPA Guide to the Palmetto State.* The Oxford University Press, New York, 1941. Reprinted, with an introduction by Walter B. Edgar, University of South Carolina Press, Columbia, 1992.

ARTICLES AND DISSERTATIONS

Baxley, Bennett, ed. *St. James Santee Parish Historical Sketches.* St. James Santee Parish Historical Society, 1996 (booklet).

Bonner, Walter. "Yellow Fever at Mount Pleasant, Charleston Harbor, S.C. in 1857, With a Review of Its Consequences." *The Journal of the South Carolina Medical Association*, 83: 262-268, 1987.

Cann, Mary Katherine Davis. "The Morning After: South Carolina in the Jazz Age." Ph.D. dissertation (unpublished). University of South Carolina, 1984.

Duffy, John Joseph. "Charleston Politics in the Progressive Era." Ph.D. thesis. University of South Carolina, 1963.

Hannum, Eleanor Clarke. "The Parish in South Carolina, 1706-1868." Master's thesis, University of South Carolina, 1970.

Kovacik, Charles F and Robert E. Mason. "Changes in the South Carolina Sea Island Cotton Industry." *Southern Geographer*, 25: 77-104, 1985.

Merrens, H. Roy and George D. Terry. "Dying in Paradise: Malaria, Mortality, and the Perceptual Environment in Colonial South Carolina." *The Journal of Southern History*, 1: 533-550, 1984.

Smith, Henry A. M. "The Baronies of South Carolina, V. The Seewee Barony." *The South Carolina Historical and Genealogical Magazine*, 12: 109-117, 1911.

Smith, Henry A. M. "The Inscriptions on the Tombstones at the Old Parish Church of St. James's Santee, Near Echaw Creek." *South Carolina Historical Magazine*, 12:153, 1911.

Stauffer, Michael E. *The Formation of Counties in South Carolina.* South Carolina Department of Archives and History, 1993 (booklet).

Thomas, John P. "The Barbadians in Early South Carolina." *South Carolina Historical and Genealogical Magazine*, 31: 75-92, 1930.

Zeigler, J. A. "Moncks Corner — A Story of a Name and Place That Has Long Intrigued Students of This the South's Most Historic Region." (Manuscript of a presentation at a meeting of the Moncks Corner-Pinopolis Book Club, October 13, 1953).

CONVERSATIONS

Richard Dawsey
Creighton Frampton
Jack Leland
Edith Dawsey Moses
Helen DuPre Satterly

NOTES AND WRITINGS

Betty Smith Bonner
Lillian Edith Lofton Bonner, "Lofton Family History"
    (unpublished manuscript).
Julie Lewis Brinkley
Suzanne Bagnal Britt
Harry Mikell Lofton
Lillian Edith Bonner Jamieson
Lillian Edith Stroman Lofton, "The Life of Henry Michael
    Lofton" (unpublished manuscript).
Nancy Shallert Lofton
Mary Lofton Lunz, "Life of John Marion Lofton"
    (unpublished manuscript).
Richard Matteson
Lloyd Johnson McClellan
Katherine Dawsey Wesselink

PHOTO CREDITS

CHAPTER 2: p. 6 1771 plat: South Carolina Archives, Colonial Plats, Volume 7, p.11; p. 7 McClellanville, 1896: Section of U.S. Coast and Geodetic Chart No. 153. Survey between 1852 and 1870, with additions in 1896; p. 8 the Richard Tillia Morrison, Jr., house: Postcard photograph courtesy of Lillian Bonner Jamieson; p. 9 Pinckney Street, 1910: from *The Visible Village*, courtesy of the Village Museum; p.10 McClellanville waterfront: From *The Visible Village*, courtesy of the Village Museum; p. 11 The Louis Augustus Whilden house: Photograph courtesy of Charles Jerry Owens; p. 11 Seaside Inn: Postcard photograph courtesy of Lillian Bonner Jamieson; p. 12 The Hamilton Seabrook house: Photograph courtesy of Lillian Bonner Jamieson; p. 16 The generator: Photograph courtesy of the Village Museum; p. 17 *The Spray*: Photograph courtesy of Judith Stroman Fortner; p. 17 Cape Romain party: Photograph courtesy of Jean Smith Stroman; p. 18 Children at Beckman's Beach: Photograph courtesy of Jean Smith Stroman; p. 18 Hunting, about 1916: From *The Visible Village*, courtesy of the Village Museum; p. 26 The Village, 1939: from *The Visible Village*, courtesy of the Village Museum.

CHAPTER 3: p. 37 Cape Romain lighthouses: Photograph courtesy of Jean Smith Stroman; p. 41 Awendaw Bridge: From *The Visible Village,* courtesy of the Village Museum; p. 44 The Kings Highway: Courtesy of the U.S. Forest Service and Bert Niemyer; p. 46 Hampton Plantation: From *The Visible Village*, courtesy of the Village Museum; p. 47 The Wedge Plantation: Photograph courtesy of Lillian Bonner Jamieson; p. 48 The Parish Church of St. James Santee: From *The Visible Village*, courtesy of the Village Museum.

CHAPTER 4: p. 59 Nathan Legare: Photograph courtesy of Rutledge Leland, Jr.; p. 70 Christ Episcopal Church: Postcard from the author's collection. p. 72 Lofton monument: Photograph 2001 by the author; p. 76 Henry Michael Lofton: Photograph from the author's collection; p. 77 Susan Ann Morrison Lofton: Photograph from the author's collection; p. 81 Laurel Hill Plantation: Photograph courtesy of Charles Jerry Owens; p. 82 Four generations of the Morrison family: Photograph courtesy of Stuart MacIntosh.

CHAPTER 5: p. 84 Thomas Lucas Lofton: Photograph from the author's collection; p. 86 McClellanville waterfront, 1952: Postcard courtesy of the Village Museum; p. 88 Workers pounding rice: Photograph courtesy of the Village Museum; p. 93 The Dawsey House: Photograph courtesy of John Dawsey Moses; p. 105 Shrimp boats: Photograph courtesy of Glenn Racine; p. 106 The *East Wind*: Photograph courtesy of Alexander Lucas Lofton; p. 107 The *Vacio de Gama*: Watercolor, Edith Lofton Bonner, a copy of an original by Richard Lofton, Jr.

CHAPTER 6: p. 123 New Wappetaw Presbyterian Church: Photograph courtesy of Lillian Bonner Jamieson. p. 124 Reverend Ludwig Beckman, Jr.: Photograph courtesy of Jean Smith Stroman; p. 127 Methodist Church: Postcard photograph courtesy of the Village Museum; p. 129 Episcopal Chapel of Ease: Photograph 2000, by the author; p. 130 McClellanville Baptist Church: Postcard photograph courtesy of the Village Museum; p. 131 Old Bethel African Methodist Episcopal Church: Photograph 2000, by the author.

CHAPTER 7: p. 136 Richard Morrison Lofton: Photograph in the author's collection; p. 136 Lillian Edith Stroman: Photograph in the author's collection; p. 138 "Around the Beach": Photograph in the author's collection; p. 142 the Lofton family, about 1906: Photograph in the author's collection; p. 143 Richard Morrison Lofton, Jr.: Photograph in the author's collection.

CHAPTER 8: p. 147 The Clubhouse, Santee Gun Club: Photograph courtesy of Jean Smith Stroman; p. 152 Post office and bank: Postcard photograph courtesy of the Village Museum; p. 157 Edith and Richard Lofton: Photograph in the author's collection.

CHAPTER 9: p. 162 Picnic party: Photograph courtesy of Judith Stroman Fortner; p. 162 Young adults on the waterfront: Photograph courtesy of Jean Smith Stroman; p. 163 Young women in horse and buggy: From *The Visible Village*, courtesy of the Village Museum; p. 167 Susie Mae Lofton Bagnal: Photograph courtesy of Suzanne Bagnal Britt; p. 170 Edith Lofton: Photograph courtesy of Lillian Bonner Jamieson.

CHAPTER 10: p. 188 McClellanville school: Photograph courtesy of Judith Stroman Fortner; p. 189 High school students and principal: Photograph courtesy of Jean Smith Stroman; p. 189 McClellanville Public School: From *The Visible Village*, courtesy of the Village Museum; p.

191 May Queen: Photograph courtesy of Jean Smith Stroman; p. 191 Maypole dancers: Photograph courtesy of Jean Smith Stroman; p. 192 Girl Scouts or Girl Guides: Photograph courtesy of Judith Stroman Fortner; p. 192 Girls' basketball team: Photograph courtesy of Lillian Bonner Jamieson p. 192 Coach David Watson and his team: Photograph courtesy of the Village Museum; p. 202 McClellanville Public School, showing wings added: Photograph courtesy of the Village Museum.

CHAPTER 11: p. 205 Lofton family reunion: Photograph in the author's collection.

CHAPTER 12: p. 231 Pinckney Street: Photograph in the author's collection; p. 233 Edith Lofton Bonner: Photograph in the author's collection; p. 234 "Short Straw": Photograph in the author's collection; p. 235 Mary "Teen" Lofton: Photograph in the author's collection; p. 239 *Captain Huck*: Photograph courtesy of Glenn Racine; p. 239 Cape Romain lighthouses, 1996: Photograph courtesy of Glenn Racine; p. 243 New Wappetaw Presbyterian Church: Photograph by the author; p. 244 The Deerhead Oak: Photograph courtesy of Charles Jerry Owns; p. 245 Jeremy Creek, 1996: Photograph courtesy of Glenn Racine.

Lofton Genealogy

The connections and interconnections of early members of the Lofton and Morrison families in the South Carolina Lowcountry

| Samuel Joseph Lofton 1798- | **m.** | Mary | | Michael Lowry 1790- before 1840 | **m.** | Suzanna Ward 1788-1865 |

| **Samuel Herd Lofton** 1819-1957 | **m.** | **Susan Ann Lowry** 1819-1857 |

Henry Michael Lofton 1840-1917	John Marion Lofton 1845-1927	Mary Ann Lofton 1847-1870	Samuel Joseph Lofton 1849-1899	Jennie Lulu Lofton 1851-1909	Robert G. Lofton 1853-1857	George E. Lofton 1855-1857
m. Susan Ann Morrison 1844-1896	**m.** Eliza Ann Morrison 1850-1920	**m.** James Graham Sams 1839-1911	**m.** Elizabeth Vinro Moore 1852-1947	**m.** Charles Rhett Taber, MD 1839-1898		

| Richard Tillia Morrison 1771-1860 | **m.** | Elizabeth Toomer Legare 1789-1845 | | Robert Murrell Venning 1789-1856 | **m.** | Eliza Whilden 1797-1862 |

| **Richard Tillia Morrison, Jr.** 1816-1910 | **m.** | **Elizabeth Ann Venning** 1817-1859 |

1	**2**	**3**	**4**	**5**	**6**	**7**	**8**	**9**	**10**	**11**
Sarah Claudia Morrison 1838-1922	Richard Tillia Morrison 1840-	Robert Venning Morrison 1842-1924	Susan Ann Morrison 1844-1896	James Brown Morrison 1846-	Samuel Morrison 1847- (died near birth)	William Henry Morrison 1849-1855	Eliza Ann Morrison 1850-1920	Elizabeth Legare Morrison 1852-1938	Eugenia Isabel Morrison 1855-1896	Mary Whilden Morrison 1857-1920
m. Louis Augustus Whilden 1832-1864	**m.** Selina Priscilla Toomer 1843-1915	**m.** Elizabeth Aletha Muldrow 1848-1937	**m.** Henry Michael Lofton 1840-1917	**m.** Eliza Hibben Leland 1847-1922			**m.** John Marion Lofton 1845-1927	**m.** Aaron Whitney Leland 1851-1912	**m.** Dr. Isaac Auld, III 1858-1923	**m.** Henry Michael Lofton 1840-1917

| Nathan Legare Toomer 1812-1873 | **m.** | Anna Maria Axon Vanderhorst 1820-1867 |

| **Richard Tillia Morrison, Jr.** 1816-1910 | **m.** | **Eliza Abigail Toomer** 1803-1906 |

12	**13**	**14**	**15**	**16**	**17**	**18**
Vanderhorst Toomer Morrison 1862-(died at 2 months)	Henry Toomer Morrison 1863-1953	Charles Wilson Morrison 1866-1895	Anna Lee Morrison 1870-1932	Mary Belle Morrison 1873-1968	Lucia Vanderhorst Morrison 1875-1887	Bonneau Ursula Morrison 1877-1945
	m. Sarah Ward McGillivray 1869-1964	**m.** Caroline Frances Price 1869-1930				**m.** Hugh Swinton McGillivray 1871-1960

Notes - 1. Henry Michael Lofton married **1st** Susan Ann Morrison **2nd** Mary Whilden Morrison
2. Richard Tillia Morrison, Jr. married **1st** Susan Ann Venning **2nd** Eliza Abigail Toomer
3. Richard Tillia Morrison, III, and Selina Priscilla Toomer Morrison had no children. Richard Tillia Morrison, IV was son of Robert Venning Morrison and Elizabeth Aletha Muldrow

**The Henry Michael Lofton and John Marion Lofton families of
Old St. James Parish and McClellanville**

Henry Michael Lofton   m.   Susan Ann Morrison
1840-1917   1844-1896

Richard Morrison Lofton 1862-1928	Elizabeth Ann Lofton 1864-1876	Louise Augusta Lofton 1867-1956	Henry Michael Lofton 1869-1916	Julia Riley Lofton 1872-1956	Samuel Joseph Lofton 1875-1960	James Armstrong Lofton 1880-1976	Thomas Lucas Lofton 1882-1959
m.		m.	m.	m.	m.	m.	m.
Lillian Edith Stroman 1867-1830		Charlton Henry Leland 1855-1887	Caroline Matilda McClellan 1879-1973	William Adolph King 1875-1917	Abana Cummings 1879-1963	Caroline Juliet Stroman 1889-1953	Mary Claudia Leland 1883-1972

Henry Michael Lofton   m.   Mary Whilden Morrison
1840-1917   1857-1920

(no children)

Children and grandchildren of Richard Morrison Lofton (1862-1928)
and Lillian Edith Stroman (1867-1930) - see following page

John Marion Lofton   m.   Eliza Ann Morrison
1845-1927   1850-1920

Abbie Morrison Lofton 1871-1950	Gertrude Lofton 1873-1956	John Marion Lofton, Jr. 1875-1949	Ernest Lofton 1878-1880	Janie Taber Lofton 1881-1965	Eugenia Isabel Lofton 1883-1974	Mary Whilden Lofton 1885-1947	Ethel Moore Lofton 1887-1922	Joseph Brown Lofton 1892-1993
m.	m.	m.		m.	m.	m.	m.	
Walter Allen Moore 1860-1943	Julius C. Seabrook 1869-1940	Harriet Gadsden Lucas 1880-1967		George Walter Hills 1874-1907	Washington Clark Hills 1874-1907	George Robert Lunz, Sr. 1882-1945	Alfred Glover Trenholm 1874-1952	

Children and grandchildren of
John Marion Lofton, Jr.   and   Harriet Gadsden Lucas
1875-1949   1880-1967

John Marion Lofton 1919-1990	m.	Ann O'Neal Watson -1968	Alexander Lucas Lofton 1919-	m.	Sara Calvin Morrison 1924-	Elizabeth Ann Lofton 1920-	m.	Thomas Leach Brown 1924-	Amy Ashburn Lofton 1926-	m.	McKenzie Parker Moore, MD 1919-
John Marion Lofton, IV 1956-			Alexander Lucas Lofton, Jr. 1948-			Thomas Palmer Brown 1950-			McKenzie Parker Moore, III 1950-		
Charles Lewis Lofton, IV 1958-			Marianne Brock Lofton 1951-			Charles Lucas Brown 1953-			Marion Lofton Moore 1952-		
			Catherine Elizabeth Lofton 1956-						Dargan Lucas Moore 1957-		

Parents, Children and Grandchildren
of Richard and Edith Lofton

Henry Michael Lofton 1840-1917	m.	Susan Ann Morrison 1844-1896		Charles John Stroman 1831-1902	m.	Caroline Juliet Millar 1839-1869

Richard Morrison Lofton
"Richard" or "Pa"
1862-1928

m.

Lillian Edith Stroman
"Edith" or "Ma"
1867-1930

Margaret Caroline ("Margie") Lofton 1886-1973	Susie May ("Susie") Lofton 1889-1981	Lillian Edith ("Weenie") Lofton 1891-1980	Frances Havergal ("Frances") Lofton 1894-1940	Louisa Augusta ("Gusta") Lofton 1898-1988	Charlotte Evelyn Lofton 1900 (died at birth)	Caroline Juliet ("Caroline") Lofton 1902-1991	Mary Evelyn ("Teen") Lofton 1905-1992	Richard Morrison ("Dick") Lofton 1908-1966
m.	m.	m.	m.	m.		m.	m.	m.
Watus Woodson ("Watus") Dawsey 1882-1953	Luther Nettles ("Luther") Bagnal 1890-1980	Walter Morse ("Walter") Bonner 1888-1969	Robert Lewis ("Bob") Kennon 1878-1948	Maurice Jefferson ("Mattie") Matteson 1893-1964		Dewey Lloyd ("Johnny") Johnson 1898-1964		Nancy Elizabeth ("Nancy") Schallert 1917-
↓	↓	↓	↓	↓		↓		↓
Watus Woodson ("June") Dawsey Jr. 1912-1975	Luther Nettles ("Luke") Bagnal Jr. 1918-1988	Lillian Edith ("Lil") Bonner 1923-	Mary Frances ("Mary Frances") Kennon 1928-1979	Maurice Jefferson ("Mattie, Jr.") Matteson 1925-		Margaret Harriet ("Harriet") Johnson 1929-1994		Nancy Schallert ("Nana") Lofton 1941-
Richard Francis ("Richard") Dawsey 1914-	Richard Lofton ("Rich") Bagnal 1919-	Henry Erskine ("Henry") Bonner 1924-		Richard Lewis ("Dick") Matteson 1928-		Katherine Lloyd ("Lloyd") Johnson 1930-		Melissa Gay ("Melissa") Lofton 1950-
Lillian Edith ("Edith") Dawsey 1915-	Suzanne Bagnal ("Suzanne") 1923-	Walter Morse ("Walt") Bonner, Jr. 1931-						
Harley Mason ("Harley") Dawsey 1919-1976	Harry Stroman ("Harry") Bagnal 1928-							

Margaret Caroline Dawsey "Margaret Caroline"
1920-1965

John Nathan Dawsey "John"
1923-1987

Marion Ellis Dawsey "Ellis"
1926-1992

James Edward Dawsey "James"
1927-1985

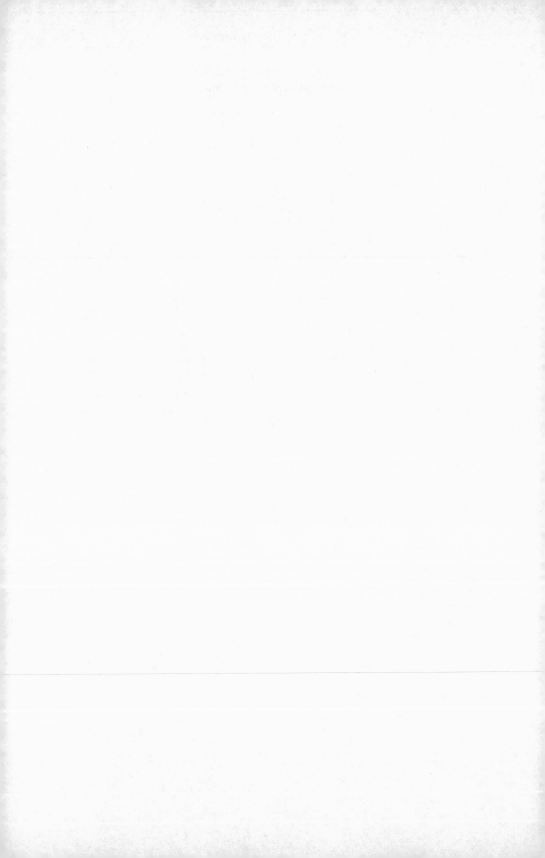

Index

137-138, 218, 239
lighthouses, 37, 238-239
Captain Huck (a shrimp boat), 239
Caribbean, 61, 84
Carmel, California, 183
Carolina, 5, 52, 57-58, 60-61, 63, 65, 83, 87, 112, 115, 117-119, 122, 185
Carolina coast, 43
Carolina, division into North and South, 120
Carolina Military Institute, 134, 148
Carolina Seafood Company, 103
Carolina Shrimp Festival, 232
Catawba Indians, 53, 54
Catholicism, 114, 117, 214
Cedar Island, 7, 65
Central America, 107
Challenger Space Shuttle, 215
Chapel Hill, North Carolina, 217
Chapel of Ease, McClellanville, 129
Charles I, King, 4, 115
Charles II, King, 52, 115-116
Charleston (Charlestown), xii, 8, 26-27, 31-32, 42-43, 47, 52-53, 55-56, 58, 60, 65, 76, 90, 94, 101, 106, 108, 118, 125, 133, 135-136, 137-138, 142-143, 146-147, 149, 166, 168, 211, 215-216, 231-232, 241
Charleston Battery, 140
Charleston City Council, 73
Charleston County, xii, 28, 50, 81, 156, 237
Council, 28
schools, 197
superintendent of education, 14
Charleston Courier, 133
Charleston District, 49, 50
Charleston Harbor, 32, 69, 70, 72-73, 76
Charleston Ice Cream Company,

31
Charleston Medical Journal and Review, 71
Charleston Naval Shipyard, 206
Charleston Presbytery, 125
Charlotte, North Carolina, 134
Cherokee Indians, 53
Cherokee Trail, 32-33
Chesapeake Bay, 101, 103
Chief Two Moons, 19-20
Christ Church Parish, 28, 50, 54, 60-61, 65, 67-69, 80, 122, 124, 133, 147, 193, 202, 240-241
Christ Episcopal Church, 70
Christ, Jesus, 121, 220
Church of England, 47, 57, 113-116, 119-120
Church of Scotland, 116
Citadel, The, 23, 74, 134-135, 158-159, 182, 210, 211
Civil War, 4, 7, 9-10, 12, 15, 21, 33, 49, 60, 62, 64-65, 67, 74, 75-80, 85, 88, 90, 98, 101, 112, 124, 129, 137, 153, 163, 169, 185, 187, 191, 193, 228
Clarke, Erskine, x
Clemson University, 98, 153
Clinton, South Carolina, 29
Club One, McClellanville's Democratic Party, 27, 147
Club Two, 27
Coast Artillery School, Monterey, California, 183
College of Charleston, 216, 206
College Park, Maryland, 223
Colleton County, 45, 60, 65
Colleton, Elizabeth Simmons, 195
Columbia, South Carolina, 74, 75, 143, 147, 168, 175, 182, 211, 221
Compensation, 176
Concord, North Carolina, 217
Confederate Army, 74
Confederate States of America, 49
Congaree River, 32

Lincoln Middle School, 238
Little Wambaw Swamp, 41
Locke, John, Dr. 118
Lockean individualism, 185
Loftin,
  Benoni, 68
  Elkannah, 68
  family, 68
Lofton,
  Carrie McClellan, 23
  Edith Stroman ("Ma"), 97, 128,
    135-137, 138, 141, 145, 148,
    149-153, 157-160, 164, 168,
    173-174, 181, 184, 190, 193,
    216, 233-235
  Eliza Ann Morrison, 10, 133-134
  Elizabeth Vinro Moore, 10, 14
  family, 9-10, 19, 27, 60, 67-75, 77,
    80, 102-103, 114, 128, 140-
    142, 157, 209, 215, 218, 222-
    224, 226-227, 233
  Frances, 144, 151, 181
  George E., 69, 71
  Harriett Ann, 68
  Harry Mikell, ix, 19, 97, 149, 158,
    164, 167, 173
    Henry, III, 241
  Henry Michael ("Captain"), 10,
    13, 23, 36, 50, 69, 74-81, 86,
    91, 121, 125-126, 128, 133-
    134, 146, 148-149, 157, 163,
    181, 194, 233, 236
  Henry Michael, Jr. ("Uncle
    Harry"), 23, 81, 92, 96-97,
    134, 166, 233
  James Armstrong, 81, 86, 92, 96-
    97, 99, 134
  Jenny Lulu, 69, 74
  John Marion, 10, 69, 74, 77, 79-
    80, 129, 163, 181, 233
  John Marion, Jr., 152
  Julia Riley, 134
  Lionel, 233
  Mark, 68
  Mary (mother of Samuel Herd), 68
  Mary Ann, 69, 74
  Mary Evelyn ("Teen"), 144-
    145, 150-152, 158-159,
    164, 168, 174, 176, 179-
    181, 205, 223, 226-227,
    235-236
  Mary ("Mame") Leland, 11,
    19-20, 22, 151, 208
  Mel, 101, 102, 104
  Melissa, 204, 227
  Nana Dee, 204, 227
  Nancy, 227
  Richard Morrison ("Pa"), 13,
    91-93, 95, 97-98, 128, 133,
    135, 137-140, 143-149,
    152-153, 155-159, 164-
    168, 173-174, 184, 187-
    188, 190, 193, 205, 233-
    235,
  Richard Morrison, Jr.,
    ("Dick"), 108, 137, 139,
    143, 151, 158, 159, 164,
    168, 181-183, 204, 227
  Robert G., 69, 71
  Samuel Herd, 67-69, 71-72,
    74
  Samuel Joseph (1798-?), 68
  Samuel Joseph (1849-1899),
    14, 69, 74, 80
  Samuel Joseph (1875-1960),
    81, 92, 96, 134
  Samuel Joseph (1910-1935),
    23
  Samuel Joseph, suicide of, 23
  Susan Ann Lowry, 68, 70, 71
  Susan Ann Morrison, 10, 76,
    77, 80, 125, 127, 128, 133
  Susie May, 137, 144, 151,
    164, 181, 209
  Thomas Legare ("Nunk"), 42,
    104, 206
  Thomas Lucas, 19-20, 22, 81,
    84, 92, 96, 134, 151
Lofton Community, 36, 93, 95,
  106, 134, 165-166, 195, 201,
  206

Whilden,
   family, 225
   John, 5
Whitefield, George, 120
William of Orange, 116, 117
Williamsburg County, 12, 75, 154
Williamsburg Township, 49
Winston-Salem, North Carolina,
   145, 168, 182, 206, 211, 215,
   224
Winthrop College, 167, 170, 173,
   193
Women's Christian Temperance
   Union, 150
Women's Missionary Union, 150

Woodville Plantation, 9
World War I, 1, 12, 15, 19, 23, 93,
   137, 153, 175, 178, 194, 229
World War II, 10, 12, 33-34, 36, 86,
   102, 120,122-122-123, 129. 141.
   168. 178. 183. 196-197. 205-206.
   212. 218
Xantippe, 193

yellow fever, 70-75
Yemassee War, 47, 54, 64
York, South Carolina, 74
Youngman, Lanie Moses, 102